Troubled days
of peace

Peter Dennis

Troubled days of peace

Mountbatten and South East Asia Command, 1945–46

Manchester University Press

Copyright © Peter Dennis 1987

Published by
Manchester University Press
Oxford Road, Manchester M13 9PL

British Library cataloguing in publication data
Dennis, Peter, *1945 –*
    Troubled days of peace: Mountbatten and
    South East Asia Command, 1945–46.—(War,
    armed forces and society)
    1. Asia, Southeastern—History   2. World
    War, 1939–1945—Asia, Southeastern
    I. Title   II. Series
    959'.053   DS526.7

ISBN 0 7190 2205 3 *hardback*

Typeset in Great Britain by
Alan Sutton Publishing Ltd
Printed and bound in Great Britain by
Biddles Ltd, Guildford and King's Lynn

Contents

List of Illustrations

Acknowledgements

In the course of writing this book I have had assistance from many quarters and in many ways. A brief mention here is an inadequate expression of my indebtedness to those who have helped me. I alone am responsible for any errors of fact or interpretation.

I began my research under grants from the Social Sciences and Humanities Research Council of Canada and the Arts Division Research Fund of the Royal Military College of Canada. I was given further assistance from the Australian Research Grants Scheme and from the University of New South Wales, which granted me study leave in 1983. Without this support I could not have undertaken this book, and I am most grateful for it.

The staffs of the libraries and archives I have worked in have been unfailingly helpful and patient, and I thank them: in Australia, the Australian Archives (Canberra); the Australian War Memorial; the Menzies Library, Australian National University; and the Library, University College, Australian Defence Force Academy; in Britain: the Public Record Office; the Imperial War Museum; the Liddell Hart Centre for Military Archives, King's College London; the Middle East Centre, St Antony's College, Oxford; the John Rylands University Library of Manchester; and the Broadlands Archives; in Canada: the Massey Library, Royal Military College; in France: the Service Historique de l'Armée de Terre (archives and bibliothèque); the Archives nationales Section d'Outre-Mer; the Archives du Ministère des Affaires Etrangères; the Fonds historique du Maréchal Leclerc; and the Institut Charles de Gaulle; in The Netherlands: the Afdeling Maritieme Historie Van de marinestaf; and the Historical Section of the Royal Netherlands Army; in the United States: the National Archives (Washington). I am especially grateful to the help I was given in those libraries and archives by Mme Berger de Normazy of the Archives du Ministère des Affaires Etrangères, and Colonel M. Courdesses of the Fonds Leclerc; Commander(rt.) F.C. van Oosten of the AMH, Dr C.M. Schulten and Dr P.M.H. Groen of the Royal Netherlands Army Historical Section; Mrs M. Travis of the Broadlands Archives; Mrs Sally Marks of the Diplomatic Branch of the National Archives, and Mr John E. Taylor of the Modern Military Branch of the National Archives.

Quotations from Crown copyright records in the Public Record Office appear by permission of the Controller of HM Stationery Office. For permission to quote from records in their care I am grateful to the Trustees of the Broadlands Archives; the Trustees of the Liddell Hart Centre for Military Archives, King's College London; the Afdeling Maritieme Historie; the Middle East Centre, St Antony's College; and to the other archives mentioned in the bibliography.

Several participants in the events I have tried to describe willingly shared their memories, and in some cases diaries and other papers, with me. I am indebted to the late Earl Mountbatten of Burma, Lieutenant-General Sir Philip Christison, General Jean Lecomte, and Professor W. Macmahon Ball for giving so freely of their time. Lord Mountbatten's tragic death came only weeks after I talked with him. He has been well served by his official biographer, Philip Ziegler, and if the tone of my book is more critical, my attitude remains no less admiring.

I wish to thank the following individuals who assisted me in different ways: Jaap Valkenburg guided me through the various archives I visited in The Netherlands; Dr Peter Romijn of the Netherlands State Institute for War Documentation readily answered my queries and directed me to important sources; Gunther E. Rothenberg assisted me with Dutch translation; Ria de Groot helped locate material in the Australian Archives; my colleagues John Robertson, John McCarthy, Roger Thompson and Jeffrey Grey gave me the benefit of different perspectives; Paul Ballard drew the maps; and my wife Iréna helped me in particular with my faltering French.

My greatest debt is to Anthony Short, who first encouraged me to examine this subject, and who has sustained my efforts through his friendship, advice and generous hospitality. I thank him above all, not least for his understanding when other commitments prevented me from completing this book as quickly as I originally had hoped.

Peter Dennis
Canberra
September 1986

Abbreviations

AA	Australian Archives, Canberra
AFNEI	Allied Forces, Netherlands East Indies
ALFFIC	Allied Land Forces, French Indo China
ALFSEA	Allied Land Forces, South East Asia
AMAE	Archives du Ministère des Affaires Etrangères
AMH	Afdeling Maritieme Historie
AOM	Archives nationales, Section d'Outre-Mer
APWI	Allied Prisoners-of-War and Internees
AWM	Australian War Memorial
BA	Broadlands Archives
CAB	Cabinet
CCS	Combined Chiefs of Staff
CEFEO	Corps Expéditionnaire Français d'Extrême-Orient
CIGS	Chief of the Imperial General Staff
CLI	Corps Léger d'Intervention
COS	Chiefs of Staff
CRS	Commonwealth Record Series
DGER	Direction Générale des Etudes et Recherches
DIC	Division d'Infanterie Coloniale
DO	Dominions Office
DSR	Department of State Records
FL	Fonds historique du Général Leclerc de Haute-clocque, Maréchal de France
FO	Foreign Office
FRUS	Foreign Relations of the United States
JCS	Joint Chiefs of Staff
JRULM	John Rylands University Library of Manchester
JSM	Joint Staff Mission
KCL	King's College London, Liddell Hart Centre for Military Archives

MECSAO	Middle East Centre, St Antony's College
MMB	Modern Military Branch
NA	National Archives, Washington
NEI	Netherlands East Indies
NICA	Netherlands Indies Civil Administration
OSS	Office of Strategic Services
PREM	Prime Minister's Office
RAPWI	Repatriation of Allied Prisoners-of-War and Internees
RAAF	Royal Australian Air Force
RAF	Royal Air Force
RG	Record Group
RL	Rear Link
RIC	Régiment d'Infanterie Coloniale
SACSEA	Supreme Allied Commander, South East Asia
SEAC	South East Asia Command
SHAT	Service historique de l'Armée de Terre
SOE	Special Operations Executive
SSU	Strategic Services Unit
SWNCC	State-War-Navy Coordinating Committee
SWPA	South West Pacific Area
VCIGS	Vice Chief of the Imperial General Staff
WO	War Office

For Andrew

Introduction

The ceremony was brief. At 10.30 on the morning of 12 September 1945 the Supreme Allied Commander, South East Asia Command, arrived at the steps of the Municipal Building in Singapore. Admiral Lord Louis Mountbatten was greeted by his commanders-in-chief, General Sir William Slim, Admiral Sir Arthur Power, and Air Chief Marshal Sir Keith Park. As Mountbatten inspected the guard of honour, made up of British, Australian and Indian land, sea and air forces, several flights of Mosquitos, Sunderlands and Dakotas flew overhead, while in the harbour more than 60 warships attested to allied naval strength. Inside, in the Council Chamber, almost every senior officer from South East Asia Command was present to witness the Japanese surrender. At 11 o'clock the Japanese delegation arrived to the distant jeers of assembled former prisoners-of-war. In the absence of the Japanese Supreme Commander in southeast Asia, Field Marshal Count Terauchi, who was too ill to attend, Mountbatten agreed that General Itagaki of the Seventh Army and Lt General Numata, Chief of Staff to Terauchi, could act for the Japanese. When the assembly was seated Mountbatten made a short speech, stressing that the Japanese had succumbed to the overwhelming military might of the allies. This was no negotiated peace, he added, but an acceptance by the Japanese of certain defeat at the hands of the forces now massed against them. With that he called on Itagaki to sign the instrument of surrender, and the war against Japan in southeast Asia was over.

The end was deceptively easy. With the exception of Burma and West New Guinea, the area under Mountbatten's command had not seen the Japanese defeated in battle; save for parts of Borneo and some of the outer islands of the Netherlands East Indies, the

Their numbers were large – estimates ranged up to 600,000 – and they were scattered over vast areas. Their former prisoners and internees, too, were thought to number hundreds of thousands, and their whereabouts were for the most part unknown. Much of the economic structure of southeast Asia had been distorted if not destroyed by the Japanese occupation, and the prospect of widespread famine hung over the region.

Despite the show of strength at Singapore, Mountbatten's forces were hardly adequate to the task of winding up the war against Japan. They were completely inadequate in terms of the conditions they encountered, which arose not only from the defeat of the Japanese but also from the largely unexpected political developments which confronted them with armed and organised nationalist opposition on a scale that had not been anticipated. Without any preparation and with very little guidance, either from their political advisers in SEAC or from London, military men were plunged into the turmoil of southeast Asian nationalist revolutions. For better or worse, the decisions that they had to take on a day-to-day basis helped shape the immediate course of those revolutions and in turn forced the hands of the metropolitan capitals. It could hardly be said that these were stirring times for South East Asia Command. The rescue of former p.o.w.s and internees was a humanitarian duty, and was willingly carried out, but beyond that there could be little satisfaction in performing tasks that seemed to be politically dictated rather than militarily necessary. Coming after a long and debilitating struggle against the Japanese, these were, as Mountbatten described them in his farewell signal to Park in May 1946, 'troubled days of peace'. How Mountbatten and South East Asia Command handled them, not in British territories but in the empires of their allies, is the theme of this book.

Chapter one
From war to peace

It was evident long before the capitulation of Japan that the re-entry of allied forces into southeast Asia would involve a series of immensely difficult operations. The enormous size of the theatre, the division of responsibility between several commands (which were often at loggerheads over strategy), lack of information about conditions in different areas within the region, the distance of the main allied forces from the vital centres of the British, Dutch and French pre-war imperial presence, and a severe shortage of shipping: all these factors combined to present military planners with a series of problems as complex as any they had faced during the war. As pressure on Japan increased, so Japanese military resistance strengthened, and there was every likelihood that it would continue to the bitter end. In purely military terms, therefore, it was a daunting prospect.

No military plan can be conceived in isolation, and this was especially true of the situation that prevailed in allied circles in 1945. Quite apart from mounting tensions between the western allies and the Soviet Union, there were growing disagreements among the democratic powers about the way in which allied military superiority in the Pacific theatre should be brought to bear on Japan, for it was well understood by all parties, even if the fact was not publicly acknowledged, that the nature and direction of the allied assaults against Japanese positions would help to shape, if not the overall future of large parts of Asia, then at least the status and place of the western powers within the region. Britain, France and the Netherlands each had imperial roles to reassert and re-establish after the disasters of 1941–2: in the case of the French to reclaim Indochina after having failed to resist Japanese pressures in 1941; in the case of Britain and the Netherlands to return in such force to their colonial territories as to diminish memories of the ignominious collapse in early 1942 that had so manifestly damaged, if not forever destroyed, the claims by which imperial control had ultimately been justified.[1]

The divergence between British and American policies had become unmistakeable well before the unconditional surrender of Germany in May 1945. By the summer of 1944, when the success of the Normandy landings put the final outcome in western Europe beyond doubt (even if the timing of the final German collapse and the best strategy to bring it about still gave rise to bitter disputes in Anglo-American circles), it was clear that Britain and the United States approached the question of post-war reconstruction from quite different perspectives. The Yalta conference in February 1945 marked Britain's public relegation to the position of a junior partner within the alliance, and demonstrated – for better or worse – that the United States, and Roosevelt in particular, was determined to assert its dominant position. For France, Yalta had an even more stark significance, for it was not represented at the conference, a symbol of its exclusion from the ranks of the power-brokers. By the time of Roosevelt's death in April, any illusions that the Soviet-American wartime alliance, whose only binding characteristic had been opposition to a common enemy, would automatically be carried over into the post-war world had all but disappeared as it became apparent that the advances of the Red Army into central Europe were to be the spearhead for Soviet political penetration.

While the battlefields of Europe were giving way to confrontation across the conference table, the war against Japan dragged on with no sudden or easy end in sight. In the Pacific theatre the dominance of the United States in allied circles was unchallenged. The Soviet Union remained out of the war against Japan until Germany had been defeated, by which time earlier American anxiety to bring the USSR had become distinctly equivocal. In the drive to cut off the Japanese home islands, American naval, land and air forces were centrally positioned and able to dictate the course of the decisive operations. The forces of other western powers were less well placed. British and Indian troops had fought a long and arduous campaign against the Japanese in Burma, and victory there had finally destroyed any threat to India. But Malaya and Singapore were still occupied by the Japanese, while the

centres of French and Dutch colonial power, French Indochina and
the vast Indonesian archipelago making up the Netherlands East
Indies, remained in Japanese hands. MacArthur's island-hopping
campaigns had moved American forces through the southwest
Pacific, converging on the Philippines and at the same time bypassing those areas in southeast Asia of greatest concern to the
European powers. His single-minded determination to retake the
Philippines by force of American arms alone relegated experienced
Australian troops who had pushed his advance through New
Guinea to a series of operations against secondary island targets,
while French offers of assistance to capture Indochina were
ignored. The Dutch, the last of the western European nations to be
liberated, had few forces at their disposal, and even less means to
put them into the field, especially in an area as far removed from
Europe as the East Indies. British forces in South East Asia
Command (SEAC), controlled from Mountbatten's headquarters
in Kandy, Ceylon, were mainly in Burma, with a major operation
required to land them in Malaya and Singapore, the latter being the
obvious headquarters for SEAC's post surrender operations.

On 15 August 1945, following brief discussions at the Potsdam
conference, the boundary between Mountbatten's South East Asia
Command and MacArthur's South West Pacific Area was changed,
and the responsibility for those parts of southeast Asia formerly
under MacArthur's control was transferred to Mountbatten, who
now, in addition to Burma, Siam, Malaya, Singapore and Sumatra
– which had been in SEAC since its creation in 1943 – had to plan
and carry out operations to liberate the rest of the East Indies,
including the most populous island, Java, and the southern part of
Indochina below the 16° North parallel. All this was to be
accomplished without any immediate increase in manpower or
materiel. While the shift in boundaries made military sense, not
least given MacArthur's commitment to the main thrust against the
Japanese home islands, it sharpened long-standing tensions over the
question of post war Asia and in particular over the position of the
western powers in the region. Throughout the war British and
American views on the Pacific theatre had diverged from the mutual
acceptance at the December 1941 ARCADIA conference of a
'Germany first' strategy, in which holding operations only would be
conducted in the Pacific until Germany and Italy had been defeated.
For the rest of the European war there were increasingly bitter

arguments between the two allies, as the Americans sought to stem the Japanese advances while still holding to the 'Germany first' strategy, a global balancing act that the British consistently interpreted as an attempt to undermine if not abandon the strategy agreed upon when the United States first entered the war.

There were several factors that had a particular bearing on Britain's perspective in the Pacific theatre. Unlike the United States, which was never in real danger of physical attack (apart, that is, from the Hawaiian islands), Britain was under the direct threat of invasion for the best part of a year and exposed to German air raids for the greater part of the war, including the V–1 attacks and V–2 threats in the last year of hostilities in Europe. Determination to protect the metropolitan centre therefore dictated the British approach to strategic questions in a way that the United States, notwithstanding the American sympathy for the British position, could never fully appreciate. Furthermore, Churchill's insistence on protecting the 'Germany first' strategy, more and more by pressing for indirect operations in the Mediterranean, merely seemed to the Americans a pretext for postponing what they saw as the unavoidable head-on confrontation in western Europe, or – even worse – an attempt to divert the Anglo-American effort from its primary aim of defeating the Axis powers as swiftly as possible so that the full might of the alliance could be brought to bear upon Japan, to the much more sinister goal of restoring British and other allied imperial interests in the Middle East, which itself would be but the prelude to a full scale return of the European powers to their battered empires in Asia.

The suspicion that Churchill was not fully committed to an all-out drive against Germany remained until the end of the war in Europe, although the worst American fears were laid to rest when he finally bowed to pressure from the United States (and from some of his own service advisers) and agreed to a cross-Channel attack in the summer of 1944. Those fears surfaced again when Churchill argued strongly for a continuation of operations in the eastern Mediterranean in late 1944 and early 1945, but by then American concerns about the imperial bias of British strategic proposals had switched to the Pacific. The United States had long been suspicious of British motives in the war against Japan. The abysmal performance of British forces in the Malayan campaign, culminating in the Singapore fiasco, had shattered Britain's imperial prestige, and

Churchill's insistence on the 'Germany first' strategy to the apparent exclusion of any significant action in the Pacific cast doubt on his commitment to pursue the war on the global scale that the Americans envisaged. In truth, Churchill's understanding of the war against Japan hardly went beyond the defence of India, which to him was synonomous with Empire. Even Singapore had little more than symbolic significance for Churchill. Not without reason did Slim's Fourteenth Army in Burma become known as the 'Forgotten Army'.

American commanders in the Pacific were dismissive of the British contribution. MacArthur, who like most Americans made little distinction between British and Dominion forces, had a low opinion of the Australian troops under his control, until the successful advance through New Guinea forced him to acknowledge the Australian skill in jungle fighting. Beyond that grudging recognition, however, MacArthur would not go: through the entire campaign in the southwest Pacific he never took any non-American officers on to his staff, while his manipulation of the press to publicise American achievements while downplaying those of allied forces was nothing short of scandalous. Admiral Ernest J. King, US Chief of Naval Operations, was unenthusiastic about a significant British naval participation in the Pacific, and in the last six months of the war against Japan, when the inevitability of the German defeat freed much of the Royal Navy for deployment elsewhere, British ships were kept away from the main operational areas in the final drive against Japan. 'Vinegar Joe' Stilwell, the US commander in China and for a time Mountbatten's Deputy Supreme Commander in SEAC, was openly contemptuous of the British in Burma. Lt General A.C. Wedemeyer, who succeeded Stilwell in China after serving as Mountbatten's Deputy Chief of Staff, was equally given to denigrating British efforts, and added to this an undisguised hostility to what he saw as the British intention to shape the course of operations against Japan in accordance with post war British imperial ambitions in Asia.

The British quickly became aware of the American attitude, but there was little they could do to change it. Churchill consistently blocked any attempts to increase British commitments to the war against Japan if that meant the slightest diminution of the effort in Europe. The victories in Burma, the one area where British arms did eventually achieve notable successes against the Japanese, were

won by British forces which had been starved of support and
largely neglected by London. Churchill's oft-repeated promise that
once Germany was defeated the full resources of Britain would be
switched to the fight against Japan was nothing more than a
rhetorical flourish to allay American criticisms. However unfair
and ungenerous much of the individual American criticism was, it
was closer to the truth than Churchill was ever willing to admit
publicly.[2] By 1944, when the Japanese were clearly on the defensive
at the same time as the defeat of Germany had become inevitable,
the American attitude had moved beyond being a source of
irritation and had become a matter of real concern. From
Chungking, the British ambassador, Sir Horace Seymour, reported
in December that 'hardly any Americans out here feel any sympathy
for the British Empire in the East', and he went on to say that 'This
fact simply has to be accepted, and our cooperation has to be, and
in fact is, solely on the basis of beating the Japs'.[3]

But of course neither the United States nor Britain, nor any of the
lesser allies in the Pacific war, was conducting the final campaigns in
particular 'solely on the basis of beating the Japs.' Not only was the
post war balance of power in Asia at stake, but the nature and timing
of the recapture of colonial possessions would clearly determine in
some measure the reception that the imperial powers could expect
from the local populations which had been so suddenly abandoned
in 1942. The particular short-term worry over American attitudes
was that the western allies depended heavily on American military
aid through Lend-Lease to support the operations required to
recover the territories lost at the beginning of the war. Esler Dening,
Mountbatten's political adviser in SEAC since 1943, warned against
Britain becoming an 'inveterate borrower' from the United States,
and urged: 'We shall have to learn to stand upon our own feet if we
are to regain our lost prestige in the Far East.'[4] Unfortunately it was
not so simple. South East Asia Command drew much of its materiel
support from Lend-Lease, and this reliance was planned to increase
if and when forces from liberated France and the Netherlands joined
the war in the Pacific. Galling as it was to the British, in SEAC, in
London, and in Washington, to be lectured on the evils of
imperialism, there was little they could do to respond officially while
their dependence on Lend-Lease deepened. Seymour in Chungking
was 'trying patiently' to disabuse General Patrick Hurley, US
ambassador to China, of the suspicion that Britain was pursuing a

colonial policy in Asia, and that in southeast Asia in particular it was reaching secret understandings with the French and Dutch to thwart American plans for a post war settlement.[5] The main American fear, according to J.C. Sterndale Bennett, head of the Far Eastern Department of the Foreign Office, seemed to be that Britain would support an 'imperialist' peace in Asia on the grounds that the creation of a strong China would threaten Britain's position in Hong Kong and Malaya, and that British military operations against Japan would be conducted with this ulterior motive in mind.[6]

Yet when the matter was put squarely to Hurley, he suggested that Anglo-American differences were over means rather than ends, that both countries wanted to see a strong and united China. The danger lay, he stressed, not in his opposition to British policy but in Roosevelt's growing suspicions about British support for French aims to Indochina.[7]* According to Hurley, trouble was looming over the question of Lend-Lease equipment being used in the recovery of colonial possessions, not only by the French in Indochina but also by the Dutch in the East Indies and the British in Malaya.[8] Dening welcomed Hurley's assurances about his own position for, as he advised the Foreign Office, 'I have on frequent occasions drawn attention to the exclusionist nature of the United States strategy in the war against Japan and to American reluctance to give credit to British effort and readiness to criticise it. . . .'[9] The greatest immediate obstacle, Dening thought, lay elsewhere, for 'in General Wedemeyer, who is after all in military control in China, we have an American who is profoundly distrustful of everything British and who is convinced that we are a bad number. He has told me so himself, and what he says should not be ignored.'[10] Dening's suspicion was well-founded: at a meeting with an American consular official in June 1944 Wedemeyer had made it clear that 'in his opinion the British are primarily interested in restoring their prestige throughout southeast Asia and secondarily interested in defeating the Japanese. . . .'[11] It was a measure of British concern over Wedemeyer's attitude that the Foreign Office was undecided whether it would welcome Wedemeyer's acceptance of a British invitation to visit London. The chairman of the Joint Intelligence Committee in the Foreign Office, V.F.W. Cavendish-Bentinck, thought that there was a danger that if he did come to London and

* See Chapter 2.

hold talks with the Foreign Office, he might become even more
anti-British on his return to China so as not 'to lay himself open to
the accusation of having been subjected to the blandishments of the
crafty British.'[12] When Wedemeyer finally pleaded that pressures of
time made it impossible for him to go to London, one member of
the Foreign Office commented: 'Personally I never thought
Wedemeyer would venture, or be allowed to venture, into the
Lion's den.'[13] Blandishments or not, Wedemeyer and other
Americans, at both the political and military level, continued to
criticise British participation in the war against Japan at the same
time as they pursued what Dening with some justification called an
'exclusionist' strategy. For all Churchill's reluctance to become too
deeply involved in the Pacific war, there was, as Sterndale Bennett
emphasised, an element of hypocrisy in the American attitude: 'The
Americans have not disdained the use of our territories, particularly
India and Burma, and the considerable resources which those
territories have made available for them in furthering their effort in
China.'[14] The restrained comment by the Foreign Secretary,
Anthony Eden, on this observation – 'Good point' – disguised a
widespread feeling in Whitehall that Britain could not take for
granted an American recognition of British rights in Asia, either in
the immediate military sense or in terms of a post war settlement.

By the middle of 1945 the allies were preparing for what it was
hoped would be the final drives against Japan. These operations, of
course, were drawn up without reference to the possible effect of
the atomic bomb, knowledge of which was confined to a tiny circle
of political and military officials. In South East Asia Command,
preparations were well in hand for the launching of operation
ZIPPER, the invasion of Malaya and the capture of Singapore. An
early – and easy – end to the war was not anticipated and previous
experience suggested that Japanese resistance would continue to the
bitter end unless a halt in the fighting was ordered by the Emperor.
In July, however, the situation changed dramatically. Mountbatten
was en route to London to confer with Churchill and the Chiefs of
Staff, when he was ordered to alter his plans and go to Berlin to
meet Roosevelt and the US Joint Chiefs of Staff. He arrived at
Berlin on 24 July, and was informed by the Combined Chiefs of
Staff that his command had been enlarged to include Borneo, Java
and the Celebes Islands, and that there would also be changes in

Indochina. This was a considerable additional responsibility, but once he had been assured that he would retain those forces already in the area he did not raise any objections, apparently thinking that the enlarged territory would not stretch SEAC's capabilities unduly.[15]

Following the Combined Chiefs meeting, General George C. Marshall, US Army Chief of Staff and the President's senior military adviser, told Mountbatten of the American plan to use the atomic bomb against Japan. Shortly afterwards Churchill also told him about the bomb, and advised him to make preparations for a Japanese surrender soon after the middle of August. Mountbatten thereupon cabled SEAC headquarters in Kandy, informing his Deputy Supreme Commander, the American Lt General R.A. Wheeler, and his Chief of Staff, Lt General F.A.M. ('Boy') Browning, that an early Japanese capitulation was possible, and that Churchill was anxious that SEAC have plans ready for a swift occupation of Singapore. Churchill, Roosevelt and Marshall had sworn Mountbatten to absolute secrecy on the question of the bomb, so that although in his cable to SEAC he stressed the possibility of an early end to the war, he was unable to refer to the new weapon that made victory a matter of weeks rather than the months that the most optimistic forecasts had hitherto predicted. The basis on which SEAC's planners were required to draw up contingency operations was rendered even more difficult by the fact that details of the new boundaries – and hence an appreciation of the increased responsibilities of SEAC – were not dispatched to Mountbatten's headquarters until 2 August.

The response from Kandy was swift. Dening advised the Foreign Office that SEAC's planners were locked into the complex time-table for ZIPPER and could not mount a 'balanced' operation to take Singapore immediately following a Japanese decision to sue for peace. The political ramifications of such a situation were considerable:

If circumstances should arise wherein we recover Malaya and in particular Singapore, not by force of arms but by an act of surrender, then we should to my mind, carry out our reoccupation with the maximum degree of efficiency and the maximum display of force. This is necessary not because the stigma which attaches to our loss of these territories is by no means forgotten, but because we must impress upon local inhabitants that we are now possessed of force and organisation which were so conspicuously lacking at the time of our defeat. Still more is it necessary to impress Japanese forces, who will ultimately be repatriated to their own country, with armed strength from

which their surrender has preserved them. . . . Politically it is vitally
important that our return to territories occupied for so long by Japanese
should take place in a manner most calculated to impress the inhabitants
with the security we are capable of providing. . . . [W]e should exert every
effort to be in a position to assume effective control as soon as possible
after a general surrender order becomes effective. But to assume control
means to accept responsibilities, and these must be planned for.[16]

At the same time that Dening was voicing his concerns to the
Foreign Office, Browning advised Mountbatten that if there was a
sudden Japanese surrender the allied commitment to ZIPPER
meant that until allied forces could arrive in strength in the various
territories the Japanese would be required to carry out certain
functions. They would have to maintain law and order, to protect
(but not man) vital installations and defence positions, and
administer the areas they occupied and be responsible for the
feeding and care of prisoners of war, internees, and the whole
civilian population. Not only was it vital that there should be no
interference with the preparations for ZIPPER, it was also important that whatever force was sent to occupy key targets such as
Singapore be a balanced one, capable of dealing with any situation,
'including treachery'. 'Finally', wrote Browning, 'it is our
considered opinion that no announcement whatsoever of capitulation should be made until theatre commanders are capable of
implementing plans simultaneous with the announcement.'[17]
Events outside SEAC's control, however, soon made it impossible to heed any of these warnings. Following the dropping of two
atomic bombs on Hiroshima and Nagasaki, the surrender of Japan
was announced on 14 August, the day that Mountbatten arrived
back in Kandy. As soon as the Supreme Commander's cable had
been received from Berlin, planning had begun to speed up the
occupation of key areas, especially Singapore. The 5th Indian
Division in Burma and the 3rd Commando Brigade in India, both
of which were scheduled to take part in later stages of ZIPPER,
were chosen to carry out the reoccupation of Singapore. Although
ZIPPER could not be abandoned, not least because it was thought
essential that a show of force be mounted in Malaya as soon as
practicable, this redeployment of two formations previously
earmarked for ZIPPER marked the first step in the reordering of
priorities within SEAC. Mountbatten and Wheeler appreciated
that a speedy response to the Japanese surrender was necessary, and

therefore planned to send a naval force accompanied by Royal Marines and several brigades of the 5th Division to occupy Penang as a staging post and then to move south to Singapore to open negotiations with the local Japanese commander which, if successful, would allow the occupation of the island to begin on 28 August.[18]

The priorities that Mountbatten laid down on the basis of his new directive from the Chiefs of Staff were first to seize strategic areas while simultaneously accepting the Japanese surrender in Burma, and later to retake the remaining areas within the enlarged boundaries of SEAC. Strategic areas, in order of priority, were Malaya, Saigon, Bangkok, Batavia and Surabaya, and Hong Kong. Detailed plans were drawn up for the deployment of units from the 12th and 14th Armies to occupy the most important points, and naval forces were already sailing for Penang to begin the landing of allied troops when MacArthur demanded an immediate halt to all activities against Japanese-held territory. His reason was that he feared that until a final surrender had been signed in Tokyo the allies risked creating a confusing and potentially dangerous situation if local commanders, at whatever level, attempted to negotiate with the Japanese. Compliance with the terms of the surrender could only be assured if unequivocal orders were sent to Japanese theatre commanders from Tokyo. Communications between Tokyo and field commanders were erratic at best, and MacArthur was anxious that sufficient time be given for the transmission of surrender orders to forces throughout Asia and the Pacific before the allies made any moves on a local or theatre basis to disarm the Japanese.

Mountbatten reacted strongly. On 20 August he protested bitterly to the Chiefs of Staff that MacArthur's unilateral ban placed in jeopardy those forces already sailing for Penang. They had been at sea for six days and if the order to suspend activities against Japanese forces in Malaya was to stand, they would have to return to Rangoon, thus risking troop casualties and vessel breakdowns. Since SEAC was decidedly short of manpower and shipping, MacArthur's order threatened to place an intolerable strain on SEAC's overstretched resources.[19] The following day Mountbatten gave further details of the effect on SEAC's operations of MacArthur's order. The surrender, he told the Chiefs of Staff, was now scheduled to be signed on 31 August, and it was

thought that a further six days would elapse before confirmed
surrender orders had reached all Japanese forces. SEAC's early
moves into Penang and Singapore would have to be postponed,
and ZIPPER, scheduled for 9 September, would become the first
operation that SEAC could mount, with allied forces not reaching
Singapore until about 11 September, almost two weeks after the
surrender ceremony in Tokyo Bay.[20]

Mountbatten's protests to London came to nought. MacArthur's
directive stood, and in the event the surrender was not signed until
2 September, the date which thus marked Mountbatten's formal
acceptance of the new boundaries of South East Asia Command.
The situation that Dening and Browning feared had become a
reality. SEAC's forces were well distant from the key areas when
the surrender came into effect, and there was little that Mountbatten and his commanders could do to enforce its terms if the
Japanese were unwilling to comply. The hiatus between the ceremony in Tokyo Bay and the return of allied forces in strength to
former colonial territories was critical in determining the atmosphere in which the allies would re-establish control. And the
contrast between the show of strength in Tokyo Bay and the dribble
of SEAC's forces into its key areas could hardly have been greater.
The limping return of the British, French and Dutch to Singapore,
Saigon and Batavia was far from the impressive, not to say
triumphant, entry that advisers such as Dening had thought
necessary. The manner of that return was to bring almost as many
problems as the debilitating military struggle that had made it
necessary.

Well before SEAC's forces reached Indochina and the East
Indies, there were signs that Mountbatten would face serious
problems whose solution was largely dependent on factors beyond
his control. The first of these arose out of the numbers of troops at
his disposal. Once the war against Germany was over, in fact even
before the final surrender, there were irresistible pressures to
demobilise troops in Europe who were no longer needed. Moreover
it had been agreed in 1944 that six weeks after the defeat of
Germany, British forces would begin to release a special priority
class, those most immediately invaluable in the immense task of
domestic post war reconstruction. At the same time it was decided
to give relief to those who had been serving in the extraordinarily
difficult conditions in Asia and the Pacific by reducing in stages the

period of service qualifying for repatriation from four years to three years. That was a decision in principle only, and could not be put into effect until May 1945, when the surrender of Germany enabled the War Office to make the first reduction to three years and eight months. Since by then southeast Asia was the only operational command, it benefited most from the relaxation in the terms of service.

Operation PYTHON, as the repatriation programme became known, had an immediate effect on SEAC. General Sir William Slim, C-in-C, Allied Land Forces, South East Asia (ALFSEA), advised Mountbatten that compliance with the terms of the new repatriation scheme would require the withdrawal of those men now due for release within the following several months, which led Mountbatten to inform the Chiefs of Staff that ZIPPER would have to be postponed until 9 September. No sooner had word of this delay been conveyed to London than the War Office made a further change in the PYTHON scheme. The Secretary of State for War, Sir James Grigg, was anxious to encourage support in Britain for the war against Japan and also to boost morale among the long-suffering troops in South East Asia Command. Undoubtedly he was also mindful of the forthcoming election, in which the service vote would play a significant role. He therefore told Mountbatten on 6 June that he intended to announce two days later in the House of Commons that the qualifying period for repatriation would be reduced by an additional four months. The overall effect on ZIPPER, he argued, would be small, and the War Office could always fall back on the 'operational clause' – i.e. that all undertakings were subject to operational requirements – if the new programme unduly hampered SEAC's activities.[21] Mountbatten was not convinced, and suggested to the Chiefs of Staff that this latest variation on the PYTHON programme might well have the very opposite effect on morale of what was intended. Furthermore, the repatriation of significant numbers of men without their replacement by fresh troops from Britain, would create a very difficult situation for SEAC:

Since morale is bound to be a delicate problem now that the war is over in Europe, I consider it would be disastrous if we made any extensive use of the operational clause or if the promise made by the Secretary of State were now to be qualified in any way. . . . I fear that we shall in any case be faced with a tricky morale situation as soon as it becomes apparent that the return of these men without relief has prolonged indefinitely the time the remainder may have to stay on without any operations to keep them occupied.[22]

Eventually a compromise was agreed upon whereby those men eligible for repatriation were withdrawn from forces earmarked for ZIPPER and concentrated in India, but were warned that the shipping situation made their speedy return to Britain unlikely. In one sense it was an unsatisfactory settlement, since although it removed eligible men from SEAC's control it merely transferred them to India Command, which had serious problems of its own.

A sizeable proportion of Mountbatten's land forces were from the Indian Army, and this proportion increased as the PYTHON programme intensified. Indian troops were no less anxious to return to their homes, and India Command was concerned that its own security needs would be sacrificed to the pressing requirement of SEAC to maintain sufficient forces for ZIPPER and the other operations planned in the event of a sudden Japanese surrender.[23] The political situation in India was volatile, as the anticipated end to the war against Japan raised expectations of political concessions from Britain. If in those circumstances, the Chief of the General Staff (India) warned, thousands of men released under the new PYTHON scheme were landed in India with no immediate prospect of movement back to Britain and with no organisation to care for them during their probable enforced stay of several months, a 'highly dangerous and possibly unmanageable state of affairs' might be created.[24] Lt General Sir Claude Auchinleck, C-in-C, India, not only stressed to Mountbatten that the maintenance of internal security was of overriding importance to India Command but added that the proposed operations to be undertaken in southeast Asia had striking political implications for India and for the troops that she supplied to SEAC. Although it was likely that he could persuade the Government of India to provide the troops that SEAC required, it was not a foregone conclusion,

as political questions, such as the future of the liberated regions, are involved, and certain important and vocal sections of Indian public opinion have strong views on the subject! . . . The whole political situation in this country is delicate in the extreme and likely to become even more so in the near future, and this, I think, makes it most important that we should be fully consulted before your staff launch out into any new projects or plans, if, as seems certain, we shall have to find the means to carry them out.[25]

Mountbatten was at pains to reassure Auchinleck that he fully appreciated the situation regarding the use of Indian troops in southeast Asia:

I fully see your point about the political difficulties which might arise about the future status of the liberated regions. As far as I am concerned, however, I do not think there is any need to be in any doubt about my policy. You know my views on the future of Burma from the many talks we have had, and I can assure you that I have equally progressive views . . . about the future of Malaya, which I intend to follow as long as I am in command in the Far East. I have been pressing the Colonial Office to put out some informed publicity about future policy, and if they will only do so I think it will be found not entirely contrary to the view of the important and vocal sections of Indian public opinion to which you refer.[26]

Mountbatten's answer understandably referred to the liberation of British territories through operation ZIPPER. These were areas in which the return of British control was largely uncontested and for which plans had long since been made. For those areas it was a question of marching back into familiar territory. In the other parts of southeast Asia it was quite a different matter. In the East Indies and Indochina, SEAC would be facilitating not a British return but a restoration of the Dutch and the French, and it was obvious, even if not fully appreciated, that this was a situation not faced before. British troops would be responsible for the installation of foreign governments whose acceptability (if not in local terms, legitimacy) was very much in question. The concerns about a return in force, raised a month earlier by Dening when referring to British territories, were doubly complicated when it was a question of non-British colonial possessions being reclaimed by British troops in the name of other masters. The delicacy of this problem escaped everyone at this stage.

In reality there were few options open to Mountbatten. The war against Japan had never enjoyed the popular support in Britain that had been the case with the war in Europe, and once Germany had surrendered domestic pressures to reduce the military effort in favour of postwar reconstruction made it politically difficult for the British government to urge an even greater involvement for purely British forces in such a distant theatre. It was even more difficult for the new Labour government, which took office in July 1945, to prolong military service in southeast Asia, especially when the atomic bombs brought the war to a precipitate end. To all intents

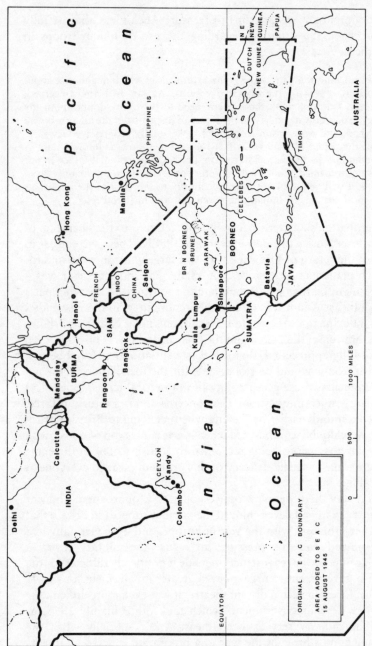

Fig. 1

and purposes, therefore, PYTHON was inviolate. The announcement by the Australian government of its intention to withdraw its troops forthwith from Borneo left Mountbatten with an even heavier burden than he had anticipated, for he had hoped to draw on Australian resources – military and material – to restore stability to an area that seemed inescapably of vital interest to Australia. It was, but that did not prevent the Australian government also from succumbing to demands to bring the troops home as soon as possible after the Japanese surrender. The American military effort had long since bypassed the area of SEAC's operations, and given the prevailing US attitude to the 'colonial' powers, there was little likelihood of any assistance from that quarter in the difficult post surrender situation. In Washington 'Jumbo' Wilson continued to hear criticism of Britain's military efforts in the Far East right up to the Japanese capitulation, on the grounds that British strategy against Japan had been directed to the recovery of colonial possessions rather than to the swiftest possible defeat of the enemy without a thought of postwar advantage.[27] It was, of course, by then a wearyingly familiar charge, but unlike similar accusations made over the conduct of the war against Germany and Italy, it was less well founded when applied to the war in Asia and the Pacific. Success in Burma would not only secure India and prevent the possible loss of the whole Middle East, but was esssential to the maintenance of India as a major supply base for the China theatre.

As long as SEAC remained an *allied* command, there were bound to be problems over the degree to which postwar considerations should influence military operations. To the British and their European allies, it was only proper that there should be a close connection, for whatever discussions there might be over the future of the colonial areas, there was no question but that political change could come only after the imperial powers had returned in force and re-established their control. That change would come was self-evident: what was much less clear was the extent to which the western powers could direct the nature and pace of that change. The British were anxious to associate the United States with themselves in that difficult post surrender period, for quite apart from their need to continue drawing on American military supplies, they did not wish to assume sole responsibility for the decisions that would eventually have to be made. It was a forlorn hope, perhaps, but they saw in a continuing joint control through the Combined

Chiefs of Staff a chance of muting American criticism of the 'imperialist' basis of British policy in southeast Asia.

For their part, the Americans were unwilling to be drawn into the difficult situation which they saw developing in southeast Asia. Early in 1944 the State Department rejected Mountbatten's request that US Civil Military Affairs officers be attached to SEAC on the grounds that their 'presence . . . would further increase the belief among the people of India and presumably throughout the Far East that our policy and that of the British in Asia are the same.' The attachment of such officers to US forces operating independently of British control was another matter, and it was possible that developments in Thailand and Indochina, in the northern parts of which Chinese forces were operating, might require the presence of American civil affairs staff.[28] But for the greater part of SEAC, the United States wanted to maintain – and to be seen to maintain – a role separate from that played by Britain and its imperialist European allies.

Once Japan had surrendered there was, in American eyes, no military reason for the United States to continue to involve itself actively in the affairs of SEAC, and every political reason for it to remain aloof from the post surrender mess that had suddenly been dumped in Mountbatten's lap. As long as SEAC remained a nominally inter-allied command, the United States could legitimately comment on developments there; and while SEAC continued to rely heavily on equipment originally supplied under Lend-Lease, the United States had the ability to bring pressure to bear on the handling by the European allies of the course of events there. The extent of its involvement, however, was for the United States alone to decide. This was power without responsibility. The last vestige of direct American involvement disappeared in October 1945 when the Joint Chiefs of Staff recommended that US participation in the activities of SEAC should cease and that US military staff assigned to Mountbatten's headquarters should be withdrawn immediately.[29] Henceforth SEAC was a joint allied responsibility in name only, at least insofar as the control of operations was concerned. Free from any direct responsibility for – or first-hand knowledge of – the complexities now confronting Mountbatten within the enlarged boundaries of SEAC, the United States nevertheless felt free to continue its criticisms of British policy, secure in the knowledge that it would not be required itself to practise what it was quite willing to preach to others.

With direct American assistance out of the question the British were forced to consider other offers for assistance that were pressed on them by their European allies who had a colonial stake in southeast Asia, France and the Netherlands. However, these offers, which in turn became requests and then demands, raised serious problems for SEAC, both military and political. Anxious as Britain was to relinquish control of non-British territories to the respective imperial powers, certain conditions had to be met before Britain's responsibility as the senior ally within SEAC could be considered to have been discharged. Mountbatten had two main tasks: to effect the surrender and disarmament of the Japanese troops within SEAC's newly-enlarged boundaries, and to locate and repatriate allied prisoners of war and internees. These duties could be fulfilled only after allied control had been imposed, but it was not at all clear that SEAC was in any position to do this in the short term. In March 1945 the Japanese had deposed the Vichy French government in Indochina and had begun to encourage Vietnamese groups to resist the return of the French; while in Java an Indonesian republic, openly supported by the Japanese, had been proclaimed on 15 August, the day of the Japanese acceptance of the terms of surrender and the day when Java formally became the responsibility of SEAC. This was an added complication for Mountbatten, since it was clear that in the absence in the immediate future of sizeable British troop deployments in the liberated territories it would be necessary to rely on the Japanese to administer prisoner camps and to control food supplies until SEAC's own forces could arrive. It soon became equally clear that the Japanese political initiatives in the final months of the war had markedly increased the hostility in some sections of the local populations to the impending return of French and Dutch control.

French and Dutch requests – later demands – to participate in the early stages of the allied re-entry into the areas of special concern to them posed a dilemma for the British. They were ready and willing to include their European allies in the sharing of the post surrender burdens, but they recognised the problems involved in that participation. First, neither the French nor the Dutch – especially the latter – had trained and equipped troops readily available. The troops they did have were based outside SEAC and would require special shipping to transport them to the theatre. Even if Britain had been willing to provide that shipping (and given the world-wide shortage

1 Mountbatten with (l) Air Chief Marshal Sir Keith Park and (r) Lt General Sir William Slim

that would have entailed a difficult choice of priorities), the decision was not hers alone to make. Allied shipping had been placed under the control of a shipping pool, of which the United States was a member. American approval was therefore necessary to divert a significant number of ships away from other duties to the transportation of French and Dutch troops to southeast Asia. Given the American attitude to the role of the imperial powers in their reclaimed colonies, it was by no means certain that the required shipping would be made available. Second, both the French and the Dutch relied heavily on US equipment, and – in the case of the Dutch – on US training facilities, and there had been many indications that the United States would raise strong objections to the use of American-supplied equipment to promote the return of the colonial powers. Third, once it was appreciated that political conditions in Indochina and the East Indies were such that SEAC's forces might well meet with active resistance from the local populations, it seemed imperative for British troops to make the initial entry in order to accept the Japanese surrender and locate the prison camps before French and Dutch troops confronted indigenous revolutionary forces.

With such huge areas and large numbers involved, it was essential that SEAC be able to operate in an atmosphere of law and order if the Japanese were to be disarmed and concentrated without incident and if succour was to be brought to the thousands of prisoners and internees who were known to be in desperate straits. But whose law and order was to be established? To that question there was no easy answer, as Mountbatten and SEAC soon found. In the process their involvement in the internal post surrender problems of Indochina and the Netherlands East Indies was to go far beyond what had originally been envisaged.

Chapter two
The allied re-entry to southern Indochina

Of all the areas for which SEAC was responsible in the postwar phase, Indochina potentially held the most difficulties for Mountbatten. Its continued status as a French colony was unclear, and was the subject of dispute between Britain and the United States.[1] The decision at the Potsdam conference to divide responsibility for the country between China and SEAC, which would carry out the essential post surrender tasks north and south of the 16th parallel respectively, was an additional complication. Unlike the situation in the NEI, allied agents – British, French and American – had penetrated Indochina during the war and were by and large well-informed on developments there. In purely military terms, Indochina was a major target for allied operations, for the headquarters of the Southern Japanese Army were at Saigon. It was feared that its commander, Field Marshal Count Terauchi, who controlled Japanese military forces throughout southeast Asia, might not obey the Emperor's orders to surrender and might do everything in his considerable power to frustrate the allies' hopes of a relatively smooth transition. The signal for that was the Japanese *coup* of 9 March 1945, which displaced the French Vichy government of Admiral Decoux. Two days later, with Japanese support, the Emperor Bao Dai proclaimed Vietnam's independence and thereby opened the way for indigenous political organisations to participate publicly in the struggle for power. By far the strongest of these organisations was the Viet Nam Doc-Lap Dong-Minh Hoi or Viet Minh, a broadly based alliance of several political groups dominated by the tightly controlled Communist Party led by Ho Chi Minh. When news came of the Japanese surrender the Viet Minh moved quickly: after a series of huge rallies in Hanoi and provincial centres, it forced Bao Dai to abdicate on 23 August and established a provisional government which within two days had taken over the three main cities of Vietnam, Hanoi, Hue and Saigon.

MacArthur's determination to accept a general Japanese surrender in Tokyo before any local or regional ceremonies could be held delayed the arrival of Mountbatten's forces in Saigon. That postponement enabled the Viet Minh to consolidate its position so that by 13 September, when a brigade of the 20th Indian Division began its fly-in to Saigon, the major points of control were already in Vietnamese hands. The British intention had been to limit their involvement to the takeover of Terauchi's headquarters and to the launching of the RAPWI programme. The French were to do the rest. But even before British forces landed in Saigon to establish the SACSEA Control Commission, it was obvious that such a restricted British role would be difficult to sustain in the absence of any sizeable number of French troops. The inability of the French to field significant forces in the critical weeks following the Japanese surrender arose in part from the deep divisions within the ranks of the allies over the postwar status of Indochina as well as from primarily military choices over the allocation of limited resources. But political considerations were paramount, to an extent that did not arise in any other theatre.

American policy towards Indochina was shaped by Roosevelt's intense dislike of French colonial policy. Although he distrusted the colonial powers in general, France was singled out for special opprobrium. Its poor performance in the early days of the war against Germany was compounded by the accommodation reached between the Vichy government in Indochina and the Japanese, which gave the Japanese bases and transit rights in Indochina without having to fight for them. (Roosevelt's stance, especially when he contrasted the moral basis of American policy with the opportunistic, self-interested outlook of other powers, sat uneasily with the fact that of all the states fighting against the Axis, only the United States had ever recognised the Vichy government in France, and had maintained an ambassador there until the American entry into the war in December 1941. That ambassador had been Admiral William D. Leahy, who later became Roosevelt's Chief of Staff and who fully shared the President's anti-French attitudes.) Roosevelt's determination to advance the cause of decolonisation increasingly centred on Indochina, where in American eyes the colonial record was least defensible and where the colonial power was least able to reassert its prewar authority. Although the United States had on a number of occasions in 1941 and 1942 expressly endorsed the return of Indochina to French control at the end of the war, there was no conviction underlying these statements, and once the landings in Vichy-controlled north Africa had succeeded, the American policy changed. By the time Charles de Gaulle emerged in mid 1943 as the leader of the Free French, against Henri Giraud, the American favourite, Roosevelt's opposition to French colonialism was implacable.

American hostility to the reimposition of French rule in Indochina was compounded by Roosevelt's distrust and dislike of de Gaulle whose imperious manner and obsession with France's position in the world provided the personal focus for the President's persistent opposition to French ambitions. The stronger that opposition became, the more de Gaulle identified with Britain, at least on the colonial question. British support for the French claim to Indochina in turn reflected their own concern for British colonial possessions in Asia. 'Our main reason for favouring the restoration of Indo-China to France', wrote one member of the Foreign Office in March 1945, 'is that we see danger to our own Far Eastern Colonies in President Roosevelt's idea that restoration depends upon the United Nations (or rather the United States) satisfying themselves that the French record in Indo-China justifies the restoration of French authority.'[2] British support also arose from London's anxiety to establish close links with a strong postwar France which would act as a western buffer to Germany. For both European and Asian interests, therefore, Churchill backed de Gaulle, though the relationship was never an easy one.[3] This unholy alliance merely confirmed Roosevelt's fears, as did constant French, and to a somewhat lesser extent British, pressure to make provision for the entry of French troops into the war against Japan. For Roosevelt, as for most American political and military figures, British military plans were always potentially tainted by political considerations, and especially by imperialist designs that had little to do with the primary goal of defeating Japan. In the case of France and its requests – and eventually demands – there could be no doubt. French aims were clear and undisguised, and a decision to allow French troops to participate in the war against Japan would, in American eyes, have been a tacit acceptance of those aims. This was especially so since it was to the United States that France looked for weapons with which to re-equip and rebuild its forces. Without American agreement to rearm the French, and in the absence of transport, the disposition of which by the Allied Shipping Pool required American approval, both the French and their British ally could do little to advance their postwar colonial aims.

Until early 1945 Roosevelt steadfastly refused to discuss the details of the postwar future of Indochina, insisting that it was a question to be settled after the surrender of Japan. He attempted to split the embryonic Anglo-French common front on southeast Asia in 1942 by having Indochina assigned to the China theatre, where the combination of the United States and China was certain to frustrate French ambitions. To counter American dominance and to provide a base for future British operations, Churchill called for the creation of South East Asia Command, from which, however, the United States excluded Siam and Indochina: those, especially the latter, were preserved for American and Chinese penetration. The choice of Mountbatten as Supreme Allied Commander in SEAC was initially welcomed by the Americans, who saw in his energy and youth some chance of reversing the sorry British record in Malaya, Singapore and Burma. But it did not take long before Mountbatten's appointment was dismissed as a public relations exercise. Stillwell spoke contemptuously of him as the 'glamour boy', and SEAC soon became known to some American critics as 'Save England's Asian Colonies.' Despite the exclusion of Indochina from SEAC, Mountbatten nevertheless arrived at an informal agreement with Chiang Kai-shek in October 1943 that allowed for the mounting of clandestine operations in Indochina from SEAC. Since this agreement was accepted by the American Joint Chiefs of Staff, Roosevelt's policy was undermined from the beginning.

The President's opposition to any discussion of the postwar status of Indochina was extended at the beginning of 1945 to include involvement in any military operations designed to push the Japanese out of Indochina.[4] However, he was already softening his position, because at the same time as he rejected an official endorsement of Mountbatten's activities in Indochina he was prepared to 'turn a blind eye' to them rather than precipitate a confrontation and force a decision on the broader issue. To Halifax, British ambassador in Washington, this was as satisfactory an outcome as could be expected at the time, and he recommended that Britain 'let sleeping dogs lie', but this was not acceptable either to the Foreign Office.[5] Sterndale Bennett protested that 'the war cannot stand still', and argued that the sort of 'blind eye' approach which Roosevelt was suggesting was open to such misinterpretation that it was 'highly unsatisfactory that we and the Americans should be fencing with each other in this way.'[6] At SEAC headquarters Dening was at first inclined to follow Halifax's advice and to push ahead with clandestine operations in Indochina in the hope that once confronted with a *fait accompli* Roosevelt would accept the situation and drop his opposition, but he soon changed his mind when Wedemeyer, who had left Mountbatten's staff in late 1944 to become commander of American forces in the China theatre, laid claim to the whole of Indochina and refused to recognise the informal agreement that Mountbatten had reached with Chiang Kai-shek.[7] The Chiefs of Staff, however, insisted that despite the pressing operational questions that had to be settled, Indochina was fundamentally a political matter that was entirely for the Foreign Office to resolve; yet they were opposed to pressure being brought to bear on the State Department to provide a clear statement on American policy towards the participation of French forces in the war against Japan.[8] The Permanent Under-Secretary at the Foreign Office, Sir Alexander Cadogan, agreed to the extent that until a decision had been reached on the political issues at stake, Indochina would continue to dog broader aspects of Anglo-American relations. Underlying the whole dispute, he added, was 'the President's sinister intentions with regards to Indo-China.'[9]

Even as Cadogan ascribed 'sinister' motives to Roosevelt's plans for the future of Indochina, the President's position was changing. Although at the Yalta conference he insisted that American ships could not be used to transport French troops to the war against Japan, the Japanese *coup* against the French Vichy regime on 9 March forced him to confront the issue squarely. Within ten days he had reversed his policy, ordered American air forces in China to assist the French resistance to Indochina if that could be done without interfering with the war against Japan, and accepted postwar French control of Indochina if the French agreed that independence was the ultimate goal of their colonial presence.[10] By early April Mountbatten and Wedemeyer had patched up their differences, and Wedemeyer had agreed not to oppose British and

French activities in Indochina if they contributed to the overall effort against Japan. When Churchill told Roosevelt that British operations in Indochina would go ahead and that Wedemeyer would simply be informed, the President did not demur.[11] A day later he was dead. American suspicions of French and British intentions continued under Truman, but the period of outright opposition to their involvement in Indochina was over, so that at the United Nations Conference in San Francisco in May, Secretary of State Edward Stettinius, Jr. could blithely assure the French representatives that 'the record is entirely innocent of any official statement of this government questioning, even by implication, French sovereignty over Indochina.'[12] The question then became one of timing, and the extent to which French participation required active American support.

French plans to mount operations in Indochina first crystallised in October 1943, when the preliminary steps were taken by the National Defence Committee to establish an expeditionary force for the Far East. Later named the Corps Expéditionnaire Français d'Extrême-Orient (CEFEO), it was originally designed to consist of two infantry brigades recruited in West Africa and Madagascar, supported by air and naval units, and to be ready for despatch to the Far East by late 1944. Two months later, in December 1943, the Corps Léger d'Intervention (CLI) was formed in Algeria. Made up of twelve hundred specialists in clandestine warfare, with the appropriate language skills for operations in Indochina, the CLI was intended to establish cadres from which expanded resistance could develop as opportunities arose. It was never used in its original role, because the United States steadfastly refused to reply to requests from France and Britain for agreement that the CLI should be moved out to the East. As long as Roosevelt was determined that Indochina should not return to French rule at the end of the war, there was no likelihood that permission would be given, or assistance provided for the transport of French forces in preparation for operations in Indochina. Britain was much more favourable towards the French desire to become involved in the war against Japan, and when in November 1944 the French National Committee sent General Roger Blaizot to establish a French Military Mission at SEAC headquarters in Kandy, he was welcomed by Mountbatten and accorded full status – at least in the eyes of the Supreme Commander and of the British government.

The United States, however, on Roosevelt's direct orders, refused to acknowledge the Mission, and withheld from French operatives any assistance from American sources.[13] Furthermore, Mountbatten's American Deputy Supreme Commander in SEAC, Lt. General Wheeler, told him that he could act only in accord with the directives issued to him by the Combined Chiefs of Staff, and since the Combined Chiefs had expressly stated that French troops were not to be despatched to the Far East, the Blaizot Mission could serve no useful purpose.[14]

It was not until May 1945, when American policy had changed to accept French participation in the war against Japan, that the CLI was moved from Algeria to Ceylon, where it arrived on 28 May. By then its usefulness as originally conceived was doubtful, and even before it left Algeria it had been renamed the 5th Régiment d'Infanterie Coloniale (RIC), a recognition of the fact that the time had almost passed when it could have been used to establish advance bases for subsequent operations in Indochina. (Dening remarked that the change of name was 'unfortunate', since it reinforced the American suspicion that the French anxiety to participate in the war against Japan was merely a pretext for restoring their empire. Part of the reason for the change, he added, was that 'no Britisher can pronounce the original title', but a more probable explanation was that since the force was to be stationed on Ceylon, with no immediate prospect of deployment in the field, it was likely to be confused with the Ceylon Light Infantry.[15]) With the end of the war in Europe, the French became more and more concerned that their troops should take part in the war in the Far East. It could, de Gaulle emphasised to Truman, have 'very important political, moral and military consequences.'[16] Rather than wait for an American proposal, the French tried to force a decision by making a firm offer. General Brosin de St. Didier, head of the French Military Mission in Washington, told Marshall at the end of May that the French government would place 'at the entire disposal' of the United States an army corps of two divisions, together with supporting troops and service units. The two divisions put forward were the 9th Division d'Infanterie Coloniale (DIC) and the 1st DIC. The 9th DIC under General Valluy had distinguished itself in the European theatre, where it had fought from 1 August 1944 until the German surrender, and it could be shipped out to the Far East by the end of June. The 1st DIC, however, had only recently been raised, but the French proposed to replace its coloured troops with white, battle-trained volunteers from the First French Army, and were confident that if it received its equipment by the end of July, it could follow the 9th DIC within a month.[17] De Gaulle maintained the pressure on the United States by naming General Jacques-Philippe Leclerc as Commander of French Forces in the Far East, heeding the suggestion of his chief adviser on Indochina that the appointment had to go to a man whose authority and standing would not be challenged.[18]

Such concrete proposals invited comment, and expressions of doubt were soon voiced. Marshall thought that the timings St. Didier had provided were far too optimistic, and that it would be 'several months' after the French timetable before the two divisions could be equipped and transported to the Far East.[19] Eisenhower urged Marshall to insist on all French troops in the Far East being white, and suggested that the 3rd Algerian Division be substituted for the 1st DIC, since the former had already experienced combat as a division and would require minimum retraining.[20] St. Didier was able to assure the Americans that the expeditionary force of some 62,000 men would be all white,[21] but the question of how the French troops were to be equipped was more difficult to settle. The CLI had been equipped by the British, but the larger forces required for the CEFEO were beyond British capabilities, and it would fall to the Americans to provide the necessary weapons and supplies. At the very time that the French raised the problem of equipment, however, Truman had tightened the criteria by which Lend-Lease material could be made available, and by restricting it to 'that which is to be used in the war against Japan, and . . . not . . . for any other purpose' had thrown up possibly insurmountable obstacles in the path of French participation. The policy was 'so sweeping and inflexible', wrote General Hull, the Assistant Chief of Staff, 'that it is questionable it should be communicated informally.'[22]

Leclerc's appointment as Commander of French Forces in the Far East attracted considerable criticism. Hero of the liberation of Paris and Strasbourg, Leclerc's leadership of the famous Deuxième Blindée (the 2nd Armoured Division) bordered on the legendary. But professional assessments of Leclerc lagged somewhat behind his popular reputation. In some French military circles, that is in the camps of his rivals, he was regarded as 'the spoiled child of De Gaulle,' and one French officer, the chief of staff to General Jean de

Lattre de Tassigny, Commander of the First French Army, observed sourly that even in Leclerc's most famous actions, 'it was the Americans who had opened the way for him'.[23] Eisenhower opposed Leclerc's appointment on several grounds:

During the past year he has indicated that his temperament is not that required for a top flight commander. He has avoided serving under the First French Army [i.e. under de Lattre de Tassigny], has insisted on being independent of French Commanders, and has fought well only when the spirit moved him.[24]

These criticisms were noted in Washington, where it was also observed that Leclerc was 'a fighting general rather than a political one',[25] and approaches were made to the French to appoint a more experienced commander, but to no avail.

Truman's delineation of the restrictions on the use of Lend-Lease materiel on 5 July did not rule out the possibility of French participation in the war against Japan, and the French pressed all the more vigorously for a firm decision since it was clear that one way or another operations in the Far East were entering their final phase. As long as the war continued, the French could make a military case for being included: once hostilities had been concluded, their future was much less certain. On 19 July, the Combined Chiefs of Staff responded to the long-standing French request which, it should be remembered, had been supported by the British since late 1944. They agreed in principle to accept the French offer of a corps subject to four conditions: that the corps would serve in a theatre to be determined under either British or American command; that the corps would not be deployed until basic questions of transport, equipment, and reinforcements had been settled; that calls on Lend-Lease would be minimised by making the greatest possible use of equipment supplied under the North African and Metropolitan programmes (i.e schemes designed to equip French forces for action in European and North African theatres); and that because of shipping priorities, it would not be possible to deploy the corps before the spring of 1946.[26]

Pleased as they were by the agreement in principle, the French could take little satisfaction from the conditions imposed by the Combined Chiefs. St. Didier pointed out that much of the equipment available under the Metropolitan and North African Programmes had been worn out in the campaigns leading to the defeat of Germany, and replacements had been cut off by Truman's decision on 8 May to suspend Lend-Lease for the European theatre.[27] Even more important, the Combined Chiefs' decision to postpone the arrival of the French corps in the Far East until early 1946 threatened to deprive the French of the ability to be on the ground at the most important stages of the war – the final operations against Japan and the immediate post surrender period. Appeals to the British were sympathetically received, but as Cadogan pointed out to the French ambassador, René Massigli, the decision was not one for Britain alone to make, and the French were urged to continue to press Washington.[28] They found little sympathy there, however. Already at the Potsdam conference it had been decided, following an American initiative, to divide Indochina into two operational spheres, one a British and the other a Chinese responsibility. Transport remained under the control of the Allied Shipping Pool, on which the United States was unlikely to change its previous endorsement of the Combined Chiefs' warning that a French corps could not be moved to the Far East before the spring of 1946. At the highest levels there was growing resistance to French claims, and a determination not to be pushed into any earlier commitment on Indochina. De Gaulle, Truman remarked testily in August, 'took himself and his ideas of French prestige altogether too seriously, and "to use a saying that we have away back in Missouri", he was something of a pinhead.'[29] The imminent collapse of Japan following the atomic attacks pushed the question of a French expeditionary force even further down the American list of priorities, and the French themselves realised that with the end of the war, different priorities would prevail. When news of the atomic bombs came through, one of Leclerc's staff wrote of a sense of unease: 'has the C.E.F.E.O. ceased to exist?' he asked.[30] The answer was not immediately clear, although Leclerc's appointment several days later as Commander of French Forces in the Far East indicated that American assistance or not, de Gaulle was not about to be deflected from his goals in Indochina. The American position meant that in the short term at least the burden would fall on Mountbatten and SEAC.

The extent of French reliance on British resources quickly became apparent. Mountbatten was told on 17 August that the French proposed to 'make available' the Madagascar Brigade, the 3rd and 9th DICs, and some 1500 non-Divisional troops, but in a practical sense the offer was little more than a paper commitment. Of the 7000 men of the Madagascar Brigade, only 2300 were Europeans: while ready to embark within fourteen days, they were fit only for occupation duties and were supplied with British equipment. The 9th DIC, 17,000 strong (all white), had American equipment, could be used in an occupation role, and could embark by mid-September. The 20,000 Europeans of the 3rd DIC had no equipment and could not leave for the Far East before mid-October; while the non-Divisional troops, also without equipment, would not be ready to embark until mid-November. The only French troops relatively close at hand were the 5th RIC in Ceylon, but with a strength of 979 (plus 17 vehicles) it could not provide a major contribution for the immediate tasks.[31] Within days of having arrived at SEAC headquarters at Kandy on 22 August, and having been briefed by his own Intelligence Branch at Calcutta (the 'Direction Générale des Etudes et Recherches', which had replaced the old Deuxième Bureau), Leclerc was convinced that the only way to restore French sovereignty in Indochina was to use a major military force. The difficulty, he advised Vice-Admiral Thierry d'Argenlieu, whose appointment as French High Commissioner had been made at the same time as Leclerc's, was that Britain's desire to assist the French, especially against the Chinese in the north (who if unchecked could pose a serious threat to Burma), was balanced by its anxiety not to disturb its relations with the United States in particular.[32] So delicate was the balance the British were trying to maintain that only moments before Leclerc was due to broadcast to Indochina over SEAC Radio, Mountbatten asked for a sentence to be added so as not to encroach on allied sensitivities. Leclerc was furious, and his staff questioned whether Mountbatten was quite as frank as he had first appeared. The French understood the problem well enough – 'The war is over for the allies, but not for us' – but in the short term could do little about it other than insist, as did Leclerc, that British forces would have to bear the entire burden of maintaining order in the southern half of Indochina until sufficient French forces arrived.[33] It was not that they were content to accept this situation: de Gaulle ordered that other units be stripped of materiel to supply equipment for the 9th DIC so that delays in moving it to the Far East would be minimised, and pressure was put on the United States to agree to provide the necessary transport from the Allied Shipping Pool, but nothing could alter the fact that at the time of the Japanese surrender, there were virtually no French troops available to re-enter Indochina.[34]

Despite the fact that Saigon had been made Mountbatten's first priority by the Chiefs of Staff, it was not until 8 September that a small British advanced party of medical and engineering reconnaissance detachments, together with No. 3 RAPWI Control Staff, flew into Saigon. Two weeks previously, on 24 August, the newly-appointed French Commissioner for Cochinchina, Jean Cédile, had been parachuted into southern Indochina on the direct orders of de Gaulle, who was anxious to have French representatives there to keep a special watch on French interests. Within hours, Cédile and his team of some 25 men were captured by Japanese troops and taken to Saigon. There, on 1 September, he escaped, installed himself in the Governor-General's palace, and persuaded the Japanese to retain their guards until the arrival of allied forces. He was therefore on the spot when the massive riots against the French broke out on 2 September, but was unable to pass on any information to SEAC headquarters because he had destroyed all his coding instructions just before being taken prisoner.[35] It was not an auspicious beginning to the return of French rule, but at least the French were in Saigon, well in advance of any SEAC presence. Mountbatten's plans to establish the Control Commission in Saigon at an early stage were hampered by MacArthur's prohibition on local surrenders before the Tokyo Bay ceremony and by transport difficulties. Although the Chiefs of Staff backed MacArthur's decision and overruled Mountbatten's protest, he went ahead with making preliminary contact with Terauchi's headquarters so that once the formal surrender had been signed, he could move his forces with minimal delay. On 27 August, his staff met with Terauchi's spokesmen in Rangoon, as a result of which it became apparent that the worst fears held by SEAC – that the Southern Army would disobey the Imperial order to surrender and fight on – would not be realised, even though there was still the possibility, soon to be confirmed, that local commanders might assist those indigenous groups opposing the return of western rule. Even with this early start, the main forces of the Control Commission were not ready to fly to Saigon until 13 September.

The redrafted directive which the Chiefs of Staff issued to Mountbatten in mid-August had laid down that SEAC should 'not occupy more of French Indo-China than is necessary to ensure the control of the headquarters of the Japanese Southern Armies.'

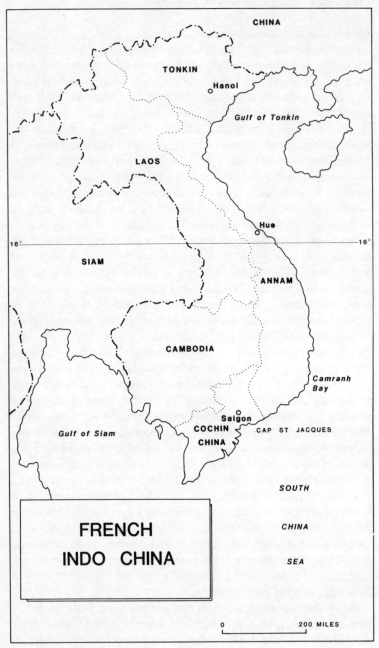

Fig. 2

When Mountbatten appointed Major General Douglas D. Gracey of the 20th Indian Division, whose troops were to form the major part of the allied occupation force to head the Control Commission, it was in the expectation that Gracey would restrict his activities in accordance with the directive of the Chiefs of Staff. Communication difficulties between SEAC's negotiating team in Rangoon, Terauchi's headquarters, and Tokyo, as well as a lack of suitable transport, forced Gracey to establish the Control Commission in Rangoon before it could be moved to Saigon. There was thus a three-way communication network dealing with the situation in Saigon, its effectiveness severely hampered by erratic and unreliable transmission and its difficulties exacerbated by the withdrawal of the small US team that had been designated to provide signals support for the Commission. Lacking his own agents on the ground, Gracey had little choice but to rely in large measure on the reports that trickled in from French and American observers (the former channelled through the DGER's Service des Renseignements in Calcutta), supplemented by press reports emanating from Hanoi and by political appreciations sent from Kandy. Gracey also served as the commander of Allied Land Forces French Indo China (ALFFIC). As head of the Control Commission, he was directly responsible to Mountbatten; as C-in-C, ALFFIC he answered to Slim. The Chiefs of Staff directive, issued through Mountbatten, had defined his role very narrowly, but Slim had given him much wider terms of reference. It was a recipe for multiplying the confusion that already existed.

Even before Gracey arrived in Saigon, he was considering a somewhat wider role than had originally been envisaged for him. Following the riots of 2 September, with their attacks on French personnel and property, he demanded that Terauchi obey the terms of the Rangoon agreement, under which Terauchi accepted responsibility for maintaining law and order until the arrival of allied troops.[36] When the Japanese compliance proved less than total, Gracey was forced to weigh up the alternatives. The French officers who discussed the situation with him came away with completely different impressions of his intentions. Lt Colonel Rivier of the 5th RIC, which was due to follow Gracey into Saigon, reported to Leclerc that he was in daily contact with Gracey, with whom he was working 'in perfect accord'. Gracey, he noted, 'strongly believes that we ought – vis-à-vis the Indochinese – to avoid all action that could – from the political point of view – be exploited against us by the anti-French elements or whoever'.[37] On the other hand, Lt Colonel Martin, head of the French mission to the Control Commission, told Leclerc that not only was Gracey well disposed towards French interests, but that he 'envisages a forceful military action to establish order in the whole of the southern zone.'[38] Whatever Gracey intended – and at that stage it was unlikely that he had any firm plans in mind other than to fulfil the terms of his directive as best he could with limited forces – there was little doubt in French circles as to the best policy. At the Tokyo Bay surrender ceremony, Leclerc, the 'fighting soldier', had been struck by MacArthur's advice to 'bring in troops, troops and more troops', and the contrast between the overwhelming display of American military power and the lack of resources that Britain had available in the Far East convinced him that pressure had to be kept on the British on two levels: in London to persuade them to provide early shipping for French military forces, and locally to act in French interests until the French were able to take over from Gracey.[39]

The main fly-in of allied troops to Saigon began on 11 September. Two days later Gracey arrived, accompanied by his staff, but the whole of 80th Brigade was not fully established in Saigon until 26 September. As important as this deficiency was, even more critical was the lack of any political adviser to Gracey who, on the basis of inadequate and conflicting reports and in the absence of any political briefing from SEAC, had to manage as best he could for ten days before his political adviser arrived. Gracey's most pressing task seemed to be to enforce Terauchi's adherence to the surrender terms and to begin disarming and concentrating the 70,000 Japanese soldiers in the vicinity of Saigon. The fragility of the local situation was vividly demonstrated by the scene at the airport at Saigon when Gracey landed. The field was ringed by armed Japanese, and the only transport available for the allied troops was Japanese using Japanese drivers. At the airport Gracey had ignored the waiting Viet Minh delegation, both because his first concern was to conclude the war against Japan and because his orders had spelled out that only French authority was to be recognised. In any case, an early interview with Cédile had not suggested that the situation was out of control. Cédile described the 2 September riot as only 'moderately serious', and while attacks

on property were increasing in the absence of any effective maintenance of law and order by the Viet Minh government, Japanese
troops retained a semblance of authority. As the incidence of
violence and atrocities grew, however, Gracey concluded that a
firm response was necessary, for even though he thought the
situation was 'not serious' he nevertheless considered the
provisional government a 'direct threat' to law and order.[40]

On 19 September, he sent his Chief of Staff on the Control
Commission, Brigadier Maunsell, to hand to the provisional government a copy of a proclamation that he intended to publish and
enforce two days later. He announced his intention to close all
newspapers, and ordered the provisional government to stop
seizing buildings or other property and to supply a list of all
Vietnamese police and armed units, together with details of their
arms and locations. The proclamation imposed a ban on all
demonstrations, processions and public meetings, prohibited the
carrying of weapons of any kind, and warned of stricter enforcement of the night time curfew in Saigon and Cholon. The Viet
Minh's immediate response was to call a general strike, but Gracey
was not unduly concerned, convinced as he was that once the
proclamation was in effect and the intimidation of ordinary
workers had been curbed, labour would return. The provisional
government's formal answer pledged its compliance with the terms
of the proclamation and asked that the restrictions on newspapers
be lifted, which Gracey agreed to consider since 'your prompt
obedience to my orders . . . has shown me that wise counsels have
prevailed.'

His authority, Gracey emphasised, came from Mountbatten,
who had delegated to him 'the command of all British, French and
Japanese forces and all police forces and armed bodies in French
Indo-China South of 16° latitude with orders to ensure law and
order in this area.' Gracey was at pains to rebut any possible
charges that he had exceeded the terms of his mission and he
explained to Mountbatten that 'I would stress that although it may
appear that I have interfered in the politics of the country I have
done so only in the interests of the maintenance of law and order
and after close collaboration with the senior French representatives.'[41] The original directive issued to Gracey by ALFSEA on 28
August had instructed him to 'secure the Saigon area', disarm the
Japanese and rescue allied prisoners of war and internees, 'maintain

law and order and ensure internal security', and 'liberate Allied territory in so far as your resources permit.'[42] Clearly on that basis he was acting perfectly properly in issuing his proclamation in Saigon and in referring to his authority in the whole of southern Indochina. However, just before Gracey left Rangoon on his way to Saigon, his directive was changed. The Chief Civil Affairs Staff Officer at SEAC headquarters, Brigadier E. Gibbons, objected that Gracey's directive was far too sweeping, and urged that his area of responsibility be much more narrowly defined.[43] Dening shared his concern, and his warning that 'we shall have to be very careful about the extent to which we commit ourselves for the maintenance of law and order' was circulated to the Cabinet, as was his advice that 'we should avoid at all costs laying ourselves open to the accusation that we are assisting the West to suppress the East.'[44] Mountbatten thereupon ordered Slim to change Gracey's directive so that he was no longer responsible for holding the whole of Saigon, as the original directive had implied, but only those 'key areas' that were necessary for the control of the Southern Army's headquarters and the disarming of all Japanese, and any other areas vital to the rescue of APWI.[45] This was a much narrower prescription, but there is some doubt as to whether it had reached Gracey's headquarters before he took the decision to issue his proclamation. If it did not, Gracey had no choice but to act according to the only directive he had received and in light of his own on-the-spot appreciation of the situation.

On the day that Gracey's proclamation was delivered to the provisional government Slim had been at the Control Commission. He subsequently told Leclerc in Kandy that the situation in Saigon was good. There were sound relations between the British and the French authorities, and the occupation of territory was proceeding steadily. Most of the fighting that was occurring was between the Vietnamese, as rival factions battled for supremacy, while for the allies there was every hope of recovering the country without bloodshed. The only 'black spot' that Slim detected was the vehemently anti-Vietnamese attitude of the local French population, which he believed had to be calmed so as not to inflame the situation further. Overall, however, it was a reassuring picture that Slim provided, and on its basis he advised Leclerc that he wanted to withdraw the 20th Indian Division as soon as possible, the implication being that given the relatively stable conditions in Saigon that could be effected in the near future. In the meantime, as long as British troops comprised the major part of allied forces in southern Indochina, i.e. until the arrival of the 9th DIC, Gracey should retain command. Slim recommended that Leclerc should take over when the 9th DIC was in place, and Leclerc agreed, but reserved the right to refuse if the political situation deteriorated.[46] Slim's additional recommendation that d'Argenlieu should not go to Indochina until he had firm proposals from the French government to discuss with the Vietnamese was passed over, for Leclerc had already advised d'Argenlieu not to spell out any offers on the grounds that whatever was mooted was immediately used against the French to extract even more concessions.[47]

Reassured by Slim's appreciation of the situation in Saigon, and by his endorsement of Gracey's actions, Mountbatten decided to defer to Gracey's judgement and to back him, even though the proclamation's assertion that Gracey was responsible for the whole of southern Indochina was contrary to his directive as amended (but apparently not received) on 12 September.[48] Mountbatten told the Chiefs of Staff that Gracey had 'acted with courage and determination in an extremely difficult situation together with, as yet, inadequate forces'. Since he judged it 'dangerous' to revoke the proclamation, there seemed to be two ways in which it could be reinforced. The first option (Course A) entailed implementing the proclamation and retaining the responsibility for civil and military administration throughout the whole of southern Indochina until Leclerc was able to take over command. The alternative (Course B) was to limit British responsibility to control of the Japanese Southern Army headquarters in Saigon, and turn all other areas over to the French. That was Mountbatten's recommendation, for it restricted British involvement to a clearly defined task whereas Course A would require a full Indian division to be used in a law and order role pending the arrival of sufficient French troops, which Leclerc stated would not be before the 9th DIC landed in Indochina in early November. In the meantime, Leclerc indicated that he would be willing to deploy his own troops in areas outside Saigon, even though they would remain under SEAC control, but this, Mountbatten emphasised, was not consistent with his own responsibility as Supreme Commander. If southern Indochina was to be part of SEAC, he had to retain operational control of all troops, just as he had to be responsible for the maintenance of law and order: if those responsibilities could not be accepted, his theatre boundaries should be redrawn to exclude Indochina and the French handed all the tasks with which the British were currently saddled. The choice was a stark one, as Mountbatten realised when he asked the Chiefs of Staff for a 'policy ruling' on which alternative was to be adopted.[49]

Gracey's proclamation was not alone in precipitating a review of the situation in southern Indochina. As soon as Leclerc arrived in Kandy in late August he had pressed Mountbatten to accelerate the movement of the two European divisions, especially the 9th DIC, to the Far East. He was anxious to avoid using the black troops of the Madagascar Brigade, since in circumstances in which 'the yellow races have lost faith in their [white] protectors who did not protect them', French prestige could only be restored by using European forces.[50] Cédile also asked for black troops to be kept out of Saigon, and there was some consternation in French circles when it was found that the British would be represented by an Indian division, although their concern seems to have been assuaged when it was discovered that Gurkhas made up a significant proportion.[51] Leclerc was disturbed by the news that much of the British shipping which he had hoped would be made available to move French forces was earmarked for the repatriation of Indian troops out of the Mediterranean theatre, and following his complaints to Paris, the French government instructed its ambassadors in London and Washington to protest on the grounds that given the lack of French shipping in the Far East, France's ability to reoccupy Indochina with French forces rested entirely on the transport assistance provided by the Allied Shipping Pool.[52]

It apppears that Mountbatten subsequently told Leclerc that he would press the British government to give priority to the movement of the 9th DIC in particular, but did nothing, which became apparent when Massigli and others in the French embassy in London tried to follow up on the promised initiative. Leclerc's reaction on hearing this was predictable: all the resentments and humiliations that he felt were poured out in an angry letter to Mountbatten. Some of his charges had nothing to do with SEAC – 'certain people wanted to throw us out of north Indochina', a reference to Chinese and American activities – but the thrust of his protest was that Mountbatten had to realise that in Indochina, unlike other countries for which SEAC was also responsible

(Burma, for example), time was of the essence. A month would make all the difference to the French attempts to regain Indochina, whereas it was less important for Mountbatten's other tasks, which should not be used as a pretext for failing to act on the major issue. 'I can assure you that if I fail in the task which has been entrusted to me of returning Indochina to France the whole French people will know the reasons.'[53] Leclerc's staff tried to soften the final accusation by translating it 'the entire French people will wish to know the reasons', but the true meaning was quickly brought to Mountbatten's attention. His Assistant Chief of Staff, Major General B.C.H. Kimmins, outlined everything that had been done to assist the French, and Browning told Mountbatten that Kimmin's 'somewhat hostile' tone reflected his staff's anger that 'they were being criticised for inaction, while actually they have worked incredibly long hours, especially on behalf of the French. . . .' Browning advised Mountbatten to make 'three things . . . absolutely clear' to Leclerc: that during the whole period in which French forces operated within SEAC he was under Mountbatten's command; that the shipping problem was complex; and third, that 'Gen. Leclerc (who after all was only a Divisional Commander a very short time ago) be made to appreciate the need for diplomatic finesse as a Commander within a theatre comprising a Supreme Headquarters [and] Allied Commanders-in-Chiefs of all three services, and the need for delicacy of inter-allied-theatre relations, which include both political and military considerations of extreme complexity.'[54]

Fortunately perhaps, Mountbatten chose not to follow Browning's advice but to ignore the insinuations in Leclerc's letter. In one sense he had little choice, for however much he and his staff might have felt aggrieved over the apparent lack of appreciation of their efforts, the fact remained, as Kimmins admitted, that the promised telegram urging an acceleration of the movement of the 9th DIC had not been sent until Leclerc made his protest.[55] At a meeting with Leclerc, Mountbatten undertook to send another telegram to the War Office on the subject of the 9th DIC, to arrange for French troops to be parachuted into Laos to guard a number of French internees (Wedemeyer had refused to allow French planes to take off from the China theatre for this purpose), and to ask Wedemeyer to close down Radio Hanoi, which the French argued was inciting revolution throughout Indochina. It was, Leclerc's staff recorded, a 'cordial' interview, and several days later, after a meeting with Slim and Kimmins, Leclerc came away satisfied that the problem of the 9th DIC was in hand. That evening – 'ambiance sympathique' – Leclerc entertained Mountbatten at dinner ('Mountbatten a apprécié particuliérement la salade et le champagne'), and their differences seemed to have been smoothed over, even if privately Leclerc thought that 'Mountbatten, a sailor, only knows a little about land forces and does not dare to take decisions without his staff.'[56]

This episode represented much more than a clash of personalities or demonstrations of pique on either side. Together with Gracey's proclamation it brought to a head the question of the British involvement in southern Indochina, especially in the critical period before French forces arrived in strength. Dening warned the Foreign Office that

a situation is arising which is even more serious than I had contemplated since objection is being taken at the very outset to the presence of British troops as supporting French imperialism. . . . we cannot escape from our duty which is to liquidate the Japanese headquarters at Saigon and the Japanese forces in Indo-China south of 16° parallel and to evacuate allied prisoners of war and internees. That object can only be attained if law and order are maintained in the areas occupied by British forces.

One way of limiting Britain's role was to issue a public statement detailing 'what our sole object is and that when it is accomplished our forces will be withdrawn.' 'By making such a statement', he concluded, 'we shall have put ourselves in the right.'[57] The problem was far more complex than that, however. It was difficult to distinguish between maintaining law and order so that the primary tasks could be accomplished, and maintaining law and order pending the arrival of French troops. The first was a proper function of the British commander, while the second, which would inevitably entail suppressing political demonstrations, could hardly be other than an expression of support for French imperialism. Certainly, the Foreign Secretary, Ernest Bevin, was happy to give that support, at least in private: he told the Chinese Foreign Minister in London that Britain 'naturally assumed that Indo-China would return to France', and noted afterwards that he 'got the impression that . . . [the Foreign Minister] would have welcomed a less unequivocal assertion of our support of French rights in regard to Indo-China.'[58] Others, however, were less sure of Britain's position. Dening reported without comment a broadcast on Radio Saigon which claimed that Slim, then visiting Saigon, had said that the British would not intervene in the 'internal quarrels' of Indochina,[59] and Mountbatten's reprimand of Gracey had been on the basis that Gracey had taken it upon himself to set his proclamation on law and order matters in the context of his authority over the whole of southern Indochina. Further, Mountbatten urged the Chiefs of Staff not to build up British forces in Indochina beyond the minimum necessary to disarm the Japanese, 'for the stronger we are the more the French will feel they can take provocative action against Annamites relying ultimately on the presence of powerful British forces. . . .'[60]

On the other hand, the French had never been in any doubt that Indochina would have to be retaken by military means. Although Rivier told Leclerc in mid-September that his goal was to maintain law and order without bloodshed, he nevertheless stressed that he would if necessary achieve it 'at any price', and even before Gracey's troops began to arrive in Saigon, the French were thinking in terms of a military campaign rather than a simple reoccupation, which made Gracey's apparent willingness, as one report expressed it, 'to do everything in his power to reinstall French sovereignty in Indochina quickly' all the more reassuring.[61] Within days of his arrival in Saigon, Gracey had confirmed the French hopes in him: 'I can only admire the wisdom of his decisions and the energy with which he executes them', wrote Rivier. 'He is rendering us services whose importance will only be properly appreciated later, in the fullness of time.'[62] Further evidence of Gracey's apparent good will towards the French cause came in the third week in September, before the Chiefs of Staff were able to respond to Mountbatten's request for a policy ruling.

Gracey's proclamation heralded an attempt to clamp down on the outbreaks of violence that had become common in Saigon. Despite the terms of the surrender, the Japanese forces did little to maintain order, while the claims of the provisional government to control Saigon and much of southern Indochina seemed ludicrous to Gracey and his staff. When the proclamation was put into effect on 21 September British Indian troops began disarming Viet Minh police and repossessing public buildings such as the Treasury, the Posts and Telegraph centre, and goals and police stations occupied by Viet Minh officials. Gracey had already decided to extend his control, and in consultation with Cédile and Rivier made detailed plans for a complete takeover in Saigon. The small numbers of the 5th RIC in Saigon were supplemented by rearmed (and only recently released) members of the 11th RIC and French civilians, and in the early hours of 23 September the British/French *coup* began. By midday the major public administrative buildings were in French hands, and the tricolour flew over the Hôtel de Ville. The Viet Minh guards and officials were taken completely by surprise, and the whole operation was carried out with virtually no casualties on either side. It was a deceptively easy victory. Gracey had reinstalled the French, the excesses of whose troops in the following days ensured that the inevitable Viet Minh reaction would be all the stronger. Far from minimising British involvement, Gracey had tied it inextricably to French attempts to reassert their sovereignty, and had precipitated the very situation that Mountbatten had sought to avoid.[63]

Chapter three

Consolidation and expansion in southern Indochina

The *coup* of 23 September was carried out with almost no loss of life and with very few casualties, and to that extent it justified Gracey's belief that a short, well planned military operation would restore the main administrative and service centres to French control at minimal cost. Gracey's hope and the French belief that a demonstration of French purpose would shatter the provisional government, cow the criminal elements that Leclerc and others thought were at the foot of the unrest, and rally the great mass of Vietnamese behind stable French rule might have had some chance of success – at least in the short term – had it not been for the conduct of French troops and civilians in the days following the *coup*. Gracey's inability to control the French made his earlier claim that British forces were not in Indochina to intervene in internal political affairs but were there to maintain law and order while discharging the responsibilities laid down by the Chiefs of Staff doubly suspect: not only was order not maintained by allied forces, but it was flagrantly broken by French troops who were ultimately under British command. The gains of 23 September were shortlived, and far from giving the French a foothold from which they could expand their area of control so that the British involvement could be correspondingly curtailed, Gracey's decision provoked a violent response and tied British forces – and British policy and prestige – much more closely to French actions than had ever been thought desirable or even likely.

In explaining his actions to Mountbatten, Gracey argued that from 16 September he had begun to disarm the Vietnamese police force and armed units using only British troops, but the task was too great for the limited numbers at his disposal. He was therefore obliged to employ such French forces as were available. If he had any doubts about the reliability of the French troops, they were apparently dispelled after Rivier had assured him that they were 'hand-picked, well disciplined, efficiently officered units' who were sufficiently well-trained to be able to disarm the Vietnamese guards and take over the control of the chosen public buildings.[1] Gracey seems to have been eager to be convinced on this point, because already he had evidence to the contrary. At the time of the proclamation he had proposed to ALFSEA that a British command and base be established at Camranh Bay, but was advised to use French forces working with the local Japanese on the grounds that the British government's policy was 'to restrict the use of British troops to the absolute minimum'. Gracey replied that 'after seeing the emotional behaviour of French troops during September and their unnecessarily provocative and undisciplined attitude' their deployment at Camranh Bay 'would provoke unrest and possibly bloodshed.' The 5th RIC, he added, who were reputed to be trained troops, in fact had little training and no experience, and were ill equipped to handle the 'tricky situation' they would encounter.[2] Even more dubious was the 11th RIC, only recently released from Japanese imprisonment, deficient in training, and determined to reassert French power and prestige after the humiliation of the Japanese March *coup*. These troops, together with the several score of French civilians Gracey had armed, were hardly likely to demonstrate restraint or 'be good enough to avoid strife', which had been his reason for arguing against the use of French forces at Camranh Bay.

It was not therefore surprising that following the successful takeover of public buildings by British troops, trouble broke out when French forces, military and civilian, moved in. Gracey reported to Mountbatten on the 'indiscipline of French troops and provocative acts of French civilians' that inevitably led to Vietnamese counter-actions.[3] Cédile gave many more details to Leclerc. The soldiers of the 11th RIC had fired into empty buildings in a show of strength to impress the crowds of women and children. They began making mass arrests, taking all the Vietnamese, including women, found in the course of searches for arms caches. All were bound, and the men were 'roughed up'. This, Cédile stressed, was completely against his orders forbidding 'unjustified acts of brutality or displays of resentment or vengeance towards the Annamites'. In particular Cédile had warned those 'certain elements' of the French population who did not appear to appreciate that everything they did was in view of foreign observers, who judged the French cause accordingly. Cédile had hoped for a 'gentle and calming' operation, but instead the impression had been created that the French were going to unleash a reign of terror. The actions of the armed French had been strongly opposed by the British, and Gracey had told Cédile that as a result of its indiscipline the 11th RIC ought to be confined to its barracks and partially disarmed, and purged of its less desirable elements.[4] The poor performance of their troops was undoubtedly a blow to the French, and one that they were understandably anxious to play down. D'Argenlieu assured Paris that the reports in the British press of French excesses were either 'pure fantasy' or 'greatly exaggerated', but his claim that the Vietnamese population showed no signs of hostility to the allied forces carried little conviction.[5]

Hopes that the *coup* would restore order to the Saigon-Cholon area were shattered within twenty-four hours. By 26 September Gracey had to report to Mountbatten that there had been a 'considerable increase' in the Vietnamese abduction of French civilians, the men usually being murdered and the women mistreated while being held as hostages. There was, he added, clear evidence of Japanese complicity, at least to the extent that despite orders from the British command, Japanese troops had done nothing to prevent these attacks, and had in some cases stood by and not fired on the kidnappers. The worst single incident occurred on the night of 24 September, when a large crowd of Vietnamese attacked French civilians in the Cité Heyraud district in the northeast section of Saigon, killing about 150 and abducting as many again, many of the latter being horribly tortured and some subsequently murdered. There were many other outbreaks of violence, but this one in particular confirmed Gracey's belief that tough measures were needed to prevent a total collapse of law and order. The successful takeover of the public utilities in Saigon had not gone unchallenged by the Vietnamese, who had managed to sabotage temporarily the power and water plants and Saigon Radio. Within the area of Saigon-Cholon, the British had been able to impose a measure of order: 'rough treatment' by 80 Brigade brought two rioting mobs under control and 'produced less keenness', but the price for this success had

been some 60 Vietnamese killed and an unknown number of
wounded, and an 'increase in hostility to British Indian Gurkha
troops.'

Outside Saigon-Cholon the Vietnamese had established road
blocks as far as 30 kilometers from the city, apparently hoping to
choke off the supply of food. Gracey planned to respond to these
developments by increasing military activity designed to prevent the
establishment of a complete blockade. Thus he intended to maintain access to Saigon from the north by using Japanese troops to
disarm the Vietnamese and 'where necessary ruthlessly enforcing
. . . [his] order', but the clearance of the southern approaches,
where the blockades were most numerous, would have to wait until
more troops became available. Within the key area of Saigon-
Cholon itself – outside of which, in reply to Mountbatten's support
of Gracey's proclamation, Gracey assured Mountbatten 'I had no
intention of deploying my forces . . . and will not do so' – Gracey
proposed to use his own troops, 'and very sparingly French troops',
to disarm the Vietnamese and to reopen the market for which he
was convinced alternative food supplies were available, thus rendering the blockade ineffective. Last, he attached particular
importance to the reopening of Saigon Radio, on which he would
urge the French to broadcast details of their 'liberal' policy for the
future of Indochina. To achieve all these goals Gracey needed
additional troops, and he therefore urged the accelerated arrival of
the rest of 20th Indian Division and of the promised French troops,
i.e. the 9th DIC.[6]

Gracey's actions in restoring French control in the Saigon-
Cholon area and his subsequent proposals to Mountbatten
following the sustained resistance put up by the Vietnamese
exposed the contradictions in the British position and the tensions
between the British and the French. Gracey had always maintained
that his role was to control the headquarters of the Southern Army
and disarm the Japanese, and that it did not extend to involving
himself or his forces in the internal affairs of the country. He
therefore ignored the Viet Minh delegation waiting at Saigon
airport when he arrived, and had no contact with them until his
Chief of Staff delivered notice of the proclamation on 19 September. In justifying the *coup*, he explained to Mountbatten that no
administrative services had been operating in Saigon, and that since
his 'brief contained instructions not to get involved politically . . .

[it] was therefore impossible to have any dealings with [the] Viet Minh Government.' In those circumstances he had no alternative but to re-establish French control.[7] Gracey's intention of applying a very restrictive interpretation to his directive contrasted with Slim's views. At a SEAC headquarters staff meeting, when the general tenor seemed to be in favour of stopping the buildup of Gracey's forces so as to prevent any widening of the British role (for example by withdrawing 100 Brigade and sending it from Rangoon to Borneo rather than to Saigon), Slim spoke out against attempts to define Gracey's mission too narrowly: besides controlling the Japanese headquarters, he insisted, Gracey was responsible for the maintenance of law and order, at least in the Saigon-Cholon area.[8] Mountbatten, it will be recalled, had referred the question to the Chiefs of Staff and asked for a 'policy ruling', but before there had been any reply, Gracey had virtually pre-empted the matter by launching the *coup*, thereby expanding the British involvement and directly involving himself in the internal political affairs of Indochina.

Certainly Gracey was no dyed-in-the-wool imperialist, and many of the subsequent attacks on him were at best ill-informed, but neither was he as free of blame as his most recent defender suggests.[9] On the basis of his own reporting of circumstances in Saigon his actions were inconsistent, and by sticking to what he saw as the letter of his directive he missed potentially fruitful opportunities to enlist the cooperation of the Viet Minh at an early stage. After the *coup* it was too late: Viet Minh distrust of British and French motives was irreversibly reinforced by Gracey's reinstallation of the French and by his evident inability or unwillingness to restrain their excesses and brutality. It must be remembered also that under the terms of his amended directive, Gracey had been made responsible for the maintenance of law and order within the key centres of Saigon-Cholon. He chose to fulfil that role by backing the French against the Viet Minh who he himself admitted were capable of exercising some control to the extent of keeping essential services running in Saigon. The end result of Gracey's actions, however unwittingly, was to emphasise the principle of non-interference in the internal affairs of Indochina (by demonstrating complete support for short-term French aims) at the expense of law and order, for the result of the *coup* was not to enforce law and order but to prolong the period of disorder.

Slim, who consistently argued for a much broader interpretation
of Gracey's role, also urged the early opening of talks between the
French and the Viet Minh. When he put the suggestion to Cédile
just before the enforcement of Gracey's proclamation, Cédile
refused on the grounds that to see any members of the provisional
government would be to imply a measure of official recognition. He
was also undoubtedly strengthened in his opposition to Slim's
proposal by Gracey's absolute refusal to have any contact with the
Viet Minh, and by his fear that the local French population, already
dismayed by the slowness of French troops to arrive and by their
alleged restraint once they had landed, would react badly to any
provocative action on his part; and he maintained this position
even after the *coup* had reinstalled the French in control of
Saigon.[10] Slim and Mountbatten put the same suggestion to
Leclerc the day after the proclamation came into effect, drawing
attention to the British experience in Burma which they claimed
provided an example for the French to follow in that the promise of
Dominion status to Burma had defused a situation very similar to
that in Indochina, where the Japanese had installed a violently
xenophobic nationalist government. The French government, they
insisted, had to do the same: de Gaulle's March 1945 statement on
the future of Indochina had to be repeated but in a more detailed
form, and it had to be circulated much more widely. Mountbatten
went on record as saying officially to Leclerc what he had already
told him in private: that he urged Leclerc to advise the French
government in turn to make a new offer of the equivalent of
Dominion status to Indochina. Leclerc agreed that the arguments
were well-founded, and undertook to put them to d'Argenlieu and
to de Gaulle, while pointing out that the French were speaking of
autonomy rather than independence, and that however good
examples might be, they could not be copied slavishly.[11]

Privately he was not convinced. He wrote to D'Argenlieu that the
two situations were not analogous. In the latter there was a state of
anarchy, and any declaration of France's intention had to be
accompanied by a show of force. The allied military weakness
merely encouraged instability, which would quickly disappear once
sufficient forces were on the ground.[12] He repeated the same
arguments to de Gaulle, stressing that the disorder in Indochina
was the work of 'looters and assassins' exploiting the hiatus in
control between the Japanese and the allies and backed surrep-

titiously by the Japanese who had not renounced their ambitions for a Greater Asia. Any signs of weakness or disharmony between the allies would play into the hands of the Japanese and risk serious consequences for whites in Asia. At the meeting with Mountbatten Leclerc had insisted that even when the Japanese had been disarmed the maintenance of law and order would 'not for a moment' be a French responsibility until he had sufficient forces at his disposal, which would not be the case until the whole of the 9th DIC had arrived, despite Mountbatten's attempts to pressure him into accepting responsibility on 5 October, by which time the French would have a little over 3000 troops in southern Indochina (including, on Mountbatten's own estimation, 1200 rearmed former prisoners of war of 'mediocre value'). Leclerc had firmly rejected Mountbatten's suggestion, pointing out that Gracey had also claimed that a full division was necessary to restore order. Since Mountbatten had earlier said that at least from a military point of view he had endorsed Gracey's actions and the reasoning behind them, he was in no position to object. Leclerc told de Gaulle that British forces would have to continue their operations against the Vietnamese until the arrival of the 9th DIC,[13] which became the question around which the problem of the handover by the British to the French thereafter revolved.

Leclerc's point blank refusal to assume responsibility for law and order in southern Indochina until he had a division to deploy lent new importance to the acceleration of the arrival of the 9th DIC. On 25 September Mountbatten asked the Chiefs of Staff to give 'overriding priority' to the provision of extra shipping to move the division to Indochina – but without interrupting the return of Indian divisions from the Mediterranean theatre. Unless this was done, he warned, 'it is likely that British troops may continue to get involved in local clashes and sustain casualties protecting the lives of French civilians'.[14] Leclerc added his own pressure, emphasising to Kimmins that the continuing uncertainty over the arrival of the 3rd DIC made it imperative to speed up the despatch of the Madagascar Brigade. 'For political reasons', he stressed however, 'I wish to bring in[to] Indo China only European soldiers', which limited the eligible number from the division to only one thousand (a significant decrease from the earlier figure of 2300).[15] When Mountbatten convened a meeting in Singapore of his senior staff together with Cédile, Gracey, and Gracey's newly arrived political adviser, H.N. Brain, he still hoped to be able to limit the British involvement. He already had reason to suspect Gracey's judgment, but once Slim, the senior military commander in SEAC, also insisted that a full division was necessary merely to carry out Mountbatten's course B (the control of the Japanese headquarters by British forces with the French taking responsibility for everything else) he had no choice but to advise that the whole of the 20th Division be sent to Saigon. In making that recommendation, however, Mountbatten significantly widened his proposal under course B. Originally he had suggested that Gracey be responsible only for controlling the Japanese headquarters in Saigon, and that the remainder of the city, as well as the rest of southern Indochina, be handed over to the French, but after discussions with Slim and Gracey, he advised the Chiefs of Staff that he would require a complete division in order to be able to control the whole of Saigon which, as Gracey had forcefully pointed out to him, covered an enormous area. Since much of Saigon had become a battlefield as a result of Vietnamese counter-attacks following the *coup*, and given the Japanese failure to act against Vietnamese firing on allied troops or harming French civilians, the British role could no longer be limited to the very restricted involvement outlined in course B but had to be extended to include the maintenance of law and order over the whole of Saigon.

That extended geographical commitment of British forces underlined the dual necessity of minimising the period in which they would be required to act in their new role and of trying to arrange a truce in the fighting. Mountbatten passed on to the Chiefs of Staff Gracey's assurance that the French would not call on British assistance in operations outside the Saigon-Cholon area, but would instead hold the Japanese responsible for the safety of allied nationals beyond the British zone. When the French were sufficiently strong, the Japanese (still bearing arms) would be marched to a concentration area near Saigon, disarmed by the British and made ready for repatriation to Japan. All this, Mountbatten stressed, made the need to accelerate the arrival of the 9th DIC 'more important than ever.' On the political level, Mountbatten persuaded Cédile to drop his former opposition to talking to the Viet Minh leaders and to agree that Gracey should try to arrange a meeting at which Cédile could explain the French March offer of autonomy for Indochina within the French empire.

It was a bold attempt to contain the overall British commitment, but the short-term price was a deepening British involvement on both the military and political level. In Mountbatten's eyes the cost was acceptable if it guaranteed an early British withdrawal.[16]

Support for that position came from Cadogan in the Foreign Office and from Brain, Gracey's political adviser. Cadogan rejected Dening's view that Gracey should limit his role strictly to the control of the Japanese headquarters in Saigon, the withdrawal of Japanese forces in southern Indochina and the evacuation of APWI. By relying on Japanese troops in areas outside Saigon, Mountbatten could not 'divest himself of the final responsibility for ensuring law and order throughout the territories embraced in his command'. Were he to state that his role did not extend beyond the responsibilities that Dening suggested were appropriate, 'the revolutionary elements would no doubt regard it . . . as an invitation to proceed with their activities and the French, who have been pressing us in vain for months for transport to carry their troops to Indo-China, would feel that their worst suspicions of our motives were confirmed.' 'We are most anxious at this juncture', Cadogan emphasised, 'to avoid any such French reaction in view of the current discussions on wider issues between the French and ourselves.' Priority therefore had to be given to the supply and movement of French forces, 'even at the cost of delaying operations elsewhere', and if a statement had to be made on British intentions in Indochina, it should be issued by Mountbatten who should stress that the fulfilment of his immediate tasks might require interference in the internal affairs of Indochina if he was hampered in those tasks by conditions of disorder and threats to security.[17]

From his personal observations of the conditions around Saigon, and especially from his assessment of the Japanese arising out of his attendance at the twice-daily meetings between the Control Commission and the Japanese headquarters staff, Brain reached much the same conclusions. Only an extended British involvement could successfully disarm the Japanese without causing the wider situation to deteriorate further. If the Japanese were ordered to march to a concentration point to be disarmed prior to evacuation, the areas they abandoned would be free to be taken over by Vietnamese opposed to French rule, thus exposing the British to the same French charges that Cadogan was anxious to avoid being raised. It was not possible to impose the responsibility for disarming the Japanese on the French for two reasons: events following the *coup* had shown that the Vietnamese reacted violently to the installation of French control, and it was by no means clear that the Japanese, who were known to be handing over arms to the Viet Minh forces, would obey orders issued by the French. The Japanese attitude to the French, Brain wrote, was one of 'veiled contempt'. 'They have had to deal with no serious resistance from the French, and they know of them only as a defeated nation. . . . To expect them to take orders from the French would . . . in my opinion be a serious provocation.' Britain therefore had no choice but to expand its involvement in order to carry out its primary task; once that had been achieved, British troops could withdraw in favour of a French occupation. The key, once again, was a speedy arrival of French forces.[18]

Leclerc had refused to endorse Gracey's proclamation on the grounds that to do so would make him equally responsible for its enforcement, which he could not do until he had sufficient French forces at his disposal. That stand was accepted by Mountbatten and the Chiefs of Staff and served to underscore the importance of moving the 9th DIC to Indochina. When the French government first offered the 9th DIC for use in Indochina, it was understood that it would be ready to embark from Marseilles by mid-September. Shortages of shipping put the date back to mid-October, with arrival in Indochina some three weeks later, i.e. early November. That delay was strongly criticised by the French who kept up constant pressure on London (and to a lesser extent Washington) to provide the necessary shipping. Massigli's representations to the Foreign Office and the War Office seemed to produce at least implicit promises that there would be no further slippages in the timetable, so that when at the end of September the French military attaché in London reported that the arrival date had been postponed yet again to the end of November, Massigli quickly reassured Paris that the attaché had misunderstood what the War Office had told him.[19] Further confirmation that all was on schedule came from Singapore, where the visiting British Secretary of State for War, J.J. Lawson, promised Leclerc that the 9th DIC would arrive on time and that the 3rd DIC would be equipped as agreed, which to Leclerc's mind contrasted with the gloomy news from Saigon where, he claimed, the British were so afraid of adverse world reaction that they lacked firmness with the result that incidents of violence were increasing.[20] The French were therefore devastated when at the beginning of October the Chiefs of Staff told Mountbatten that his calculations had been wrong, and that instead of early November the 9th DIC would not arrive before the end of December.[21]

The new date arose out of a study by the Joint Planning Staff in London, which concluded that an earlier arrival of the 9th DIC could only be achieved at the expense of personnel movements on the Britain/India route, which would break the government's commitments under the PYTHON programme (which Mountbatten had also strongly endorsed) and delay the arrival of new drafts in India to replace those troops repatriated back to Britain. The alternative was to rearrange shipping schedules on the Britain/Australia route, but that would affect the repatriation of Australian and New Zealand troops and, more important, it would delay by some three months the arrival in the NEI of some 5000 Dutch troops from Europe, thus postponing the date at which British forces on Java and Sumatra could complete their tasks and hand over to the Dutch. Since French troops would not arrive in force until the end of 1945 at the earliest, the Joint Planning Staff emphasised that the British buildup in Indochina, including a Spitfire squadron and a Mosquito squadron, had to continue, and it suggested that as an 'interim policy' Mountbatten be told that while his primary responsibility was to control the Saigon area, he could assist whatever French forces were on the ground to establish law and order throughout the rest of the country 'to the limit of our ability provided that, in the judgment of the local commander, this can be done without prejudicing the local security of Saigon'.[22] The Chiefs of Staff accepted all the recommendations of the Joint Planning Staff, and instructed Mountbatten 'to stress to General Leclerc the importance we attach to the earliest acceptance of responsibility by the French', which it agreed could not take place until the arrival of the 9th DIC, now pushed back to the end of December at the earliest. They also authorised him to announce that while he did not wish to interfere in the internal affairs of Indochina, he might be forced to if the evacuation of the Japanese and APWI was hampered by unstable conditions, which was far less precise guidance than the 'detailed instructions' Dening had asked be sent to Mountbatten to explain 'how far he can go'.[23]

When news of the postponement of the arrival of the 9th DIC reached SEAC headquarters Mountbatten reported that Leclerc was 'absolutely horrified'. 'He is extremely distressed at this delay,' he wrote to the Chiefs of Staff, 'and has expressed his protest in the most emphatic terms.' Mountbatten was barely less distressed, and pointed out that the longer British forces had overall responsibility in southern Indochina 'the more difficult it will be for us to avoid being drawn into fighting, if only to rescue inadequately trained French troops attempting to restore order outside the Saigon area.' (So much for his faith in Gracey's guarantee that the French would not call on British assistance when operating beyond the British Saigon zone). The only way in which SEAC could prevent British troops from becoming involved in an ever-widening role was to rely on the Japanese to maintain order, but that meant not disarming and concentrating them, which had always been the primary task that had brought the British into southern Indochina in the first place. If there was to be a delay in disarming the Japanese until the 9th DIC arrived they would be left alone for three months by which time all former prisoners and internees would have been evacuated, thus leaving the British with no real reason for maintaining troops in Indochina unless to interfere in the internal affairs of Indochina. 'In fact', Mountbatten warned the Chiefs of Staff, 'we shall find it hard to counter the accusations that our forces are remaining in the country solely in order to hold the Viet Nahm [sic] Independence Movement in check.' Already, the Viceroy, Lord Wavell, advised him, protests had been made in India about the use of Indian troops to quell disturbances in Indochina and Java, and these were likely to develop into 'considerable agitation' unless Indian forces were quickly withdrawn. 'From my point of view', Wavell added, 'the sooner . . . the better'.[24] Auchinleck also had consistently objected to the prolonged use of Indian troops in southeast Asia, and shortly after the decision on the arrival of the 9th DIC became known he registered a strong protest against the suggestion that their withdrawal from Indochina might be delayed, 'particularly', as he noted (with Wavell's concurrence) 'after the recent visit of the Secretary of State for War who has personally assured British troops in Indian Command that he would do everything possible to have more transport allotted to their speedy return home.'[25] At his staff meeting Mountbatten made it even clearer that he had no doubt how the continued deployment of British troops beyond the time needed to fulfil the primary tasks would be interpreted:

'British forces would patently be holding resistance movements in check until the arrival of the French.'[28]

There were other objections arising out of the delay in the arrival of the 9th DIC. The use of Japanese troops raised questions about Britain's adherence to the terms of the surrender and to the tasks which had been allotted to Mountbatten by the Combined Chiefs of Staff. Even though the United States had withdrawn from active participation in the affairs of SEAC, it nevertheless retained formal powers over its activities, and it was privy to the main signal traffic between SEAC and London. Were Mountbatten to leave the Japanese armed and at liberty for three months pending the arrival of the 9th DIC, American suspicions of British intentions in southern Indochina would be confirmed. But on a more general level, there was widespread and growing disapproval of the fact that for reasons usually not understood British troops in Indochina (and in the Netherlands East Indies) had to rely on the Japanese for the maintenance of law and order. British forces had gone into these countries, so the argument ran, to accept the Japanese surrender and to disarm and evacuate Japanese forces following the allied victory in the war in the Far East; whatever problems the allies faced in winding up the war, the solution did not run to employing the hated Japanese. When Cadogan suggested that Mountbatten would be 'extremely reluctant to call upon Japanese troops to use violence against the inhabitants of any of the liberated territories', he was echoing the expressions of repugnance that were appearing more frequently in the British press – together with photographs of armed Japanese soldiers at liberty in the streets and markets of Saigon.[27] At best the need to rely on Japanese forces to carry out essential post-surrender tasks sat uneasily with Mountbatten's insistence in the Singapore surrender ceremony that the Japanese had been defeated by the military might of the allies.

Once it was clear that the 9th DIC would not arrive until the end of 1945, the Chiefs of Staff, following the recommendation of the Joint Planning Staff, urged Mountbatten to consider using the Madagascar Brigade, most of whose troops were black. Leclerc and Cédile had already rejected these on political grounds, Leclerc arguing that the introduction of black troops to Indochina would be a 'catastrophe' – they would be 'fire to the powder', he wrote – and even the announcement of the delay affecting the arrival of the 9th DIC was not enough to make him change his mind.[28] Cadogan

2 Lt General Leclerc with Major General Douglas Gracey in Saigon

agreed that the French were right to insist that their first troops in Indochina should be white, and Mountbatten replied to the Chiefs of Staff that quite apart from Leclerc's objections, he did not have the personnel shipping within SEAC to move the Brigade, even though it seems that earlier he had asked only for cargo transport, the implication being that sufficient personnel shipping was available.[29] When Mountbatten refused to accept the Madagascar Brigade as a partial substitute for the 9th DIC, he was told by the Chiefs of Staff that the arrival of the latter could only be achieved by delaying by three months the repatriation of 12,000 Indian troops who were due to leave the Mediterranean in October or by delaying over a three month period the despatch of 6000 British drafts to India to replace men released under the PYTHON scheme. 'What priorities do you recommend?' they replied,[30] knowing that since Mountbatten had wholeheartedly supported the PYTHON programme, to the extent of refusing to allow 'operational necessity' to be used as a reason for postponing or altering its implementation, he was unlikely to agree to the conditions that his insistence on the early arrival of the 9th DIC would entail.

The announcement that the arrival of the 9th DIC would be delayed for several months beyond what had originally been envisaged made the question of a political understanding, and possibly a truce, between the French and the Vietnamese all the more important for the British, for that was the only way that the British involvement, extended as it automatically was by the prolonged absence of French troops, could be limited in terms of fighting. The prognosis was not good. Whatever Cédile's personal inclinations – it appears that when he first arrived in Indochina his views were liberal – he was determined first to assert French sovereignty. The events of September confirmed him in his belief that the Viet Minh lacked popular support, and that the great mass of Vietnamese, at least in Saigon, wanted little more than stability and order. Much as Gracey may have agreed with Cédile's assessment, he was increasingly convinced that Cédile was incapable of pursuing the firm line that was necessary, especially after the *coup*, when much of the local French population went on an orgy of violence and destruction against the Vietnamese. Cédile's instructions to the French community in Saigon were widely ignored, which strengthened him in his belief that the whole local French population would have to be evacuated. 'They do not

understand the situation', he advised Leclerc, 'and are unaware that
the present state of international relations has created obligations
more than rights. They think they have only rights.'[31] That was a
view shared by Brain, who described the local French as 'one of the
greatest obstacles to the institution by the French of a liberal policy
and its acceptance by the Annamites'. 'They combine an almost
hysterical fear of the Annamites (which to my mind denotes a guilty
conscience) with an intense hatred and desire for revenge', he
noted, urging their removal from Indochina as soon as possible. [32]

Cédile's position was a difficult one, caught as he was between
the local French who thought him weak and the Vietnamese who
saw him as the architect of the *coup* and the representative of the
metropolitan government intent on maintaining French control.
Isolated in Saigon and without direct communications with Leclerc
in Kandy and d'Argenlieu in Chandernagor near Calcutta (all
French signal traffic went through SEAC headquarters in Kandy),
Cédile was under intense pressure. He had neither French military
forces nor top level political advice at his disposal, and he lacked
the personal stature or political authority to impress either side in
Saigon. Within several days of the *coup*, Gracey and Brain thought
that he could not last. 'It is possible that Cédile may collapse',
Gracey warned Mountbatten. 'His task is really beyond him.'[33]
'[He] is a well meaning and liberal minded man, but he is entirely
unfitted to cope with the very difficult situation here', Brain added.
'It was felt by all of us who saw him when the situation was at its
worst two days ago that he was on the verge of a complete
breakdown.'

What was needed, Brain suggested with Gracey's support, was a
'strong man with a reputation of fairness who will represent the
new France and who will not refuse to give the Annamites a
hearing'.[34] That was an outsider's assessment; de Gaulle had his
two men ready to take charge in Indochina – d'Argenlieu, twenty
years a Carmelite monk and a senior naval officer passionately
attached to France's imperial role, and Leclerc, the 'fighting general', sent to restore French power in Indochina just as he had
spearheaded the liberation of Paris, and convinced that a military
solution had to precede any political concessions. Neither had any
first-hand knowledge of conditions in Indochina – Leclerc did not
arrive until early October (much to the astonishment of de Gaulle,
who had assumed that Leclerc had gone to Saigon soon after

Gracey's arrival[35]), and d'Argenlieu not until the end of October. During the critical weeks of September the two men had no direct contact, but relied instead on the patchwork of French intelligence services and occasional reports from the beleaguered Cédile to keep in touch with developments in Saigon. They exhorted Cédile, but were unable to advise him in any realistic sense. He was therefore thrown back on local advisers, but these were not impressive, at least to Gracey and Brain. Gracey instructed his political adviser to forward a list of 'French officials here who are useless and should immediately be removed', and Brain wrote critically of Rivier, the senior French military officer in Saigon, who was rumoured to be at odds with Cédile and who, in Brain's view, lacked 'personality and leadership'.[36] Both militarily and politically British personnel moved in to fill the gap.

The first talks between British and the Viet Minh were held on 1 October. Brain emphasised that British troops were not in Indochina for any political purpose, and certainly not with the intention of restoring French rule by force. As things had developed, the Japanese were the only beneficiaries of the violence that had broken out: while their wartime victims fought among themselves, 'the real culprits – the Japanese themselves – stand by and smile'. Brain then invited the Viet Minh representatives to meet Gracey (who was waiting in another room) and listen to his offer to arrange a meeting with the French. Gracey prefaced his remarks by stating that he did not intend to discuss policy, but to find a way of restoring order and curbing violence. Either the Viet Minh could cooperate, or they could face the consequences that would follow from Gracey's use of his entire division, 'with tanks, guns and the finest infantry in the world'. The Viet Minh representatives undertook to hold discussions with the French, with Brain standing in for Gracey, which was somewhat less than the Viet Minh's initial request that the British act as arbitrators but which was as far as Gracey, under firm instructions from Mountbatten not to get involved in political matters, was prepared to go. A ceasefire was agreed upon, to take effect from the evening of 2 October, and a meeting between the French and the Viet Minh was arranged for 3 October. Gracey had every reason to be satisfied with the results, at least as far as the Viet Minh were concerned. His more immediate worry was the French. From the reaction of Cédile and Lt Colonel

Repiton (Leclerc's representative in Saigon) to his account of the meeting, he told Mountbatten, '[I] cannot be optimistic.' Leclerc's early arrival, he stressed, had become all the more important, both for restoring law and order and in political terms.[37]

A second meeting on 3 October produced few results, except to convince Brain that the Viet Minh negotiators, led by Pham Noc Thach, were limited in the response they could make to the French by popular expectations that had been aroused and by the extremists within their own ranks who were unlikely to obey a ceasefire if it was shown to be on the basis of political cooperation with France rather than the independence they sought. 'Both sides', Gracey told Mountbatten, 'place great hopes on our mediation', and while no real progress had been made, the truce at least was continuing.[38] Although Gracey undertook to protect Vietnamese civilians during the truce, he did not call a halt to his military buildup. Just before the first meeting with the Viet Minh he had asked Mountbatten for permission to use Spitfires against roadblocks and fortified positions that could not be cleared without substantial casualties to British land forces. Mountbatten approved the request, subject to careful restrictions. Spitfires could be used only if 'overriding operational purposes' required Gracey to keep the roads clear and were not to be used against large crowds of Vietnamese where heavy injuries would result. When Spitfires were about to be used, two hours' warning had to be given by means of dropping leaflets over the proposed target, and the text of the leaflet had to be telegraphed back to SEAC headquarters so that the inevitable anti-British propaganda (much of it emanating from Radio Hanoi, which repeated requests to Wedemeyer had failed to have closed down) could be countered by official British sources in London and Washington.[39] Mountbatten was reluctant to approve the use of air power, fearing that large casualties would invariably result, but others saw in it an effective and powerful weapon when ground troops were in short supply. In Paris, General Juin personally stressed to the British Air Mission to France the 'paramount importance' of moving two Spitfire squadrons to Indochina, especially in light of the new delay to the arrival of the 9th DIC, and asked that the possibility of providing an aircraft carrier to transport the squadrons be investigated 'at the highest level'. The Chiefs of Staff had no objection in principle to the use of aircraft in an offensive role in Indochina; their only concern was whether the French request could be accommodated without undue interference with the overall trooping programme.[40]

An uneasy calm settled over Saigon, although isolated incidents of violence still occurred. Neither the French nor the Viet Minh budged from their established political positions, though equally neither broke off the talks. Distrusting Gracey's judgment, Mountbatten had sent his own political officer to Saigon to make a personal assessment. Brigadier E.C.J. Myers, who had previously served as Head of Mission to the Greek Resistance, was told by Mountbatten to investigate the situation and recommend ways for SEAC to achieve its primary goals without it becoming involved in internal politics. His report on 3 October, the day of the second British-Viet Minh talk, made gloomy reading. The old French administration, he told Mountbatten, was 'rotten to [the] core', while those who had followed Cédile to Saigon had already alienated the Vietnamese by their high-handed attitude. Cédile was 'not big enough for the job', and had serious differences with Rivier who was ineffective. What was needed was a 'firm but progressive policy defined in detail' by the French and backed if possible by the United Nations. If the French did not act with urgency, he warned, they would create a 'running sore' that would last for years.[41]

That sense of urgency was lacking in the imperial capitals. When Leclerc transmitted to de Gaulle Mountbatten's suggestion that a new French declaration on Indochina was needed, de Gaulle refused. It was 'out of the question', he told Leclerc. The statement of March 1945 was quite sufficient, and to issue another would have the appearance of a retreat. Mountbatten's disquiet, de Gaulle suggested, could be explained in terms of a reaction to his own lack of foresight in failing to make provision for the earlier despatch of the 9th DIC, or – more sinister – it could perhaps be explained in terms of Britain's ulterior motives in the Far East. Whatever the reason, de Gaulle rejected the British pleas to take the political initiative in Indochina.[42] In London the British government did not seem unduly worried either. Mountbatten's objections over the delay to the 9th DIC made little impact, perhaps because he refused to consider the alternative of the Madagascar Brigade. Prime Minister Attlee summed up the Defence Committee's view when he remarked that the situation 'did not appear to warrant any precipitate action to alter the present scheduled movements for

French forces to Indo-China'.[43] That was not the assessment of the
men on the spot, either in Saigon or in SEAC headquarters.

Chapter four
The Netherlands East Indies: first encounters

Following the enlargement of SEAC's boundaries at the Potsdam conference, Mountbatten reordered his priorities. Except for Hong Kong, far removed from SEAC's Kandy headquarters, Java was ranked last, and it was expected that apart from preliminary work in aiding prisoners of war and internees (the Repatriation of Allied Prisoners of War and Internees programme – RAPWI), Java could be left until more important areas had been returned to allied control. Even this order of priorities, which would have involved SEAC's forces moving progressively eastwards from Ceylon and Burma, was not adhered to, for in the case of Hong Kong it was felt essential to have the Japanese surrender accepted by British rather than by Chinese or American forces if the British claim to sovereignty was to be re-established. A British naval task force arrived at Hong Kong on 29 August, one day after released British internees had assumed control and begun the process of reinstituting British civil government.

There were few such pressures acting on SEAC when it came to Java. Dutch control of the East Indies was not in dispute among the allies, not even in the case of the United States, which viewed the Dutch colonial record more benignly than that of either the British or the French. Even if it did not produce any material advantage for the Dutch, this attitude did at least gain them a favourable hearing in high Washington circles. Admiral William D. Leahy, Roosevelt's Chief of Staff, for example, sympathised with Dutch requests for shipping to transport their troops to the Far East, whereas similar French pleas had been coldly received.[1] In the case of the East Indies, however, there did not seem to be any overriding urgency once Japan had surrendered. Not only was Mountbatten determined to hold back until it was clear that local Japanese forces intended to abide by the terms of the surrender and to follow the procedures for the transfer of control, but there was also lack of any intelligence indicating that Java would pose undue problems for SEAC. Neither the scale of the RAPWI task nor the radically changed political and military conditions in Java were as yet appreciated, either by SEAC or by its Dutch advisers.

The Dutch had long been pressing for steps to be taken to facilitate their return to the East Indies. In October 1944, at their urging, the Combined Chiefs of Staff had agreed that Britain should train and equip 15 Dutch battalions for internal security purposes in the liberated territories of the NEI. That was an agreement in principle only, and when in March 1945 the Dutch proposed that the first 4000 troops be moved to Australia, two problems arose. The Supreme Commander in Europe, Eisenhower, argued that he already had insufficient Dutch troops for his immediate needs, and there was the long-standing shortage of shipping. The Foreign Office appreciated that the non-military pressures on shipping would increase once the war was over, and therefore suggested that as many Dutch troops as possible should be moved out to the East Indies while military priorities prevailed.[2] When the Lieutenant-Governor of the NEI, Dr Hubertus van Mook, visited Washington in May 1945 to plead with the CCS for additional shipping to move Dutch Marines to the US for special training and to concentrate other Dutch troops in Australia before their return to the Indies, he made no impression. Speaking for the British Chiefs of Staff, Wilson was unable to offer any support to Van Mook's proposal which, if granted, would have disrupted SEAC's plans for the progressive reoccupation of key areas in the theatre.[3] Nevertheless the Dutch continued to press for early operations against Java in much the same terms as Dening had argued for the pre-surrender attack on British territories. 'It is considered essential for the rehabilitation of the Western Powers in the Far East', advised the Netherlands Staff Section at SEAC headquarters, Kandy, 'that the most important point of the NEI, ie West Java with Batavia and Bandoeng, be recaptured before the enemy's surrender.'[4]

The British determination to proceed on an orderly basis was doubly tested by the decision to enlarge SEAC's boundaries and by the precipitate end to the war against Japan. On the one hand Mountbatten now had additional territories to liberate and occupy, and on the other he came under pressure from allies to provide for their early return to their colonial possessions. No less than the British over Malaya, Singapore and Hong Kong, the Dutch were concerned that their forces reach the NEI as soon as possible to assert Dutch sovereignty. Once Japan had surrendered the Dutch became increasingly impatient over the delay in mounting operations against the main island of Java. Mountbatten told the Chiefs of Staff that he was prepared to assume responsibility for the whole of the NEI provided he was given sufficient forces and logistical backup. If that were the case he would establish a single command structure for the whole of the Indies, which would go some way towards satisfying the repeated Dutch requests that their commander-in-chief, Admiral C.E.L. Helfrich, be placed directly under the Supreme Commander.[5] Mountbatten was advised by his own staff that it was far preferable to retain the system whereby Dutch forces were under the control of the Commander of Allied Land Forces, Southeast Asia (ALFSEA), who exercised that control through an allied commander in the NEI. The Dutch, however, wanted to establish a self-contained organisation completely under their own control, with authority over shipping, civil affairs, personnel, relief supplies, and units already in the theatre.[6]

That was hardly a practical proposition, given the lack of available or suitable Dutch troops. At the beginning of September there were no trained or equipped Dutch forces ready for immediate deployment. Five battalions of infantry, each of 800 men, were due to arrive from Europe in late September, followed by a further five battalions in early October and another seven a month later,[7] but no troops were available immediately to satisfy the request of the Dutch Army commander in the NEI, Major General L.H. van Oyen, that Dutch troops should, as far as possible, re-enter the liberated areas simultaneously with British and Australian forces.[8] Even less was it possible to meet Helfrich's recommendation that Dutch units be flown into Batavia to take up positions there *before* the arrival of British troops.[9]

Dutch hopes that they would be able to transport European units quickly to Java had already foundered on the allied unwillingness to release Dutch shipping from the pool in which it had been placed for the duration of the war. These hopes were further dashed by an American decision in September 1945 to reject Dutch requests for additional marines to be trained in the US. A year previously, the

Americans had agreed that the initial Dutch Marine Landing Force of 5000 should be increased by 2000, since experience had shown that combat units could expect to incur heavy casualties in the Pacific. However, once the fighting had ended, there was no military justification in American eyes for training the extra 2000 marines,[10] and this position, which had been foreshadowed by the Joint Chiefs in May, was formalised by the President in September, when it was decided that 'training of foreign troops . . . already undertaken may be continued to the nearest practicable stopping point.' Once the initial 5000 marines had been trained, the US acknowledged no obligation to provide training for any other Dutch troops. All that it would undertake to do was to furnish equipment for the original Marine Landing Force and to despatch it to the East Indies in mid November,[11] well beyond the time that the Dutch estimated would be critical for the smooth re-establishment of their control. For the United States, the decision was a convenient one. Just as the Potsdam realignment of SEAC's boundaries had removed the potentially troublesome European colonial areas from South West Pacific Area's control, and hence from a primarily American responsibility, so the termination of training agreements with the Dutch put an end to the possibility that the US might become militarily involved, however indirectly, with the post surrender reassertion of imperial control. Lacking ambitions itself in these areas it was unwilling to be involved in promoting or assisting the ambitions of others.

As well as the major allies, the Dutch had also looked to Australia for help in preparing Dutch forces to retake the Indies. In September 1943, the Dutch had tried to bypass the Combined Chiefs and the opposition they knew would come from both London and especially from Washington by making a direct approach to the Australian military staff in London to see if arms and equipment could be obtained in Australia for eventual use in operations in the Indies.[12] The Australians had no choice but to insist that all requests be channelled through the Combined Chiefs, and the Dutch dropped the matter for the time being. A year later they asked the Australian government to agree to the 'arrival, accommodation, training and maintenance of a force of about 30,000 men' in Australia.[13] The Australian reaction to the request was mixed. The External Affairs Department, which hoped that Australia would be able to play a greater role in the region in the postwar period, supported the Dutch,[14] not least because the Australian position in the forthcoming talks with the Dutch on a range of issues would thereby be improved. The Defence Committee, however, opposed the request on the grounds that Australia's limited resources would better be used to support British operations, especially as there was a suspicion that the Dutch intended to raise the troops for internal security purposes rather than as frontline forces who would contribute directly to shortening the war against Japan.[15] For the moment the views of the External Affairs Department prevailed, and the War Cabinet approved the Dutch request 'in principle'.[16] Perhaps because it realised that further examination would reveal the burden which the Dutch would ultimately impose on Australia, External Affairs tried to lock the Australian government into the decision by announcing to the Dutch representatives that their request had been approved.[17] Perhaps also in an attempt to commit the Australians to a course of action which had been approved only in principle, the Dutch began preparing to send several thousand troops from Britain to Australia. The British were persuaded to provide initial training and transit accommodation, while the External Affairs Department waived passport requirements.[18]

In the following April the Combined Chiefs rejected the Dutch proposal to send 30,000 troops to Australia, and ruled that until additional commitments in Europe had been fulfilled only 4000 internal security troops (who required a much lower level of training and were therefore less of a burden on allied resources) together with some air force and civil administration personnel could be sent to Australia.[19] Despite this setback (which was temporary since the Combined Chiefs had suggested that once the manning levels in Europe had been met additional troop movements to Australia might be approved), support for the Dutch request was growing in Australia. The Joint Administrative Planning Sub-Committee reported in March that the Dutch requirements could be accommodated within the government's manpower plans on which were based the programme of gradual demobilisation of Australia's military forces and the return to a peacetime economy.[20] In June, General Blamey, C-in-C, Australian Military Forces, told General van Oyen that although the details had yet to be worked out, he considered that there was no longer any question about the arrival of the Dutch troops, and he agreed to support Van

Oyen's and Van Mook's attempts to persuade MacArthur to press Eisenhower to relax his position on the release of Dutch troops from Europe for service in the Indies.[21] Military and diplomatic opinion in Australia seemed to agree that the Dutch scheme should receive encouragement and support from Australia.

That support did not last long. Domestic political pressures on the government to speed up the demobilisation programme resulted in a considerable manpower shortage in the armed forces. By the second half of 1945 the requirements for some 4000 Australian personnel to back up the Dutch troops were no longer the negligible commitment that they had seemed in March. Secondly, the long-standing problem of shipping took on new dimensions. The end of the war in Europe brought the inevitable demands for the speedy repatriation of Australian prisoners of war, and it was decided that when it came to allocating shipping, Australian p.o.w.s were to have 'absolute priority' over Dutch troops being sent to Australia.[22] There were also demands on shipping to return to Australia RAAF aircrew in Britain who were no longer needed there but who were required in the Pacific to make good the losses sustained by the RAAF in operations in SWPA. Again, the Australian government was determined that Australian demands should take precedence.

At the end of June the Australian government decided not to proceed with the training of Dutch troops in Australia, apparently on the basis that the manpower situation did not permit Australia to accept the additional burden which the Dutch plan would have involved.[23] During the two weeks before the Dutch were informed of this change of heart, they continued to push ahead with their arrangements to despatch further troops to Australia (by mid June almost a thousand had already sailed from Britain). When the government's decision was relayed to the Dutch, they were outraged, and complained bitterly that they had been let down badly by the Australian government, whose *volte face* had caused them to waste both time and money. Their hostility was further deepened by the Australian decision not to participate in the post surrender occupation of Borneo. Having been denied the opportunity to train their own troops in Australia, the Dutch justifiably felt doubly betrayed by the Australian failure to assist in the recovery of the NEI. Prime Minister Chifley's letter of explanation of the Australian decision, and his suggestion that the 'advice tendered to you on a lower level [i.e. External Affairs] could not take into account the overall picture . . . [and that any] assumptions which you may have reached on such advice would therefore not be competently based',[24] did little to assuage Dutch feelings. Mountbatten's representative in Melbourne, Major General Harrison, warned SEAC that because of increasing friction between the Dutch and the Australians on the 'higher political plane' the 'going is very heavy.'[25] From this point on Australia was seen as hostile to Dutch interests.

The only forces immediately available to the Dutch were troops of the Royal Netherlands Indies Army (*Koninlijk Nederlands Indische Leger* – KNIL). The Netherlands Staff Section at Kandy reported that in Java there were about 18,000 prisoners of war who could be used in a military role within a short time of being released from captivity. A significant proportion of these were Ambonese and Menadonese who had customarily received extra pay for 'foreign service' in Java and Sumatra and who, remaining loyal to the Dutch, had been imprisoned by the Japanese at the same time as other native troops had been disarmed and allowed to remain free. These loyal troops, it was thought, were capable of handling any disturbances that might arise before the arrival of Dutch European forces in late September.[26] Anxious as the Dutch were to return to the Indies, there was not at this stage the overwhelming sense of urgency that developed by late September. Ignorance and self-delusion were a potent mixture, and the Dutch were yet to appreciate the enormity of the situation facing them and the limits of their own power.

Three weeks after the Japanese attack on Pearl Harbor, Van Mook was appointed Lieutenant-Governor of the NEI, official recognition of the critical situation in southeast Asia. On 6 March 1942, two days before the fall of the Indies, he left for Australia, where he was charged by the Governor-General with establishing offices to protect the interests, especially in banking and commerce, of the NEI for the duration of the war. It was not envisaged either by the Dutch government-in-exile in London or by the besieged NEI administration that Van Mook would establish an Indies government-in-exile in Australia, even though such a proposal made sense. London was far removed from the theatre, and until the very end of the war Java fell under the aegis of South West Pacific Area, commanded by General MacArthur who was based

first in Melbourne and then in Brisbane. It was to the bounty of the
United States, already gearing up to pour huge amounts of supplies
into Australia and the southwest Pacific, that Van Mook naturally
looked, rather than to the metropolitan centre, now based in a
struggling Britain that was quite incapable of offering any
assistance in the fight to regain the Indies.

The Dutch government in London viewed Van Mook with some
suspicion. His request to establish a fully-fledged government-in-
exile in Australia was rejected, and in May 1942 he was removed
from his post as Lieutenant-Governor and immediately appointed
Minister of Colonies, a position that was designed to bring him
more closely under the control of the London government. Although he had thereby been denied on-the-spot access to the source
of military power in SWPA, his new appointment brought him on
to a wider stage, and enabled him to play some part (a considerable
one, according to his own account) in the drafting of Queen
Wilhelmina's historic speech on the future of the Dutch colonial
empire. American approval of Dutch colonial policies and their
future application was the *sine qua non* for access to American
military largesse, and when Roosevelt suggested that the Dutch
make some announcement about the postwar status of the NEI and
other Dutch colonies, Van Mook was among the ministers consulted on the thrust of the speech.[27]

It was timed to coincide with a meeting in Quebec of the
influential Institute of Pacific Relations, which had organised a
conference to discuss the postwar colonial situation. When she
broadcast on 7 December 1942, the Queen promised to convene a
conference as soon as possible after the end of the war to discuss the
reorganisation of the Kingdom of the Netherlands into a Commonwealth in which relations between the four component parts (the
Netherlands, the East Indies, Surinam and Curacao) would be
based on the twin principles of 'complete partnership' and 'self-
reliance' and freedom of conduct for each part regarding its internal
affairs.[28] Although Roosevelt and American public opinion seemed
reassured by these promises, the speech merely stored up troubles
for the Dutch. It offered little concrete information about the
postwar status of the East Indies, and gave even fewer substantive
concessions to reformist let alone nationalist opinion. Van Mook's
attempts to spell out the details to a number of American journalists were purely personal; others, including the Dutch prime

minister, Professor P.S. Gerbrandy, maintained in private that the speech in no way represented any diminution of the powers of the central government over colonial affairs.[29] Promises of a postwar conference locked the Dutch government into the vagueness of the speech and prevented them from advancing further initiatives as the wartime situation unfolded. The speech was delivered in English – for primarily American consumption – and thus was largely unknown to the very audience to which it was theoretically designed to apply. When the Dutch finally straggled back to the NEI in September 1945, they were no longer part of an American-dominated theatre, but were clinging to the coat-tails of the hard pressed British, who had colonial problems of their own. Furthermore, all the Dutch had to offer was a shadowy plan for reform that was almost three years old. Conditions in the NEI had changed dramatically since 1942, and had rendered the vague promises of the Queen's speech all but irrelevant.

The Dutch, however, did not realise this. Throughout the war information on the NEI was scanty and, as later events showed, often completely unreliable. Special Operations Executive (SOE), the British organisation charged with undercover activities in occupied territories, coordinated the work of Helfrich's *Corps Insulinde* which operated as an intelligence service, employing fewer than a hundred men. According to Helfrich's chief of staff, Rear Admiral L.G.L. Van der Kun, its lack of success was the result of the British policy of doing nothing to disturb the Japanese on Sumatra for fear that they would respond by strengthening their forces there.[30] In addition to this British brake on the *Corps Insulinde's* activities, there were other factors that prevented it from achieving very much. Its senior staff was inadequate to the task, it lacked sufficient submarine transport facilities to land significant numbers of agents, and even if it had been provided with those facilities, it was unable to recruit enough competent agents. Those who were landed ran into strong hostility from the indigenous population, which ought to have signalled to the Dutch that their eventual return might not be greeted with complete favour, but it seems not to have produced in Dutch circles any questioning of their oft-repeated claim that apart from a few unrepresentative political activists, Dutch rule was largely accepted, indeed welcomed, by the great majority of the people.

It was not until June 1945 that a permanent undercover force
was established in Sumatra.[31] Three small parties of agents were
sent ashore by the *Corps Insulinde*, now renamed the 'Anglo-Dutch
Country Section'. One of the agents who landed in Sumatra later
told the Dutch Parliamentary Commission investigating wartime
policies that his British superior, Major A.G. Greenhalgh, had
strictly forbidden him to gather political intelligence, stressing that
his role was to be limited to seeking information about the location
of camps housing allied prisoners of war and internees.[32] Van
Mook's verdict on the work of the *Corps Insulinde* was damning:
its staff was well-intentioned and brave, but the practical value of
its activities was little or none.[33]

The situation regarding Java was no better. The Dutch
authorities in Australia had established two intelligence-gathering
organisations.[34] The Netherlands Indies Government Information
Service was a civil secret service responsible to the NEI Committee
for monitoring Japanese broadcasts and spreading subversive
propaganda in the occupied territories. Given that the Dutch were
so out of touch with developments in the Indies since the Japanese
conquests, it was hardly surprising that their efforts in the latter
area were a complete failure. Nevertheless, Van Mook resisted
attempts by Helfrich to have the NIGIS amalgamated with Helfrich's Netherlands Forces Intelligence Service (NEFIS), as he
wished to retain a separate and specifically civil organisation to
keep him apprised of conditions in the Indies. The NEFIS was
controlled by SOE until April 1943. Then, at the urging of
MacArthur who was planning his great offensives through the
southwest Pacific, Helfrich reorganised the NEFIS and put it at the
disposal of SWPA command. Section III of the NEFIS organised
sabotage and intelligence-gathering forays into the occupied Indies,
but as with the *Corps Insulinde*, its efforts met with little success.
Insufficient transport, a lack of good agents, and the hostility of the
local population combined to thwart its attempts to place permanent parties in those areas of the NEI that fell within SWPA's
boundaries. In September 1943, for example, following Helfrich's
reorganisation, 13 groups were landed in various parts of the NEI,
but within a short time all but two (in West New Guinea) had been
captured.[35]

In any case, the Dutch did not place much importance on
potential political problems in Java. The head of Section III of the

NEFIS, Commander L. Brouwer, later told the Parliamentary Commission that it was not his responsibility to gather political intelligence and that because of this it was not until after the Japanese surrender that he and his staff had become aware of the strength of the nationalist movement.[36] Van Mook complained to the Commission that this failure to provide him with political intelligence had put him at a great disadvantage in his relations with Mountbatten,[37] but he was hardly blameless himself for the inadequacies of the information that was fed to him. He had insisted on a wasteful duplication of effort that overstretched the very limited Dutch intelligence resources, and he had not given intelligence operations the priority that he later saw as having been necessary. Furthermore he had expected that Sumatra would present greater problems for the return of Dutch control than Java,[38] which as the heartland of the empire in the East Indies had been most exposed to the prewar panoply of Dutch power. A general warning had been sounded by Ch. O. van der Plas, Netherlands Indies Chief Commissioner in Melbourne, who predicted as early as February 1944 that 'when an evacuation approaches, . . . [the Japanese] will suddenly grant independence to some sort of Government of Quislings, hoping thereby to prepare a comeback in the future.'[39] The Dutch government in London did not welcome independent assessments, fearing an ultimate loss of central control: Van der Plas, already suspected of being too sympathetic to local opinion in the Indies, was ignored, and plans went ahead for the progressive return of Dutch rule. Only in early September 1945 did the NEFIS draw attention to the nationalists, but in a report of the 3rd, it suggested that though the Republican Army might be able to field between 40–45,000 men, its opposition to the Dutch reoccupation was likely to be ineffective.[40]

Mountbatten himself did not appreciate the paucity of intelligence on the Indies. He had told Marshall at the Potsdam meeting that before he could assume responsibility for the areas that MacArthur wished to shed from SWPA command, he would require 'adequate advance intelligence' on the new territories.[41] He never got it, because it did not exist. MacArthur had been supplied with virtually nothing from his Dutch intelligence services, and his own were scarcely more productive. In early 1943 he had suggested that the Office of Strategic Services (OSS) be used to gather information in the NEI, but when an OSS officer arrived at

MacArthur's headquarters to go into details, he found that Mac-Arthur's staff were totally opposed to the intrusion of an organisation that might rival their own intelligence service (marginally useful as the latter was). Within a month it seemed that MacArthur too had changed his mind, for his staff told the OSS officer that the OSS was not welcome in the Pacific theatre, and that MacArthur did not care to discuss the matter further.[42] That position was maintained for the rest of the war, and the OSS operated from its Chinese base. By early 1945, MacArthur's eyes were fixed on the Philippines: Java was entirely peripheral to his strategy and there was no longer any military reason to collect intelligence about conditions there.

If ignorance, self-delusion and neglect marked the allies' understanding of the realities of the situation in the NEI, agreement nevertheless had been reached over the means by which Dutch control would be reasserted. In December 1944, following the partial liberation of the Netherlands, Van Mook was reappointed Lieutenant-Governor of the NEI and sent back to Australia, where he arrived in March 1945. A Civil Affairs agreement had been concluded on 10 December 1944 between the Dutch and SWPA Command under which all matters relating to the civilian population in liberated territories were to be the responsibility of the Dutch exercised through the Netherlands Indies Civil Administration (NICA). This arrangement suited the Americans, who had no civil affairs branch in the theatre and who were primarily concerned with problems of the battle front, and it allowed the Dutch to plan for an orderly return of Dutch control as the Japanese were pushed out of New Guinea.[43] It also enabled the Americans to avoid involvement in any potential problems arising out of the reimposition of colonial rule. Expectations that this convenient division of responsibility, which had the added attraction of giving the Dutch access to American supplies, would apply to the centre of the East Indies, Java, were rudely destroyed by the sudden transfer to SEAC of Java and the other parts of the NEI formerly within the American theatre. Not only did this deprive the Dutch of US material largesse and require them to become an added burden on the already overstretched resources of SEAC, but it made it necessary to negotiate another civil affairs agreement because unlike the Americans, the British in SEAC had a civil affairs branch within which NICA henceforth had to operate.

Sumatra had been part of SEAC since the latter's creation in 1943. Throughout 1944 discussions were held in London and Kandy on the problems that would arise over the restoration of Dutch control in the wake of basically British military operations. Planning on the assumption that the Japanese would gradually cede control in the face of allied offensives, it was decided that NICA would follow behind the forces of military occupation, filling as soon as possible the vacuum created by the Japanese withdrawal. NICA personnel, headed by the Chief Civil Affairs Officer (who was to be known as the Commanding Officer, NICA), would fall under the authority of the Supreme Allied Commander, Mountbatten, and through him, of the local allied military commander. Once allied forces had landed in Sumatra, Mountbatten would issue a notice indicating his readiness to accept a Japanese surrender and maintain law and order pending the return of Dutch control. Military administration was therefore to be a transitional stage – and hopefully a short one – before the restoration of civil government. During the period of military administration all personnel involved in the occupation were to come exclusively under the control of the military authorities whose wide powers, it was thought, would only need to be exercised for the brief period following the progressive occupation of recaptured Dutch territory.[44]

This agreement did not come into force until 24 August 1945. By then SEAC's boundaries had been enlarged and it was decided on 4 September that the civil affairs agreement for Sumatra should be extended to include those territories transferred from SWPA. Once Batavia had been occupied, NICA would come under the control of Van Mook, who would thus have a dual responsibility, to The Hague as head of the NEI government, and to Mountbatten as Chief Commanding Officer of NICA. Van Mook himself had proposed this agreement, arguing that 'the spheres of action in both functions are sufficiently demarcated ... in the civil affairs agreement to avoid any difficulties in the execution of the two functions.' In any case, since Van Mook also recommended that all available NICA personnel move in 'directly' with the occupation forces, the period during which this dual responsibility would operate would be minimal. Mountbatten accepted these proposals, and at the same time rejected Helfrich's request that NICA be placed under his control.[45]

The implications of these arrangements were not immediately apparent, or rather, in the absence of a clear appreciation of the political situation in Java, it did not dawn on Mountbatten or the British government that SEAC's occupying forces had virtually placed themselves at the disposal of the Dutch. Mountbatten's directive from the Chiefs of Staff required him in the first instance to disarm the Japanese in the NEI and to enforce the terms of the unconditional surrender; to locate and repatriate prisoners of war and internees; to concentrate the Japanese in readiness for their eventual return to Japan; and lastly, to 'establish and maintain peaceful conditions preparatory to handing over the territories to their respective civil governments'. The interpretation of this final task quickly led to strained relations between the British and the Dutch, both in SEAC and beyond. By what standards were 'peaceful conditions' to be established; whose 'law and order' was to be enforced? The civil affairs agreement was based on the assumption that the transition from an essentially British military occupation to the restoration of full Dutch civil government would be accomplished swiftly, especially since NICA personnel would move in with British military forces. As well it was assumed that the only major resistance to the reimposition of Dutch control might come from the Japanese, for it was not certain that local commanders would comply with the surrender terms agreed to in Tokyo. If they did follow orders, however, there was little reason to anticipate undue problems in reimposing Dutch control. As long as the transition period was short, the potential conflict arising out of Van Mook's divided responsibilities was unlikely to be realised, but if SEAC's forces encountered unexpected difficulties, the civil affairs agreement might well complicate the situation. Under the terms of the agreement, Van Mook as head of NICA was subordinate to Mountbatten, but as the local representative of the government to whom Mountbatten was directed to hand over the pacified territories of the NEI, he could claim the right to advise the Supreme Commander and, if necessary, to appeal over his head if he considered that the conduct of military affairs was hampering the re-establishment of Dutch control.

In the absence of significant numbers of Dutch troops, British forces would be responsible for establishing and maintaining those 'peaceful conditions' that were a prerequisite for the transfer of the NEI by British military authorities to Dutch civil government.

Speed was essential if British involvement was to be limited, both to minimise the interregnum between the Japanese surrender and the landing of allied troops, and to minimise the period before the arrival of Dutch forces to relieve the British. But in neither case was the necessary speed thought to be possible without disrupting carefully worked out schedules. The dawning realisation in early September that the Japanese surrender had left not a vacuum but some sort of independent republican government in Java not only underlined the need for swift action but led to the very situation that Van Mook had argued would be unlikely to arise.

On 17 August 1945 the Republic of Indonesia was proclaimed by Indonesian nationalists led by Sukarno and Muhammed Hatta. Several months previously the Japanese had initiated moves to establish a quasi-independent Indonesia, and as Japan's military position crumbled in late July and early August, steps were taken to speed up the process by appointing an Independence Preparatory Committee and nominating 24 August as the day on which independence would be conferred officially on the East Indies. Rather than appear to accept independence as a favour from the defeated Japanese, Sukarno and Hatta took matters into their own hands and advanced the date to 17 August. The Japanese were not inclined to resist: on the contrary, despite the terms of the surrender agreed to by the authorities in Tokyo, local Japanese forces began handing over their weapons to the nationalists and interned themselves in camps to await the arrival of allied troops. By the end of August, the greater part of Java, including the main cities and towns, was in the hands of the nationalists, backed by large, well armed if poorly trained military forces. To all intents and purposes, the vacuum created by the Japanese collapse and withdrawal was filled almost immediately by a functioning nationalist government determined to oppose the return of Dutch rule.[46]

News of this turn of events did not of itself force Mountbatten to change his plans. On 3 September he informed the Chiefs of Staff that it was not intended to occupy Java until early October, when the 26th Division would arrive by sea – but only if the Japanese had complied with the terms of the surrender and had assisted in the mine-sweeping of the approach channel to Batavia, and if the Division was not required to act as a reinforcement in areas with a higher priority.[47] The following day he met Van Mook and Van der

Plas at his headquarters in Kandy, and it was only then that the problems awaiting the allies began to emerge. Originally it had been proposed that a leaflet should be dropped over the key areas óf Java to advise the local populace of the impending arrival of the allied forces, and warning them not to obey either the defeated Japanese or the self-proclaimed republic. Since the allies were not due to land for several weeks, this was clearly a recipe for complete confusion, and after some discussion it was decided to direct the commander of the Southern Army, Field Marshal Count Terauchi, to continue to maintain law and order until the allies were capable of assuming control. Van Mook went further, and insisted that Mountbatten issue an unequivocal directive forbidding any recognition, even a *de facto* one, of the 'so-called Republic of Indonesia': no steps were to be taken, even by RAPWI teams, that might imply any sort of recognition of the 'puppet' government.[48]

Mountbatten was unwilling to accept this. It was now clear that the reoccupation of the East Indies was not going to be a purely military operation, however difficult or prolonged that had been envisaged. He cabled the Chiefs of Staff for guidance, arguing that 'as this is a political matter affecting the Dutch Government, I do not feel it would be proper for me to issue such a statement in my own name' and requesting the Chiefs of Staff to 'give me instructions if you wish me to enforce this.'[49] Dening followed up Mountbatten's appeal to the Chiefs of Staff by warning the Foreign Office that 'the Supreme Commander's view is that he cannot entirely divorce himself from his British nationality and that were he to make statements of a political nature at the request of the . . . Dutch, he would, at any rate to some degree, be committing His Majesty's Government.' What was needed, and needed quickly, was a ruling from London.[50] This was more easily said than done. Mountbatten and his political adviser had admitted that the question was a political one; for their part the Dutch could point to the civil affairs agreement which specified that the 'Force Commander in the N.E.I. will be advised by his NICA Staff and will act in accordance with the provisions of an agreement between His Majesty's Government and the Netherlands Government.'[51] To the Dutch the position was clear: the Sukarno 'government' had no legal status whatever, and Van Mook, both as head of NICA and the representative of the Netherlands government at Mountbatten's headquarters, had advised the Supreme Commander not to do anything that would imply recognition of the Republic. Mountbatten, however, recorded in his diary after the meeting with Van Mook that the situation in Java would require 'very careful handling.'[52]

Meanwhile reports were trickling in from the Indies about the state of p.o.w. and internee camps, the numbers of which quickly surpassed the original estimates on which the RAPWI programme had been based. At the 4 September meeting in Kandy, Mountbatten therefore agreed to despatch an advance naval force to make preliminary contact with the camps and to assess their precise needs. Four days later, on 8 September, a small SOE/Force 136 party of seven officers led by Major Greenhalgh was parachuted into Batavia to gather information about the p.o.w. situation. Given that Greenhalgh's task was limited to locating the camps, it was not to be expected that his report would dwell on the political situation, but it is nevertheless surprising that he dismissed as insignificant the change in conditions. 'The bulk of the native population in Java are indifferent to all political movements', he advised. 'All indications are that the Nationalists are confused in their aims and badly organized. . . .' His apparent lack of concern over the nationalist movement was all the more remarkable given that he predicted that once the problems of security and transport had been solved, the repatriation of p.o.w.s and internees was likely to be a straightforward operation.[53]

Greenhalgh's comments on the state of the camps' inhabitants reinforced Mountbatten's determination to send an advance naval force to Java. Accordingly, on 15 September, Rear Admiral W.R. Patterson of the Fifth Cruiser Squadron, commanding the cruiser HMS *Cumberland* and accompanied by a frigate and four minesweepers, arrived at the port of Batavia. On board were members of No. 6 RAPWI Control Staff and Van der Plas (representing Van Mook) whose task was to make contact with allied personnel in the camps. Shortly after the ships' arrival, Major Greenhalgh boarded and brought with him the recently released British p.o.w., Lt Colonel Laurens van der Post, whose comments on the overall situation – political, military and economic – were in sharp contrast to Greenhalgh's earlier more favourable assessment. That the position was quite unlike what Mountbatten and his staff had been led to expect was underlined by the report given to Patterson by Major General Yamamoto, Chief of Staff of the Japanese Military

Government in Java, who warned that only a British recognition of the new Indonesian Republic led by Sukarno and Hatta would avert bloodshed. Meanwhile, Yamamoto advised, anti-Dutch feeling was high, and the flying of the Dutch flag would be seen as a provocative act. Given Mountbatten's strictly – and at that stage quite properly – limited interpretation of the Chiefs of Staff directive, Patterson had little choice but to order Yamamoto to observe the terms of the surrender and to take all necessary steps to maintain control in Java until allied forces could relieve and disarm the Japanese garrisons.[54]

Though the Japanese complied as best they could with these orders, the situation was already out of hand. Patterson's orders to Yamamoto failed to acknowledge that to a large extent control had passed from the Japanese to the nationalists, and that the latter, well armed and determined, were not about to give up their newly proclaimed freedom without a struggle. On 18 September Patterson warned Mountbatten that the deterioration would be irreversible unless allied forces landed quickly, and three days later he reported that Japanese efforts to restore control had met with 'little success'.[55] So concerned was he not to inflame what was clearly a delicate situation that he requested Van der Plas and Van Straaten, the head of the NICA team, to abandon the quarters they had established in Batavia and to return to the *Cumberland*. Apparently he did not want the essential RAPWI work to become embroiled in the impending confrontation between the Dutch and the nationalists, which was likely to be the case if the nationalists looked upon the RAPWI personnel as some sort of vanguard of the Netherlands government. Van der Plas agreed but Van Straaten refused, first on the grounds that such a move would be interpreted as a retreat in the face of danger but also because by staying ashore he would be able to prevent the head of the RAPWI group, Lieutenant Colonel Dewar, from approaching Sukarno to grant his staff free passage through Batavia. Patterson himself, Van Straaten reported, was genuinely pro-Dutch and was convinced that Dutch troops would have to be used, but since he would not be in command of the land forces, there was no certainty that his successor would be as sympathetic to the Dutch point of view.[56] As they looked on helplessly the Dutch noted with mounting dismay that the Japanese had been able to do little more than remove Indonesian flags, while at the same time discouraging the display of the Dutch flag, up to that time the only visible symbol of Dutch authority.

Meanwhile, pressure was mounting on Mountbatten from two sides. Bevin urged Mountbatten to provide greater information about the numbers and whereabouts of p.o.w.s and internees in the NEI: the 'almost complete absence' of details about British Europeans, he complained, was causing 'great concern'. Bevin sought an assurance from Mountbatten that SEAC would take steps to locate and help prisoners 'at the earliest possible moment and in advance of complete occupation', and that priority would be given to British prisoners.[57] From Java, reports continued to reach Kandy that the situation was deteriorating. The medical director of the RAPWI team in Batavia stressed that 'serious repercussions' would follow unless 'speedy military relief' was sent to Java.[58] On the other side, the Dutch were insisting that the British government 'instruct' Mountbatten not to do anything that would imply recognition of the republic: local British commanders, the Dutch ambassador in London requested, should be told that wherever possible they should act in accordance with the advice of the Dutch authorities.[59]

These various demands could not easily be reconciled. Mountbatten's reply to Bevin laid out for the first time the enormity of the RAPWI task. In Java alone, figures were available for only three areas (Batavia, Bandung, and Magalang), but even the known p.o.w.s and internees there totalled more than 68,000. To give priority to British prisoners (which in Sumatra, for example, amounted to less than five per cent of SEAC's estimated responsibility) would entail the reversal of the Chiefs of Staff directive, which had given higher priority to prisoners in Malaya, Indochina and Siam.[60] Leaving aside the question of British prisoner priority, it was difficult to see how relief could be more quickly organised, given the paucity of resources at Mountbatten's disposal. It was even more difficult to contemplate a relief mission on the requisite scale without some form of contact and cooperation with the republican forces who maintained *de facto* control of the key areas of Java. Initially the British military authorities tried to stick to the letter of the several agreements governing the post-surrender situation. On 13 September, Slim emphasised to the RAPWI team in Batavia that it was 'essential to deal only with [the] Japanese Military Authorities so that no grounds [will be] given for a further claim that this Independence is recognised in any way by ourselves.'[61] At the same time Mountbatten was advised by Patterson, who had not yet even arrived at Batavia and who therefore lacked any first-hand information about conditions there, to expedite the despatch of Dutch troops to Java to maintain law and order as Patterson had 'no intention of landing British personnel to intervene.'[62] The Dutch took the opposite view. The Dutch Minister for Foreign Affairs, Dr E.N. van Kleffens, told the British ambassador at The Hague, Sir Nevile Bland, that the Dutch government had given Van Mook the discretion to issue a proclamation in the NEI, and that should Van Mook decide to exercise that discretion he could request Mountbatten to 'lend the cooperation of the services under his command for its dissemination and enforcement in Java.' Again the Dutch government urged that Mountbatten be 'instructed' to comply with such a request from Van Mook should it be forthcoming.[63]

There was mounting evidence that the position in Java differed strikingly from what various intelligence reports had led SEAC to expect. London was becoming edgy over the apparent lack of a sense of urgency in the RAPWI programme. The Dutch government, now confronted by the unavoidable fact that its return to the Indies would be resisted by armed nationalists, fell back with increasing vehemence on both the spirit and the letter of its agreements with the British who were the senior power in what was still an inter-allied command. Mountbatten had little choice but to reconsider his plans for a gradual resumption of allied control throughout the vast areas of SEAC, and to give a much higher priority to Java. He decided to advance the arrival of allied troops in Java by sending two brigade groups from 23rd Division in Malaya: the first, including divisional headquarters, was ordered to leave for Batavia by 1 October, the second was to follow soon after for Surabaya, the other stronghold of the nationalists on Java. To command this force, Mountbatten appointed Lt General Sir Philip Christison, who had distinguished himself with the 15th Indian Corps in the Arakan campaign.

There is some discrepancy in the accounts of Christison's appointment. The official historian records that Christison was 'warned' by Slim on 22 September that he was likely to be appointed Commander, Allied Land Forces, NEI, whereas Christison's own account puts his appointment several days earlier.[64] More important, Christison later recalled that he had been approached by Browning, Mountbatten's Chief of Staff:

'Christie', he said, 'things look pretty rum in Java and Sumatra. Dickie is determined not to risk his reputation in what may well be a very tricky situation. Are you prepared to carry the can for Dickie? If things go wrong he'll back you from the wings, but full responsibility would rest with you. You are not being ordered to take this on, but if you are prepared to carry the can for Dickie you will go as Allied Commander, NEI, and command your old 15 Corps with 2 or 3 divisions and a Tank Brigade. . . . Think it over, Dickie is most anxious you should take it on.'

The following day, Mountbatten himself put the proposition to Christison in much the same terms.[65] Mountbatten's official biographer, Philip Ziegler, rejects this account as 'unconvincing' and unreliable, written as it was some years after the event.[66] According to Ziegler, although Mountbatten was capable of 'appalling frankness', he never sought to evade responsibility, and indeed assured British political and military figures who were visiting Singapore at the time that he was involved in every decision that was taken affecting the NEI. Ziegler also rejects the suggestion that in making this proposal to Christison Mountbatten was acting on his determination to vindicate the memory of his father, forced to resign as First Sea Lord in 1914, by rising to the top of the Navy himself, and argues that to imply that Mountbatten was capable of letting someone else 'carry the can' underestimates the character of the man. Yet Ziegler's biography is a testament to Mountbatten's 'unbridled' ambition (to use Ziegler's own description), and to this author Christison's account rings true. Mountbatten was understandably anxious to bring his Supreme Allied Command to a successful conclusion, and while no-one yet foresaw just how difficult the situation in Java would become, it was already clear that the allied reoccupation would not be the straightforward operation originally planned. At the same time there was no reason to think that it would become SEAC's major post surrender preoccupation. Mountbatten's canvas had always been the larger one, the grand strategic design, the magnificent gesture, the sense of theatre: it was left to his subordinates to execute the local details. Java fell into the latter category, a nasty imbroglio that was threatening to unbalance the whole of SEAC's post surrender planning, but one that still could not claim the greater part of the Supreme Commander's attention, which at this stage was fixed on

Indochina. Whether it was Mountbatten or Browning who spoke to Christison (and it is quite possible, indeed likely, that both broached the subject in much the same terms: the two accounts are not at all incompatible), Christison's appointment marked a new phase in SEAC's involvement in the East Indies.

Chapter five
Deeper into Java

On-the-spot reports from Admiral Patterson convinced Mountbatten that SEAC's plans for Java would have to be changed. According to Van der Plas, Mountbatten had told him that Britain 'would on no account be drawn into internal troubles in Java' and that the Dutch could not rely on British troops to put down any 'revolts or riots'. This decision, Mountbatten stressed, was an 'irrevocable governmental one'.[1] In fact no such decision had been made, nor could it have been made within the terms of the Civil Affairs agreement between Britain and the Netherlands, under which SEAC was responsible for the maintenance of law and order, which presumably included suppressing at least riots if not revolts. Nevertheless, confirmation of this interpretation of the British government's policy came from the Secretary of State for War, J.J. Lawson, who at a meeting of Mountbatten's staff in Singapore said that it was a 'fundamental policy . . . not to interfere in the internal affairs of non-British territories', although he recognised that such a policy made things very difficult for the military forces involved in those areas.[2] Mountbatten's version of Lawson's statement was rather stronger: according to Mountbatten, Lawson said that 'Britain's obligations to her Allied [sic] will not involve fighting for the Dutch against the Nationalists in Java or for the French against the people of French Indochina.'[3] It was presumably this comment (in either version) to which Van der Plas was referring when he told Van Mook that the 'irrevocable' decision not to become involved 'has been borne out personally to me by the British Secretary of State for War.'[4]

At a subsequent press conference Lawson spoke on the same subject, and according to Reuter's Singapore correspondent (whom the Reuter's head office in London described as 'reliable and

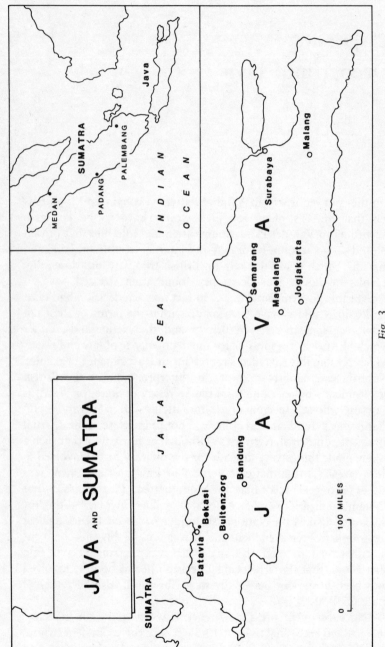

Fig. 3

trustworthy'[5]), said that Britain had no intention of intervening in Java. When this was reported in the world-wide press, the Dutch were understandably appalled, and the British government deeply embarrassed. Attlee's reprimand of Lawson – 'Statements on policy should not be made by Ministers travelling abroad without first seeking guidance from home'[6] – avoided the fact that Britain in effect had no policy, or at least had none that took account of what was actually happening in the Indies rather than being based on wartime projections that no longer corresponded with reality. Lawson replied: 'I have never in public or in private made any statement that we should not intervene. I could not avoid meeting the press at Singapore but I resisted every attempt to press me to talk about Java and other such territories.'[7] Bevin commented drily that it was 'certainly mysterious how if he never said anything on the subject, the reports circulated.'[8] When Lawson returned to London he told the Cabinet Defence Committee that all he had said to Van der Plas (having refused to speak to the press) was that 'British Commonwealth forces were going into Java to disarm the Japs and keep the peace. It was not our concern to interfere in domestic problems.'[9] Van der Plas, however, told Mook that in the presence of Lawson he had been advised that 'no British soldier would be used for the restoration of Dutch authority' and that the sole task of British military forces was to aid the RAPWI programme in Batavia and Surabaya, beyond which areas British troops would not be sent.'[10]

Lawson's comments in Singapore were for the Dutch at best an unwelcome indication of the general drift of British thinking on the NEI, but much worse was the attitude betrayed by Christison. On 28 September a battalion of the Seaforth Highlanders, accompanied by some five hundred marines and naval personnel, were landed at the port of Batavia. The same day Christison left Singapore. Just before his departure he gave a press conference (in accordance with orders he had received to that effect, he claimed in his memoirs). He briefly outlined the three tasks before him – to disarm the Japanese, to recover prisoners, and to keep law and order in the main cities until the Dutch could reclaim their colonial empire. The next day, together with an ADC, he flew to Batavia and there gave another press conference. He announced that his forces would occupy only key areas, and would hold them pending the return of Dutch control. According to reports which the Dutch accepted, he went on to say that no Dutch troops were included in the initial landings because the nationalists had threatened to oppose them. He intended to meet the nationalist leaders to explain his role, and he said he would convene a round table conference so as to bring them face to face with the Dutch, 'something which the Dutch have steadfastly refused to do hitherto'.[11]

His remarks, or rather the garbled accounts of them that subsequently circulated in the press and on the radio, caused a sensation. From Brisbane Van Mook angrily cabled Mountbatten: 'If newspapers and broadcast reports are true your commander in Batavia created impression of virtually recognizing the Indonesian republic. I can hardly believe this public action taken without your consent and without even previous notice to my government or myself.' The whole Civil Affairs agreement between the Dutch and the British in SEAC was now at risk, and Van Mook warned that he would have to await instructions from The Hague.[12] Mountbatten moved quickly to limit the damage, and told Christison:

Although the general line you have taken up about not getting embroiled is in accordance with the policy of His Majesty's Government, it is certainly not their policy to accuse the Dutch publicly of an intransigent attitude and to indicate that the British sympathies are with the Indonesians. I have shown this to the Secretary of State for War and to my Dutch Staff and we all feel that unless you can put out a suitable correction our position with the Dutch government will become impossible.[13]

Christison duly issued a statement that he had been misquoted, grotesquely in places, but the Dutch were not mollified. There was enough truth in the original reports of Christison's views to offset subsequent denials of specific comments. Before leaving for Batavia, Christison had been told by Lawson:

Mr Bevin has asked me to make it quite clear to you that HM Government are determined that nothing should be done to suggest your troops are going to reimpose Dutch colonial rule. You must not take sides. Carry out your role; it may be up to 6 months before Dutch troops can be trained and sent from Holland. The Dutch and any rebel factions must sort things out for themselves. You may, though, use your good offices to arrange meetings if this seems necessary.[14]

On the day that Christison departed for Batavia, Mountbatten met with two former prisoners of war who gave him an up-to-date and realistic picture of conditions in the Indies. Their information, which was completely at odds with the reassuring assessments that the Dutch had been providing, convinced him that it was essential for the Dutch to begin talks with the nationalist leaders. Not only was this necessary to safeguard the interests of the Dutch, but it was vital for the protection of the prisoners of war and internees whose condition Lady Mountbatten had witnessed in the course of her visit to camps in Sumatra and Java and subsequently described in graphic terms to the Supreme Commander. Purely on the basis of the Chiefs of Staff directive, therefore, Mountbatten could justify pressure on both sides to open negotiations. Later the same day Mountbatten discussed the situation with Van der Plas, and urged him to meet Sukarno and Hatta on the grounds that lack of contact between the Dutch and the Indonesians was aggravating tensions in Java.[15] To Van Mook Mountbatten suggested that the Dutch government at once issue a 'clear cut statement about the future status of the Netherlands East Indies . . . . and the possible time by which such a status shall be attained.'[16] To the Chiefs of Staff he appealed for backing: '[I have urged that] the Dutch Government should make an immediate pronouncement on their future intention with regard to some degree of independence for the Netherlands East Indies. I hope you will be able to support this.'[17] This was a bold, not to say outrageous, assumption of political authority on Mountbatten's part, and one that the Dutch justifiably resented.

Van Mook replied that it was Mountbatten's responsibility to maintain law and order until the Netherlands government was ready and able to assume control: in the meantime, and in the absence of Dutch troops, the Dutch would have to rely on the military force of the British to undertake that 'resolute action' which alone could prevent 'complete chaos and unnecessary bloodshed'. For his part Van Mook was prepared to enter into discussions with the Indonesian leaders 'so long as this does not imply direct or indirect recognition of the so-called Republic of Indonesia which would leave no base for discussion.'[18] Given the welter of confused and confusing reports, details of which had not been passed on to Van Mook, Mountbatten could hardly have expected indications of greater willingness to accommodate the nationalists' demands. For Van Mook the Civil Affairs agreement was still the basis of cooperation between the British and the Dutch, and under that agreement Mountbatten was to be advised by the representatives of the Dutch government, rather than the other way round as Mountbatten now seemed to be suggesting. Van Mook's approach to the Republic was an intensely legalistic one,[19] and for him the difficulty was how to combine a refusal to recognise the Republic with his acceptance of the need for some degree of cooperation with the forces in control in Java if prisoners and internees were to be rescued quickly.

This degree of moderation did not last long. Even as Van Mook replied to Mountbatten's extraordinary political initiative – the more astonishing in light of his earlier stated reluctance to be drawn into overt political actions – the Dutch attitude was hardening. They were bitter and resentful. Their bitterness arose out of what they considered to be their shabby treatment at the hands of the allies, and the British in particular, at the end of the war. The Dutch war effort against Japan had been taken for granted, or worse, not even acknowledged. The fact that the Dutch had put up the strongest resistance of the colonial powers seemed to count for nothing. They had readily offered assistance to British Malaya and to Australia in their hour of need, but now that it was the Dutch who looked to their allies for help, none was forthcoming. Instead, the British seemed intent on appeasing Sukarno and his collaborationist followers, whose 'so-called government was not the outcome of a spontaneous and wide-spread popular movement, but represented a Japanese attempt to continue the war in the Netherlands East Indies under another guise.'[20] It was intolerable to the Dutch that the Anglo-American Combined Chiefs of Staff should control Dutch shipping through the Allied Shipping Pool, especially when the Americans then used the Dutch liner *Nieuw Amsterdam* to repatriate US troops from Europe. Anglo-American control of shipping was thus responsible in Dutch eyes for preventing them from transporting their own troops to the east, at the same time as the British claimed to be incapable of holding any but two key areas because they were intent on pushing ahead with their own accelerated demobilisation programme. It particularly galled them to see British troops actively assisting France in the restoration of French rule in southern Indochina. The Dutch felt, quite justifiably, that on the basis of their respective contributions to the war against Japan, their own case was much more deserving of British support than that of the French, whose colonial administration loyal to the Vichy government had not been displaced by the Japanese until March 1945. Active identification with the allied cause seemed to the Dutch to carry a very real penalty.[21]

Dutch bitterness was compounded by their resentment over the attitude displayed at first by Mountbatten and later by most of the British. At the meeting with Van der Plas on 28 September, Mountbatten impressed on the Dutch the necessity for them to deal with Sukarno just as he had dealt with Aung San in Burma. This was a theme to which Mountbatten often returned in the following weeks, and each time he did so, far from convincing the Dutch, he entrenched their opposition to dealing with those nationalist leaders tarred with the collaborationist brush. Mountbatten's tendency to lecture the Dutch on Sukarno reflected – among other things – his belief that the situations in Burma and Java were analagous. They were not.

The Burma National Army (BNA) had been established by the Japanese in 1942. By early 1945, in the wake of Japanese defeats in Burma and following disillusionment with Japanese policies, the BNA switched to the allied side. Mountbatten was persuaded by Force 136 that the BNA could be a useful addition to allied operations against the Japanese, and promptly overruled his Commander-in-Chief in Burma, Lt General Sir Oliver Leese, who had accepted the advice of his civil affairs staff that to embrace the BNA would carry political risks. Mountbatten insisted that the decision to rearm the BNA was ultimately a political one, and therefore fell within his purview as Supreme Allied Commander.[22] As long as the Japanese remained undefeated Mountbatten could argue that the military situation dictated a course of action that might otherwise have been unacceptable.

By May 1945 he could point to political imperatives as well. The release of the White Paper on the future of Burma, with self-government as the ultimate aim of British policy, enabled him to insist that it was unrealistic to exclude from discussions any significant element in Burmese life. His position as Supreme Commander made it possible for him to act on that belief. Intensely conscious of his position and prerogatives, he was quite prepared to ride roughshod over anyone in whom he detected a hint of opposition. In June 1945 he issued instructions on the policy that was to be adopted towards the Burmese population. 'The guiding principle which I am determined shall be observed', he directed, 'is that no person shall suffer on account of political opinions honestly held, whether now or in the past, even if these may have been anti-British, but only on account of proven crimes against the criminal law or actions repugnant to humanity.' He went on to insist that a distinction be made between honest patriots who may have been 'politically confused' by Japanese promises of Burmese independence and those who participated in war atrocities or who 'actively opposed our return'.[23] Several weeks later at a staff meeting he spoke out against those who favoured a much harder line against collaborationist Burmese, and claimed that his policy 'had been repeatedly sabotaged by certain people who had not come into the open and directly opposed it, but had tried to whittle it away by procrastination in implementing it and by various other subter- fuges.' He threatened to take disciplinary action against anyone found acting contrary to the spirit of his directive, and would have preferred to go even further: in his notes for the meeting, he wrote that he would see to it that offenders were court-martialled.[24] As he was apparently accusing certain members of the Civil Affairs branch, this was a drastic threat to make, even if technically within his competence. Mountbatten's critics were not impressed by this display of overweening authority, because the directive had not yet been circulated to most of them, and in the following week Mountbatten apologised for his intemperate accusations.[25]

It was a different matter in London. When the Director of Intelligence in SEAC, Major General W.R.C. Penney, attended a meeting of the Chiefs of Staff in October, he noted that when the discussion turned to Java, the First Sea Lord, Admiral Cunningham ('the Old Man of the Sea'), made two contributions: '(a)Give them a whiff of grapeshot. (b)It's no use talking of Aung San as more than 50% of people in England would like to have seen him shot.'[26] In his own territory, however, Mountbatten did not have to worry about such sentiments. He explained to Tom Driberg, the left-wing Labour MP who was visiting the Far East: 'I can assure you that if I was left as free a hand in French Indochina and the Netherlands East Indies as I was left in Burma, I could solve both these problems by the same methods; though it is heartbreaking to have to leave the political control to other nations when we are really in military control.'[27] In view of the military problems that SEAC was experiencing in these areas, this display of self-assurance can only be described as breathtaking, but then Mountbatten was never one to be over- whelmed by circumstances.

Despite some superficial similarities with Burma, the situation in the NEI was in fact quite different. The nationalists in Java did not emerge as a real force until the Japanese surrender, so that there was no military reason to enlist their support. Sukarno and other nationalist leaders had collaborated with the Japanese, and had accepted arms from the defeated enemy. While the nationalist leaders had proclaimed their willingness to accept British but not Dutch troops in the NEI, they had not maintained control – either through unwillingness or inability – over the various armed groups in Java, where the p.o.w. and internee camps were increasingly subjected to intimidation and in some cases murderous attack. In a real sense, therefore, the nationalists were guilty of hampering the fulfilment of Mountbatten's objectives as defined by the Chiefs of Staff directive.

In a more general sense, Mountbatten's approach showed a remarkable ignorance of Dutch sensitivities. Burma was a British colony, the East Indies were not. Much as he liked to fall back on his status as the Supreme Allied Commander, he was seen by the Dutch as a British commander who was given to interfering in internal Dutch matters. In the White Paper of May 1945, the British government had committed itself to eventual self-government for Burma. No such undertaking had been made by the Dutch. The only pronouncement on the future of the NEI was that in Queen Wilhelmina's December 1942 speech, and even its vague suggestions of political autonomy had been rejected in private by leading Dutch politicians. It was not a case therefore, of keeping local officials on a course which had already been determined. In his insistence that Van Mook and others meet Sukarno and his followers, Mountbatten was pushing the Dutch along a path they had not yet decided to follow. However reasonable, and indeed inevitable, that course seemed to Mountbatten, pressure on them to take it appeared to the Dutch to be an unwarranted, even outrageous, trespass upon prerogatives that were theirs alone to exercise.

Burma was not the centrepiece of the British empire in the way that the NEI was for the Dutch. It was India that aroused the greatest passions in British circles, whereas the question of Burma was much less controversial. Once Labour took office in July 1945 the way was open for substantial political concessions which, moreover, the British could offer from a position of strength. By the end of the war against Japan, the British had in Burma seven infantry divisions, 250 tanks, and a considerable number of aircraft. The capital, Rangoon, fell in May, and when the Japanese

surrender was announced, not only did the British have control of
the country but they had won it by dint of prolonged battle. In
Burma alone did the allies achieve the crushing victory in a former
colonial territory that was thought to be the necessary precondition
for the restoration of imperial power. Once restored, that power
could be surrendered, in the words of the official British historian,
'as an act of grace and not of duress.'[28] It could not have been more
different for the Dutch in the NEI. Not only had they failed to drive
the Japanese out by force of arms but when they returned they came
on the coat-tails of the British. Concessions to the nationalists, they
believed therefore, would be interpreted not so much as a sign of
weakness – for that was evident – but as an acknowledgement and
acceptance of that weakness. The Indies were seen as critical to the
prosperity of the Netherlands, itself the most war-damaged country
of western Europe. To relinquish their claim to the NEI was to
condemn the home country to a protracted period of recovery, or
even worse, to a permanent reduction in its economic status. As well
there were political considerations. Unlike Britain, the Netherlands
had been occupied by German forces for five years. At the end of the
war there were some 80,000 Dutch collaborators awaiting trial, the
prospect of which was daunting to a government anxious to heal the
wounds of the war years. The fate of scores of thousands of Dutch
prisoners and internees in the Indies was still unknown. In those
circumstances, how could the government put Dutch citizens before
the courts on charges of collaboration while in the eastern empire it
was willing to treat with those who had done no less and whose
failure to control their wilder supporters was endangering the lives
of those who had fought to protect Dutch interests and paid for
their service with years of imprisonment at the hands of the
Japanese.

Reports of the statements by Lawson and Christison impelled the
Dutch government to seek clarification of British policy. The reply
that it got was not wholly reassuring, but neither was it wholly
discouraging. The public furore over comments made by men on the
spot, and the subsequent Dutch protest, forced the British government to define its position. But that did not come immediately, and
in the process Anglo-Dutch relations further soured.

   At the end of September the Dutch Ambassador in London met
Bevin to discuss the attitude of the British government towards

events in Java and to find out if the statements of Lawson and Christison accurately reflected British policy. The initial reaction of the Foreign Office was sympathetic to the concerns expressed by the Dutch. After a preliminary talk with Dutch officials, Wilson Young recommended that Britain should respond favourably to Dutch requests for greater assistance in the NEI. 'However anxious we may be to avoid being drawn into internal politics in the countries of South East Asia,' he wrote, 'it is submitted that Admiral Mountbatten cannot divest himself of the responsibility for maintaining law and order through out his theatre.' When the record of Dutch participation in the war, the allocation of Dutch shipping to the allied pool, and the overall responsibility of SEAC to maintain law and order were taken into account, the Foreign Office was justified in asking the Chiefs of Staff to 'instruct' Mountbatten 'to meet in the furthest degree practicable Dr Van Mook's requests for assistance in Java.' This was clearly a matter that would require discussion at the highest level, but in the meantime, Wilson Young suggested, it could be impressed upon the Dutch that 'we are sure that the War Secretary's statement was not intended to preclude use of British troops for putting down any revolt or riots involving serious risk to life and property.'[29] Sterndale Bennett was of a like mind, adding: 'the Dutch stood by us in 1940–41 when things were very black in the Far East and were we now by inactivity to favour the schemes of these people who have been collaborating with the Japanese we should do great harm to Anglo-Dutch relations.'[30] The Dutch could hardly have put their own case more concisely.

Nor could they have had a more sympathetic listener than Bevin, who at his meeting with the Dutch Ambassador and the Minister for Overseas Territories accepted that any appearance that Britain was avoiding its responsibility to maintain law and order and was in any way encouraging 'the consolidation of a movement which has been collaborating with our enemies' would have a 'very harmful effect' on Anglo-Dutch relations. Bevin promised to look into the possibility of speeding up the movement of Dutch troops to the NEI, although he cautioned that this was ultimately a matter for the Chiefs of Staff.[31] The Dutch could not realistically have asked for a stronger endorsement of their position. The Minister of Coordination of Warfare for the Kingdom, W. Schermerhorn, assured Helfrich that after the talks with Bevin 'it became evident that statements of Lawson and Christison only give their personal opinions and are not based on directions from the British Government.'[32]

Far from settling anything, the meeting between Bevin and the Dutch representatives merely pointed up the hollowness of the British position. Neither the Foreign Office nor the War Office knew what to do. Even less did they know what advice or instruction to give Mountbatten. Bevin emphasised that it was of the 'utmost urgency' that Mountbatten be told by the Chiefs of Staff of 'the manner in which he is to employ his troops'[33] and that he also be cautioned against making any statements without prior approval 'that might be taken as reflecting His Majesty's Government's opinion in the political affairs of foreign countries.'[34] In effect, in the absence of any clearly defined government position, the Foreign Office left it to the War Office to set the practical limits to Mountbatten's intervention, wherever it was to be made.

The only immediate suggestion that the Foreign Office could make was that Christison should be provided with a political adviser. 'Lt Gen Christison seems quite unable to avoid making undesirable statements', noted Wilson Young. 'He appears to have gone to extreme lengths in annoying the Dutch.' 'Ought not urgent steps be taken to attach a political adviser to General Christison?' asked another member of the Foreign Office. 'Otherwise he may wreck Anglo-Dutch relations for the next 20 years.'[35] Two days later H.F.C. Walsh was appointed to give political guidance to Christison. Within the Foreign Office, however, there was some confusion over Walsh's intended role. Orme Sargent, the Deputy Under-Secretary, was concerned to ensure that while he acted as adviser to Christison Walsh would still be answerable to the Foreign Office whose representative he would be while acting as Consul General in Batavia.[36] These precise circumstances did not arise since it was subsequently decided not to give Walsh any consular duties, but the more general question remained. Given that SEAC still operated as a military command under a supreme commander, were all political decisions ultimately his responsibility? Mountbatten claimed that they were, but Dening – and the Foreign Office – thought otherwise. The Chiefs of Staff were quick to advise Mountbatten to 'warn your commanders that it would be better to refrain from making public statements without prior approval. However well meaning such statements may be, there is [a] liability for misconstruction at a time when feeling is running rather high.'[37] Slim put it more succinctly to Mountbatten: 'He [Christison] has now been told to shut up.'[38] Mountbatten in turn warned Christison that the furore over his alleged statements to the press was 'well on the way to becoming an international incident and was no longer a "storm in a tea cup".'[39]

The onus was now on the Foreign Office and the Chiefs of Staff to delineate a clear policy. Dening felt that it was unlikely that the British and the Dutch would ever agree on the desirability of holding talks with the nationalist leaders, but since it would be British troops who would bear the initial brunt of the occupation of Java ('and in no great strength') Britain was entitled to ask the Dutch not to take any action that would make the British position more difficult or more dangerous. Again, the lack of reliable information about precise conditions in Java was a handicap, and Dening urged that no firm decisions be taken until the seriousness of the situation could be authoritatively assessed. 'But the principle of intervention or non-intervention requires to be outlined', he concluded, 'and my own view is the latter is the only safe course to pursue both from the point of view of our own position in the Far East and world opinion.'[40]

While that question was being decided at the highest level, Dening suggested that the military commanders on the spot had to be given considerable discretion to take whatever actions they thought necessary to maintain law and order and to protect their own troops, and conversely, they had to have the right not to be forced into actions at the behest of the Dutch that might 'prejudice beyond recovery our own attempts to restore our own position in the Far East. . . . [Furthermore] we should use such influence as we have with France and the Netherlands to ensure that they do not imperil the general position of European powers in the Far East.' The use of force to maintain law and order had to be seen as a last resort, and should not be provoked by Dutch irresponsibility or obstinacy. Gracey's intervention to arrange talks between the French and the Vietnamese, for example, had at least produced a temporary ceasefire: nothing had been settled, but the breathing space had enabled Gracey to increase his force level in Saigon. A similar situation might well arise in Java, and clear advice had to be available to Mountbatten:

As you are aware the Supreme Commander has never received any instructions on the political implications of the task which has been allotted to him by the Chiefs of Staff. I would strongly advise against him being so instructed as to become involved in political complications in French Indo-China or Netherlands East Indies. But I do suggest that [it] is only fair to him that he should receive a clear indication of the policy of His Majesty's Government in this matter.[41]

No such policy yet existed, and neither the Foreign Office nor the Chiefs of Staff had come to grips with the complex military/ political problem that confronted SEAC.

Mountbatten's own Joint Planning Staff pointed out that with the forces at his disposal, Mountbatten could do no more than occupy the key areas of Java. If the Supreme Commander was to be made responsible for the maintenance of law and order throughout the whole of the island, substantial reinforcements would be required. The movement of Dutch troops from Europe could not be accelerated, and even if Dutch troops did arrive, their level of training was such that it was unlikely that they would enable Mountbatten to expand his areas of control. The only alternative source of reinforcements was from British and imperial troops stationed elsewhere in SEAC, but their deployment in the NEI would necessitate the sacrifice of other operations, especially in British areas.[42] Bevin quickly appreciated that the only way to limit British involvement in the NEI was to accelerate the despatch of Dutch troops. This became even more urgent after the Dutch made it plain – and public – that they were not about to amplify the general proposals made in Queen Wilhelmina's 1942 speech, which in their view 'sufficiently explained their intentions.'[43] Their dismissal of Sukarno as a 'mere opportunist' with 'fascist tendencies' who had 'systematically preached hatred against the allies',[44] and their repudiation of Van der Plas, who under pressure from Mountbatten had agreed to meet the Republican leaders, were clear indications that they were not about to make any willing accommodation with the situation that prevailed in Java. Unless the British commitment was to become even greater, it was vital that Dutch troops be sent to the NEI more quickly. Again, the question turned on the problem of shipping. The War Office explained that 3200 Dutch troops in Britain were due to leave for the NEI between 20–24 October. Their departure could be advanced only by interfering with the arrangements to ship 7000 French troops to Indochina, or by delaying the release and repatriation of British troops in India. French Indochina, the War Office contended, had at least as strong a claim as the NEI for special consideration, while the British repatriation programme was politically too sensitive to be touched.[45] Anxious to pass the military responsibility on to the Dutch, Bevin said that he was prepared to consider the use of British warships or of American ships to move Dutch forces to the NEI.[46]

But even by drawing on other sources of shipping, the Dutch would be in no position to assume control for at least some weeks. In the meantime British forces would bear the brunt of the deepening imbroglio. What were to be the limits of their role? Bevin thought it was essential that either the Government or Mountbatten make a public statement.[47] Mountbatten had already made his position quite clear: he was there to carry out policy, not to initiate it. The Chiefs of Staff asked him for an estimate of the number of troops he would need to extend his control outside Batavia and Surabaya if he encountered strong Indonesian resistance, a request that implied an enlargement of their original directive to him. They also approved of Mountbatten's action in issuing a proclamation on the occasion of the landing of British troops in Batavia in which Mountbatten had stated that the role of those troops was to maintain law and order.[48]

Mountbatten had little enough guidance on policy. What he did receive in these early days of the reoccupation tended to be confused and confusing. Despite his stated reluctance, he felt that as the man on the spot he had no choice but to take matters into his own hands. The Chiefs of Staff instructed him to provide all the facilities necessary for the widest possible distribution throughout Java of the proclamation which Van Mook had drafted on 26 September (i.e. before the full extent of the Republic's strength and determination to resist the return of the Dutch had become apparent).[49] Several days later, also in response to requests from the Dutch, they ordered Mountbatten to take 'such steps as may be practicable' to control Radio Bandung whose broadcasts the Dutch regarded as offensive and inflammatory.[50] Mountbatten chose to ignore both these orders as inappropriate to the situation. He thought that Van Mook's proposed proclamation, with its heavy emphasis on the illegality of the Republic and its refusal to acknowledge the changed conditions that the war had brought, was itself inflammatory. He directed Van Mook to make changes to it, and he advised Christison to so word his reports back to SEAC

3 Mountbatten greeted by Lt General Sir Philip Christison in Batavia

headquarters that military conditions could be used as a pretext for suppressing the proclamation.[51] Much to Mountbatten's relief, it was subsequently withdrawn. As for Radio Bandung, there were no 'practicable steps' that could be taken against it.

It was an unsatisfactory position for Mountbatten to be in. His commander-in-chief of land forces, Slim, argued that the terms of the limited directive issued by the Chiefs of Staff, the maintenance of law and order, could only be achieved by two methods: either the British had to suppress the nationalists or cooperate with them. The first course implied a military confrontation; the second some sort of political recognition, if only a *de facto* one. Mountbatten was inclined to agree, and directed that the choice be put squarely to the Chiefs of Staff *and* to the Foreign Office so that a 'clear-cut decision' could be prised out of London.[52] In a subsequent cable to the Chiefs of Staff, Mountbatten rejected any criticism of his pressure on Van der Plas to meet with Sukarno. He emphasised that he had not given any 'advice on political lines' or suggested 'any modification to the policy of the Netherlands Government' (both of which claims were less than wholly true); on the contrary his suggestion to Van der Plas had arisen purely out of the military fact that British, not Dutch, forces, would have to cope with any situation that developed from a Dutch refusal to meet the nationalist leaders. In seeking 'clear guidance on policy', Mountbatten outlined the alternatives open to the British. If they decided to take a restricted view of their responsibilities, and limit themselves to disarming the Japanese and recovering prisoners of war and internees, it was necessary only to hold the key areas of Batavia and Surabaya for the introduction of Dutch troops who would then establish law and order in the rest of Java. If, however, the wider view was taken, and SEAC assumed the responsibility for the whole of Java (and the rest of the NEI), there either had to be an accommodation 'between the Dutch and the Indonesian Republic' so that troop levels could be kept at a relatively low level, or Britain had to allow the Dutch to declare the Republic illegal and to embark on a campaign of forcible suppression, which would involve a sizeable commitment of troops.

Each of these alternatives had unpalatable features. The first would require SEAC to rely on the Japanese outside the key areas, but their record to that point was such that they would be capable only of maintaining a minimum of order by dispensing with the

observance of law. Successful control therefore depended on the
harmony that could be established between the Dutch and the
Indonesians, and especially on the attitude that the Dutch population and troops took towards the Republic. The military implications of the second course were such that Mountbatten spelled
them out in detail. The movement of 23rd Indian Division would be
accelerated so that the whole division could be deployed in Java by
the end of November. RAF Headquarters NEI with two fighter
bomber squadrons and a squadron of Dutch Catalinas would be
available in Java by the middle of October. Course 2(b) required
the use of additional forces – 26th Indian Division and an extra two
fighter bomber squadrons from India, and an armoured brigade
from Malaya. The second division was earmarked for Sumatra,
and its deployment in Java would entail delays in the disarming of
the Japanese and the RAPWI programme on Sumatra. There would
also be delays in providing relief personnel for the garrison on
Hong Kong, the occupation of SEAC's territories east of Borneo,
and in the arrival of British forces in Chinese ports and in Hong
Kong. 'It is not for me to make recommendation [sic] on political
grounds which course is to be adopted', Mountbatten wrote, 'but
the military implications of adopting course (2)(b) would in my
opinion be more serious. I therefore request a clear ruling from
H.M. Government whether I am to adopt (1) or (2) and if course
(2) a further clear ruling if I am to adopt course (2)(b) if the Dutch
insist.'[53]

In later life, Mountbatten was inclined to suggest that he alone in
SEAC understood the nature of the problem facing him, that he
had to contend with subordinates who were unable or unwilling to
confront the political dimensions of the situation in Java.[54] This
was typical of the gloss which he applied to the past, sometimes
subconsciously, sometimes deliberately, especially where his own
reputation was at stake. In fact, many of his officers quite independently reached conclusions that were very similar to Mountbatten's
and their support for his position undoubtedly strengthened his
hand when dealing with London. From Mountbatten down, there
was little sympathy in military circles in SEAC for the Dutch
position, none of the expressions of practical support which the
Dutch felt were their due as a wartime ally. Slim's Chief of Staff,
Major General H.E. Pyman, visited Java in early October, and
came away disturbed by the approach of the Dutch – military and

political – to the problem there. On the basis of talks in Singapore he concluded that by their provocative actions, the Dutch had inflamed an already tense situation. Whereas British troops could move around Batavia without hindrance,

> Dutch troops can go nowhere except in strength, and they are then like red rags to a bull. The Dutch are behaving like reactionary exiles or neurotic prisoners of war and internees. The former refuse to admit that Indonesians did declare their independence and assume power on 17 Aug, the latter are hysterically frightened that they will all be massacred if some statement of policy is not made at once.

(So much for the prospects for course (1), which Mountbatten had stressed depended on the attitude that the Dutch civil population and troops adopted towards the Indonesians.) It was one thing for Pyman to describe conditions in Java, even in terms that showed a remarkable inability to appreciate, if not to accept, the Dutch perspective: they were exiles and former prisoners and internees. The former had gone through the war in almost complete ignorance of the changes that had taken place in the Indies; the latter were anxious to the point of distraction over the fate of their families, most of whom were still in camps controlled by nationalist forces. 'Reactionary' and 'neurotic' they might have been, but not without cause. It was quite another thing for Pyman to make recommendations on political matters, yet he had no hesitation. 'The following is required', he advised Slim:

(a)   Van Mook should fly to Holland to give the Dutch Government the true picture. He must be realistic. Soekarno Cabinet has run Java since 17 Aug 45.
(b)   Dutch Government should authorise Van Mook to make a preliminary statement on behalf of the Government before he goes to Holland.
(c)   The Dutch Government must make their policy statement as soon as they have been put in the picture by Van Mook.
(d)   The following subjects must be covered:-
Degree of self government to be given.
Currency.
Flag and national anthem.
Treatment of independence movement leaders and adherents must be liberal.
Netherlands East Indies Civil Affairs must be called Indonesian Civil Affairs, or at least by some other name.

The Dutch, he suggested, 'have a splendid opportunity to make a generous declaration of policy and restore their prestige in [the]

NEI and assure themselves of the lasting loyalty and co-operation of the Indonesians.'[55]

In Singapore Pyman had described his relations with all Dutch officials, civil and military, as 'excellent'. It was a different matter when he arrived in Batavia. He was 'disagreeably surprised' by Van Mook's hardline attitude towards the nationalists, and even more by his criticisms of the level of British support:

Clearly, he could not have followed the course of the *European* war with any intelligence or gratitude. He was very rude with regard to our actions in Java, and he will require a very firm handling. . . . As we are operating at present, Van Mook considers that we are an embarrassment to him. I am sure that Van Mook's present policy is an embarrassment to our Commanders.

Pyman advised Slim to discount Van Mook's belief that the nationalists could be suppressed with little force: on the contrary, Pyman reported, both British and Dutch military commanders thought that 'many lives would be lost over a long period'.[56] Several days later, back in Singapore, Pyman was invited by Mountbatten to comment on a letter he had received from Van Mook. Describing it as making 'impossible requests' and showing a 'complete lack of gratitude', Pyman advised Mountbatten 'to knock Van Mook for six and ensure that he arranges a meeting and comes to terms with Soekarno and his party'.[57]

Slim was more circumspect in his language but no less firm on the proper course of action. In the face of directions from London that had been 'somewhat involved and at times contradictory', he recommended to the Chief of the Imperial General Staff, Field Marshal Sir Alan Brooke, who had been in Singapore in late September, that Britain should limit its role to holding a few key areas and rely on Japanese troops to protect Dutch nationals in the rest of the Indies. The movement of Dutch forces to the NEI should be speeded up, and once they had arrived the NEI should be excised from SEAC's area of responsibility except for the task of disarming and repatriating the Japanese. At the same time pressure had to be put on the Dutch to make 'real, honest, definite, offers of self-government' to the nationalists.[58] To Mountbatten, Slim urged that Christison should not send troops outside Batavia, with the possible exception of Surabaya, a significant narrowing of the generally accepted minimum areas that British troops would have to hold. He also suggested that in the event of a Dutch refusal to negotiate with the nationalists – a likely proposition – the British should undertake to open talks with them on purely military grounds, i.e. that Britain did not recognise them as a government but 'demanded' their cooperation 'as influential private individuals to prevent chaos, famine and bloodshed.' This was truly, as the DQMG at SEAC headquarters, Major General R.A. Riddell, remarked, 'sailing rather close to the wind' but, as Slim concluded his letter, the situation was 'fraught with great danger'.[59]

Christison also shared most of these views. He advised Slim that the only practicable course was to recover Java by 'goodwill', a course that would entail 'generous advances in self government based on equality of opportunity and cooperation between the Dutch, Eurasians, Indonesians and Chinese.'[60] Van Mook, he assured Mountbatten, 'has quite come round to my way of thinking', a marked change from their initial meeting which had been very frosty and which had only been rescued, according to Christison, when he promised that Van Mook could take up residence in the vice-regal palace in Batavia.[61] Even Helfrich, thought Christison, was becoming a 'realist', though 'a bit of a nuisance. I no longer press for his removal, but think he might keep on the move!'[62]

Charm and social graces were overrated as weapons in the arsenal of diplomacy. Van Mook was not the sort to be swayed quite so easily, no more than he – or Helfrich – was likely to be seduced by Mountbatten's confident technique. After a party at which the two were seated next to him, Mountbatten wrote in his diary that he had 'worked on them like mad throughout dinner.'[63] Both could detect when they were being patronised and simply became more determined to resist what they saw as British efforts to undermine their own prerogatives and Dutch control of the Indies. Helfrich in particular was wary of any attempt to bypass his authority over Dutch forces. Memories of the critical days of 1942 still rankled, when in the collapse of the American-British-Dutch-Australian Command he had been left in the lurch by the British who withdrew their remaining ships to India rather than obey his orders as the senior naval officer to fight on.[64] He spent the rest of the war in Kandy, essentially on the sidelines of what was in effect a British theatre. His first chance to establish his independence came in September 1945 when he unilaterally moved his own headquarters from Kandy to Batavia, so that, as he wrote to Mountbatten during the shift, he could control the deployment of Dutch troops.[65] Once in Batavia he was in a difficult position: he shared the feeling of frustration and anger of his fellow countrymen, and both by virtue of his seniority and his nationality he expected to be consulted fully on all matters concerning the operational use of Dutch troops. When Christison decided that the presence of Dutch troops would make a tense situation explosive, he ruled that they should not accompany British forces in their occupation of the area around Batavia. Helfrich protested that this was 'no less than an insult to his Government and to his country',[66] but Christison insisted that strictly military considerations should prevail.

The appropriate course of action was not easily decided upon in London. The Chiefs of Staff thought that there was no military solution to the situation in Java, and recommended that the Dutch be persuaded to make 'some political gesture',[67] thereby virtually accepting what their commanders in SEAC were urging. The Foreign Office was not so sure. Sterndale Bennett complained that Mountbatten was going 'much too far to one extreme'. True, the Dutch would have to grant 'some form of Indonesian independence', but he warned against 'virtual surrender to the Indonesian Republicans'.[68] Sargent agreed that notwithstanding Dening's criticisms, the Dutch government did have 'considerable grounds for complaint', and commented that until the impasse was resolved, Anglo-Dutch relations would continue to sour.[69] The delay in reaching a policy decision, he noted, a delay which he attributed to the Chiefs of Staff, put the British government in an 'invidious position'.[70]

The whole question of the British role in Java was first discussed by the Defence Committee of the Cabinet on 10 October. The division between the Foreign Office and the Chiefs of Staff quickly became apparent. Bevin accused the Chiefs of Staff of 'oversimplifying' the issue, in that they had never spelled out how their narrow directive to Mountbatten – to hold the key areas of Batavia and Surabaya – could be reconciled with their instructions that he was to effect the repatriation of prisoners of war and internees, the vast majority of whom were in camps outside these two cities. If Dutch troops were to be landed progressively in Java as they became available, their small numbers would expose them to risk at the hands of the nationalists, and if they came under attack, British forces could hardly refuse to help them. In other words, Bevin suggested, the Chiefs of Staff had not defined how Britain's responsibility was to be limited, nor how British forces were to disengage themselves. On a wider level, they had 'passed over in silence the difficulty of defending any differentiation between the present problem in the Netherlands East Indies and that of the analogous problem in Indo-China.' In reply, General Sir Archibald Nye, the VCIGS, urged a political solution to the problem. Mountbatten should restrict his operations to the recovery of prisoners and internees and the disarming of the Japanese; once that had been done, he should hand over the key areas to the Dutch. In the meantime, it was necessary for the Dutch to make political concessions in order to prevent the situation from deteriorating. There was a risk that British forces would clash with Republican troops in rescuing prisoners, and it was unclear whether Mountbatten had sufficient forces to accept that possibility.

Opinion was divided over the best course to adopt, but it was agreed that nothing could be decided until more precise information had been obtained from Mountbatten on the force levels he required, in the first instance, for carrying out the most narrow interpretation of his directive. The implication was that even on that basis, additional British forces would have to be sent to the Indies. But as Bevin cautioned the Committee, that in effect meant Indian troops, which added to the difficulties of the situation. The only way to limit their use was to accelerate the arrival of European Dutch troops who could supplement and perhaps even replace local Dutch troops, whose attitude of 'shoot up the nigger' was thought by British forces to be '20 years out of date'. Simultaneous with this probable temporary increase in the British military commitment the Dutch would have to publicise their new willingness to move beyond the political programme announced in 1942.[71] Everything depended on Mountbatten's assessment. The Foreign Office and the Chiefs of Staff approached the problem from widely differing perspectives: the former were not yet ready to dismiss a solution based on British military power; the latter saw the limits of that power and urged a political settlement. Neither fully comprehended the difficulties faced by the men on the spot.

Chapter six
To Surabaya and beyond

Mountbatten did not wait for further instructions from London but held a top-level meeting in Singapore with Christison, Van Mook, Van der Plas and Helfrich on 10 October. The record of that meeting shows how far he was prepared to go to pressure both his own government and the Dutch to approach the problem of Java realistically. Far from declining to shape policy, as he claimed in his cables to London, he sought to impose sensible military and political guidelines within which an acceptable solution might be found. Convinced that his own actions in Burma showed what could be achieved by flexibility and moderation, he urged the Dutch to make similar concessions. All his powers of persuasion, authority and charm were exerted to make Van Mook see that if the Dutch continued to refuse to talk to Sukarno and Hatta, the only result would be to ensure the emergence of extremist elements with whom any peaceful settlement would be impossible. But Van Mook and Helfrich were implacable (the latter the more so), and their resistance to any compromise was perhaps strengthened by Mountbatten's unfortunate opening statement, when by way of explaining why the meeting had to be held in Singapore rather than Batavia, he said that 'the Foreign Office discouraged visits by him to Allied territories in SEAC, because incorrect conclusions could so easily be deduced, before Government policy was firm, by such visits.' This merely confirmed to Van Mook what the Dutch feared: that despite assurances that the British upheld their original policy of returning the NEI to Dutch control, they were in fact looking for a way out. Nor did Mountbatten inspire confidence in his willingness to see the matter through when he admitted that he agreed with Van Mook's wish that Java had remained part of South West Pacific Area.

Much of the long discussion centred on the question of

negotiating with the republican leaders. Mountbatten hammered the analogy with Burma,* and more recently with Indochina, where he claimed that negotiations between the French and the Annamites, brought about by pressure from Gracey, had at least resulted in a truce and furthermore had put France in a good and liberal light in the circles of world opinion. The same would happen for the Netherlands, he suggested, if Van Mook insisted on his right to talk with whichever leaders he chose. Queen Wilhelmina's 'most liberal' speech provided a useful starting point in the discussion of the Dutch 'progressive policy'. It had to be explained to the nationalists that they would achieve independence peacefully in a few years whereas if they resisted the full force of the allies would be brought to bear upon them. 'If that were done, they would surely cooperate with the Dutch and there would be an end to the troubles in the NEI, as in Burma.' Privately, Mountbatten and many others in SEAC thought that the 1942 Dutch proposals were quite inadequate, but Mountbatten had little choice but to extol them as a 'magnanimous spontaneous gesture' that had luckily been made not 'under the duress of rebellion'.

Van Mook would not be budged by this flattery. He described the anti-Dutch elements in Java variously as a 'terrorist so-called Government', backed by an organisation 'comparable to the Hitler Jugend' (Helfrich compared it with the SS), 'Fascist terrorists' and 'looters and robbers'. It was unthinkable that their leaders should be included in any negotiations. He preferred to search out the moderates and deal with them on the basis of the 1942 proposals. When Mountbatten returned again to the parallel situation in Burma, and insisted that his signal to London specifically include mention of invitations to Sukarno and Hatta to attend future meetings convened by Christison, Van Mook bridled. 'To try and force this point on to his government would only serve to antagonize them', he protested – just as clearly it had already antagonized Van Mook.

---

* A much less comfortable parallel had been raised in late September by Helfrich, who compared Sukarno and Hatta with Chandra Bose of the Indian National Army. For all its lack of success, the INA struck at the very heart of British rule in India. Despite the cruelties inflicted by members of the INA on Indian soldiers who remained loyal and refused to join the INA, Indian public opinion had considerable sympathy for the three INA officers who were put on trial in late 1945. Mountbatten huffily dismissed the case of Chandra Bose as having 'no bearing on this matter.'[1]

The Dutch refusal to countenance any meetings with the nationalist leaders put Mountbatten in a quandary. He had stressed to
Van Mook that he could only recommend any widening of Britain's
military role to the British government if he could assure London
that the Dutch were prepared to be flexible and realistic – and the
acid test of that was their willingness to negotiate with Sukarno.
Van Mook repeated his refusal to do so several times, but
Mountbatten did not give up easily. After explaining why it had not
been possible to land stronger forces more quickly in the initial
phase of the reoccupation of the NEI, he suggested that any offer on
the part of the Dutch to open discussions with the nationalist
leaders should be accompanied by the threat that force would be
used if the offer was refused. Christison would have to be present at
any such discussions to explain the forces at the allies' disposal, and
to demonstrate that if a reasonable Dutch proposal was rejected by
the nationalists, they would have only themselves to blame for the
resulting military action. Concessions on the Dutch side would
surely be matched by the nationalists, for 'if they were the least
intelligent, they would see that, once British/Indian troops were in
possession of the port and airfield of Batavia, they were powerless
to interfere with a build-up of Dutch troops from Holland which
could only end in overwhelming them.'

Van Mook, however, disagreed. For him, and for the Dutch
government, military strength was the base from which all considerations of political reform and even discussion had to begin. To do
otherwise would be to harm Dutch 'prestige'. Without a build up of
British and Dutch forces, there could be no round table conferences,
because the moderate elements would not attend in the face of
extremist pressures. Mountbatten had already decided that in order
to carry out his limited directive he would need additional troops,
and had put his requirement to the Chiefs of Staff. But in the
meeting with Van Mook he explained his decision to move the 23rd
Division to Java as a response to Dutch complaints that the forces
initially sent had been inadequate – inadequate in Dutch eyes, that
is, not to disarm the Japanese and recover prisoners and internees,
but inadequate to the task of suppressing the nationalists who were
actively opposing the return of Dutch control. Christison stressed
that the safety of the prisoners and internees and the disarming of
the Japanese – the limited objectives laid down by the Chiefs of Staff
– made it necessary to expand British control beyond the key areas

of Batavia and Surabaya, and he argued that the sight of Japanese troops being rounded up by British forces would have a 'deep effect' on the local population. Van Mook and Helfrich thought differently. They insisted that the safety of the prisoners and internees could best be guaranteed if the additional British forces were used to suppress the nationalist troops, for then the Japanese, under threats of delayed repatriation, would carry out their required policing role until the allies had sufficient strength to take complete control.[2]

Mountbatten informed the Chiefs of Staff that 'complete agreement' had been reached at the meeting over the immmediate action to be taken and asked that approval be given for a widening of his original directive which limited the deployment of British forces to key areas so that when the 23rd Division had arrived detachments could move out to occupy Buitenzorg, Bandung, Surabaya, Semarang and Malang, where there were known to be large concentrations of Japanese and allied prisoners and internees. The knowledge that additional forces were available in the event of a total breakdown of nationalist control would strengthen the hand of the moderates and compel them to negotiate with the Dutch. On the other hand it was 'militarily essential' that the Dutch make 'imaginative and generous pronouncements' on the future of the NEI and that Van Mook be given complete freedom by the Dutch government to meet with anyone he wished. Christison's presence at any such meetings would serve a dual purpose: he could satisfy himself that the Dutch were prepared to discuss political matters with the Indonesians, and once satisfied, he could publicly substantiate the threat to use military force if the nationalists showed themselves to be unreasonable or incapable of maintaining control. To avoid unnecessary provocation, Mountbatten and Van Mook agreed that concessions should be made to the nationalists; no action would be taken to prevent the use of the Indonesian flag and anthem, although the Dutch flag would continue to be flown in areas under SEAC's control; greater use would be made of those Indonesian officials in control of various services; and NICA, which had been established as the spearhead of the return of Dutch authority, would be kept in the background until it could be merged with a civil administration, at which point the name NICA and the organisation would disappear.[3]

Mountbatten's assurance of 'complete agreement' disguised the fact that Van Mook had conceded far less than had Mountbatten. At the Singapore conference, Van Mook had remained adamant

that neither he nor his government were prepared to number
Sukarno and Hatta among the moderates whom Mountbatten
insisted be included in negotiations. Even if The Hague gave Van
Mook a free hand in choosing the Indonesians he would meet, Van
Mook had made it clear that he would refuse to enter into
discussions with Sukarno. The agreement over the need to avoid
provocation simply accepted the reality in Java: there was little that
Christison or the Dutch could do to stop the use of the Indonesian
flag or anthem, while it had very early become apparent that there
was a functioning Indonesian government that was maintaining
essential services without the help of the despised NICA with which
the greater part of the population refused to cooperate. Mountbatten implied that these were significant concessions on the part of the
Dutch in Java, a softening of their hitherto implacable hostility to
every manifestation of the Republic, but this was merely putting the
best possible face on the fact that between them the allies were
forced to accept a situation they were unable to change. As opposed
to these concessions, the Dutch had wrung far more out of
Mountbatten. Although he couched it in terms of military necessity,
the fact was that he had agreed to recommend a widening of
SEAC's military involvement for two purposes: to secure the safety
of allied prisoners and internees (and to round up the Japanese),
and also to provide a military backing for Dutch political initiatives. The second purpose was contingent on the Dutch making
reasonable proposals and negotiating with the representative
nationalist leaders, but even if the Dutch proved unwilling or
unable to do that, the first requirement remained. There *was* a
military argument for a greater military commitment, but in tying it
as well to a political imperative, Mountbatten had given away more
than he gained. He had in fact been outmanoeuvred by Van Mook.

Indications that the Dutch would not agree to Mountbatten's
conditions for Britain's willingness to use the threat of force in Java
came immediately from The Hague. On the day that Mountbatten
reported on the meeting in Singapore, the Dutch Minister for Foreign Affairs told the Foreign Office in London that Van Mook's
authority to meet Indonesian leaders did not extend to Sukarno and
his followers but only to those nationalists prepared to cooperate
within the policy lines laid down by the 1942 speech. Secondly, he
insisted that the authority given to Van Mook to open negotiations
with moderate Indonesians was 'inseparably bound up' with the

rapid increase in allied military forces in Java, since talks could not proceed in an atmosphere of lawlesssness. The concessions that Mountbatten thought he had won from the Dutch were promptly quashed. Van Kleffens was at pains to stress that any proposals the Dutch might make on the future of the Indies would not be new but merely represented long-planned steps to implement the 1942 declaration.[4] This position came nowhere near the 'imaginative and generous pronouncements' that Mountbatten thought he had brought Van Mook to accept. The Dutch insistence on an increased military presence in Java coupled with their absolute refusal to allow discussions with Sukarno undercut Mountbatten's intention of linking British military support to fresh Dutch political initiatives as a means of limiting the extent of British involvement.

Dening's first lengthy report on conditions in Java reached London at the same time as Mountbatten's recommendation to widen SEAC's military involvement. Although he supported much of what Mountbatten and Van Mook had agreed on at their meeting in Singapore, especially the need for the Dutch to make political concessions to the Indonesians if the British were to avoid being accused – 'and not entirely without reason – of holding the lists until the Dutch could do the shooting', the balance of his report differed markedly from Mountbatten's assessment of the strength of the nationalist movement. Cautioning against the tendency to exaggerate the support which the nationalists claimed to enjoy, he suggested that limited concessions, if appropriately presented, might be enough to secure the Dutch position:

Sympathetically handled the Indonesian independence movement is not sufficiently potent to constitute a menace to the future well-being of Indonesia. On the contrary it might well be absorbed. But occupying as it does key positions, it can create a very serious situation if driven to do so by unsympathetic handling. The Dutch have an opportunity but their present attitude is not encouraging. The remedy lies with them but if they do not apply it, and soon, we will also become involved.[6]

Support for this view came from Van der Post, whose understanding of the NEI had been commended by Mountbatten to London. Van der Post described Sukarno and Hatta and their close supporters as 'rather pathetic figures. If they are only seen and spoken to and tactfully handled', he wrote, 'in three or four months time they will be ignominious and forgotten figures in the life of the country.' Once they had been cut down to size, the charges of collaboration against them could be fully investigated.[6]

Attlee described Dening's telegram as the first 'really authorita-
tive' assessment that London had received.[7] It now seemed possible
that a solution could be found to the problem in Java, one that
would neither involve Britain in an open-ended military commitment nor rupture Anglo-Dutch relations on the much more important European level. Unfortunately neither Mountbatten nor the
Dutch shared this view. On receiving a copy of Mountbatten's
recommendations to the Chiefs of Staff, Van Kleffens objected
angrily to the Dutch Ambassador in London. Mountbatten's
suggestion that the mere presence of the necessary forces in Java
would be enough to bring the nationalists to the negotiating table
was a 'lighthearted view' to which the Dutch government took the
'greatest exception'. Furthermore, Mountbatten's proposals that
the Dutch offer new political proposals were little more than
conditions which The Hague was unable to accept. While Van
Mook had 'almost full authority' to see whom he wanted (the term
'negotiations' was deemed 'objectionable') that did not include
Sukarno and other 'irreconcilables'.[8] In private, the Dutch were
even less flexible. The Dutch Ambassador told Major General
Penney that if in fact Van der Plas had negotiated with Sukarno, he
should be tried for treason, while the subject of the status of the
Indonesian flag brought the comment that it would be recognised
'over his [the Ambassador's] dead body.'[9]

To Mountbatten, these Dutch objections seemed to be reflected
in the reaction of the Chiefs of Staff. When the latter requested
further information before acting on Mountbatten's recommendation to accelerate British troops movements to Java, Mountbatten
complained to Christison that 'it only goes to show how little the
folks at home appreciate the situation.'[10] A more accurate comment would have been that London's appreciation differed from
SEAC's. The Foreign Office distrusted Christison's judgment, and
Mountbatten's constant harping on the Burma parallel lost some of
its force when Dening independently advised the Foreign Office
that the two cases were 'not entirely analogous.'[11] Attlee welcomed
Dening's views, and the Defence Committee which he chaired
overrode Mountbatten's order that Dening limit his time in Batavia
to two days so that he could keep in close touch with negotiations
over the future of Siam. Dening was instructed to give top priority
to the situation in Java, and to remain in Batavia until cleared by

the Foreign Office to return to Kandy.[12]

Suspicion was growing in London that Mountbatten and SEAC were proposing unbalanced and unnecessary courses of action. The Joint Planning Staff gave short shrift to Slim's recommendations on the grounds that they were made without a full knowledge of the situation, especially regarding the availability of reliable Dutch troops.[13] The CIGS, Brooke, told the Defence Committee that the fifteen Dutch battalions due to arrive in the NEI by February lacked full training and might not be able to maintain law and order. The Committee agreed that British forces would have to continue to play the major role: Mountbatten was therefore authorised to send a second British/Indian division to Java as a matter of priority over the demands of Hong Kong, Indochina and Sumatra, and arrangements were to be made to continue the use of Indian troops. To this extent Mountbatten had prevailed, but the Committee was not willing to press the Dutch to negotiate with Sukarno, despite widespread feeling that the proposed announcements by Christison on the force available to the allies should be contingent on a Dutch undertaking to include Sukarno in any talks. Attlee in particular was reluctant to force the issue: if the Dutch refused, the situation might deteriorate further and Britain would be locked into a wider role which would be beyond its resources to control. In place of Mountbatten's urging of a resolute approach London preferred a policy of wait and see.[14]

This cautious reaction was greeted with dismay by the military in SEAC. According to Penney, the government lacked the determination to force a decision: faced with the conflicting advice of the War Office, the Chiefs of Staff and the Foreign Office, it made no decision at all but allowed matters to drift.[15] Mountbatten protested that in the absence of significant Dutch military support, British and Indian troops would bear the military consequences of the Dutch refusal to negotiate, and that since the Dutch military commander in the NEI, General van Oyen, had estimated that it would take eighteen months for thirty to fifty thousand troops to subdue Java, Britain had every right to dictate terms to the Dutch.[16] The Defence Committee had decided that at any meeting with the nationalists Christison should announce SEAC's willingness to use military force in the event of a breakdown of law and order, but Mountbatten rejected that, and told the Chiefs of Staff that he had ordered Christison to make such a statement only to nationalists who were capable of enforcing compliance on their own followers. He had long since made it clear that Sukarno alone met that test, but he felt compelled to add:

I would like to assure the Chiefs of Staff that I have adopted no attitude which has not been in strict conformity with the military tasks entrusted to me and that I have at no time expressed any opinion whatever regarding the honesty or dishonesty of any personalities in the Indonesian Independence Movement.[17]

There is no record of how this claim was received, but we can deduce from previous reactions to Mountbatten's policy suggestions that it was unlikely to have been taken at face value.

Military perspectives differed vastly between London and SEAC. The Defence Committee had been told that there was some question about the reliability of Dutch troops being prepared for the NEI. Penney had no doubts: he advised SEAC that they were 'indifferent and semi-trained', and added that their arrival in the absence of any conciliatory action by the Dutch would be 'worse than useless'.[18] Christison had more immediate concerns. After several incidents of 'provocative and aggressive' actions by Dutch troops in and around Batavia, he ordered that apart from those engaged on static duty, all Dutch forces would be concentrated in reserve where they could be controlled. A typical incident was that in the afternoon of 10 October. Four Indonesians in an open car had driven slowly past Van Oyen's headquarters and when the car backfired, the Dutch guards opened fire, killing the driver and sending the car out of control. All Indonesians living on the street were rounded up for questioning.[19] Christison was not prepared to tolerate this sort of aggressive behaviour by Dutch troops. 'I must insist that *not* one single further Dutch soldier is to land in Java until [the] situation is clarified. If any further Dutch troops are landed here, civil war in which British Indian troops must become involved is inevitable', he warned.[20] Within a week his position had hardened. Impressed by the support that the nationalist movement enjoyed, which he described as 'far stronger than even we thought', he now called not only for a halt to the movement of additional troops to Java and their diversion to Borneo and 'Christian Islands' [i.e. Ambon and Menadon], but for the removal of all Dutch forces already on Java to the same holding areas. He also recommended that NICA be completely demilitarised, and that the Dutch be excluded from all RAPWI work, which would be undertaken exclusively by the British and the Indonesians, since

'RAPWI at the moment is being discredited owing to [its] alleged use by [the] Dutch to import arms and carry agents.' If these conditions were met, Christison guaranteed to fulfil the three tasks laid down in the Chiefs of Staff directive. On the other hand, he predicted, any move to associate Britain with the limited political concessions promised by the Dutch would 'discredit us in the eyes of Indonesians and may lead to hostilities.'[21] Not without reason did the War Office describe his recommendations, especially those calling for a complete Dutch military withdrawal, as 'pretty tough'.

The growing disenchantment with Dutch troops in SEAC made it all the more necessary to be able to rely on an increased British commitment. The Defence Committee had decided to deploy additional Indian troops, but this provoked a strong response from Auchinleck, who feared that in the inevitable confrontation between British and nationalist forces, Indian troops might be so influenced by political agitation from within India that they might refuse to obey orders. This was a possibility that had to be avoided 'at all costs', not least because, purely in terms of SEAC's own operations, the British position 'depends almost entirely now on the stability and loyalty of Indian troops.'[22] The Indian government backed Auchinleck, and suggested that the 2nd British Division, due to be moved to Malaya, instead be deployed in Java,[23] but this was unacceptable to Mountbatten. The 2nd British Division, he told Auchinleck, was required for possible occupation duty in Japan and Hong Kong. More important, it was not fully trained or equipped, and was unsuitable for an operational role. The 5th Indian Division, on the other hand, was available for immediate transfer to Java, using local and Japanese shipping supplemented by RAPWI air lift. Mountbatten stressed that while he was alive to the political sensitivities of increasing the number of Indian troops in Java, it was not for him to make that decision.[24]

It remained for the Defence Committee to choose. The Chiefs of Staff rejected Mountbatten's assessment of the unpreparedness of the 2nd British Division, preferring instead to accept Auchinleck's assurance that the Division would be ready to be deployed in Java by early December if it was decided to send it there. The crux of the problem was the relative weight to be given to two political considerations. The movement of the 2nd British Division to Java could be accelerated only by interfering with the PYTHON repatriation programme, while the deployment of the 5th Indian Division

4   The car in which Brigadier A.W. Mallaby was killed at Surabaya.

raised the political objections that Auchinleck and the Government of India had raised so strongly. Lawson suggested that Wavell and Auchinleck had exaggerated the danger of disaffection among Indian troops, and pointed out that when he had been in SEAC in September, Slim, the most senior Indian Army Officer there, had not seen fit to mention this possibility. The Defence Committee therefore decided that on balance the dangers inherent in a one month delay outweighed the risk of political unrest, and endorsed the Chiefs of Staff recommendation that the 5th Indian Division should be sent from Malaya to Java to be replaced in Malaya by the 2nd British Division from India.[25] This was essentially a political decision arising out of the unspoken understanding that the PYTHON repatriation programme was inviolate. To that extent, Dutch complaints that domestic British pressures to 'bring the troops home' had outweighed any sense of a common task yet to be completed were well founded.[26]

The direct military confrontation between British troops and the nationalist forces that Mountbatten had long feared came at the end of October, just as the 5th Indian Division was preparing to move to Java. On 25 October, two Indian battalions of the 49th Brigade, commanded by Brigadier A.W.S. Mallaby, began landing at Surabaya in eastern Java. Perhaps taken by surprise, the Indonesians at first offered no resistance, but as the battalions moved to occupy key positions in the city, barricades were thrown up by the nationalists. Their leaders insisted that no more troops were to be landed, but a show of force – twelve Thunderbolt P–47s from HQ RAFNEI in Batavia – convinced them not to oppose the British deployment. By the end of the first day, British forces were in control of the port and its facilities, although the nationalists still held a key bridge, the power station and the airfield. At a conference the following day between Mallaby's deputy, Colonel L.H.O. Pugh, and the Indonesian leaders, it was agreed that the nationalist forces would be responsible for disarming the unruly mobs while being allowed to retain their own arms. Steps were taken at once to begin the concentration and evacuation of prisoners and internees, and it appeared that a viable, if shaky and suspicious, *modus operandi* had been established between the British and the Indonesians.

It was shattered almost immediately and in circumstances that gave rise to charges of bad faith on both sides. From his headquar-

ters in Batavia Christison had approved the dropping from the air of
a leaflet describing the aims of the allied operations and instructing
the local population to obey whatever orders were issued by the
British military authorities. Throughout October RAF units had
distributed hundreds of thousands of leaflets progressively
eastwards from Batavia. It was unfortunate – and coincidental – that
the day after Pugh's constructive meeting with the local nationalist
leaders, RAF planes appeared over Surabaya and dropped leaflets
that had been prepared with the general situation in Java in mind and
which took no account of local conditions. Indonesians were
ordered to surrender all arms on pain of death, and the British
Military Administration was deemed to have replaced the nationalist
government which had, in fact, been running the city since the middle of August. Not unnaturally, this declaration was seen by the
Indonesians as high-handed and contrary to the agreement into
which they had entered with Mallaby only a day before. The
moderates who had met Pugh were displaced by extremists, and on
29 October nationalist attacks began on positions held by the 49th
Brigade and also on internee convoys. As British military and Dutch
civilian casualties mounted, Christison ordered Sukarno to be flown
to Surabaya to meet the local leaders, but the truce that was subsequently arranged lasted little more than twenty-four hours. Brigadier
Mallaby, accompanied by moderate nationalist leaders, attempted
to calm the crowds, but was shot and killed. Shortly afterwards the
bodies of his Brigade Major and a Force 136 representative on
Sukarno's staff were discovered: they had earlier gone to the nationalist headquarters but had been captured by extremists, tortured and
killed. The small British forces, some 1500 troops, were now faced
by a hundred thousand armed Indonesians whose weapons included
light tanks and armoured cars, largely supplied by Japanese garrisons in defiance of the terms of the August surrender. In the middle
were several thousand internees, mainly women and children.

The nationalist resistance at Surabaya inflamed the situation
throughout the whole of Java. Christison reported to Mountbatten
that the 49th Brigade was 'more or less besieged', and was
sustaining heavy casualties. At Magalang in Central Java, the
3/10th Gurkhas (less one company) were surrounded by Indonesian
forces equipped with field guns and mortars and reinforced by
troops from Jogjakarta. Their position became so threatened that
on 1 November Christison ordered the first air strike against the

nationalists. In Jogjakarta itself, the nationalists had control of the airfield, where they were reported to have captured twenty service-able Japanese aircraft, and of the local radio station, which earlier experience in Batavia and Bandung had shown was a potent weapon in whipping up local sentiment against allied troops. In western Java the situation was largely under control, although there were signs that extremists were attempting to oust the moderate leaders, and minor skirmishes continued in Batavia.

The 5th Indian Division under Major General E.C. Mansergh arrived off Surabaya on 1 November, but was not fully landed until 9 November. Even with these additional troops at his disposal, Mountbatten's forces were fully stretched throughout the length of Java. The result was that while p.o.w. and internee camps in the western part of the island were protected by garrisons and naval evacuation was being prepared for some 4000 women and children, camps in central and eastern Java were in grave danger of attack from extremist nationalists. The number of camps in the Surabaya area was unknown, and it was thought that at best they might have 'half hearted' Japanese garrisons of the sort protecting camps near Semarang. The condition of the 11,500 inmates of a large camp at Ambarawa was serious, and headquarters of the 23rd Division had recommended their evacuation, but this was impossible: all avail-able military transport was being used to build up the British military presence while civil transport was in the hands of the nationalists.[27] In the growing confrontation between SEAC's forces and those of the nationalists, the p.o.w.s and internees were vulner-able hostages: as long as they remained outside allied control and protection, SEAC's mission could not be fulfilled; while they were liable to nationalist attack, their safety could be used as a bargaining counter in talks with the allies, and especially with the Dutch.

A show of force was unavoidable if control was not to pass irre-trievably to the nationalists. On 31 October with the approval of Dening, Christison warned that unless attacks on British forces ceased, the full weight of allied land, sea and air forces would be deployed against the extremists and their supporters. Surabaya was to be the point at which allied resolve would be demonstrated. Following Mallaby's death, 49th Brigade withdrew from its exposed positions in the city and concentrated around the docks and the airfield, and in the vicinity of the main internment camps. In a leaflet dropped over the nationalist areas, Mansergh called for the immediate surrender of the nationalist leaders, the handing over of all unauthorised weapons, and the cessation of attacks on p.o.w.s and internees. When there was no response the British attack began. The 9th and 123rd Indian Brigades from the 5th Indian Division advanced into Surabaya in the face of Indonesian machine-gun, mortar, artillery and tank fire. Casualties were so heavy and the progress so costly that Mansergh called for additional fire support from air and naval units. A composite flight of eight Thunderbolts and two Mosquitos had been sent from Batavia, and Mansergh could also call on the naval artillery of the two cruisers and three destroyers that had arrived at Surabaya on 1 and 2 November. Mountbatten had been reluctant to deploy air power against Indonesian forces, and placed tight restrictions on its use, but the danger to the internees in the Surabaya area constituted a 'special case'.[28] Bombing and naval artillery attacks began on 10 November and continued for several days. By the end of the first day's fighting, a third of the city had been occupied, but it was not until 28 November that the British controlled the whole of Surabaya. Even then, sporadic resistance continued, and only in late December, in the words of the official historian, had 'comparative peace . . . descended on Surabaya.'[29]

Before the battle for Surabaya broke out, there was widespread concern that Mountbatten was losing control of the situation. At a meeting of the Defence Committee on 5 November, Attlee asked querulously whether Mountbatten was not stretching his forces too thinly in an attempt to guard all internee camps, and whether the time had not come to press him to concentrate his troops in several key areas where internees could be brought and given adequate protection. This criticism ignored the fact that Mountbatten's ground forces did not control the transport system or the communication routes between the outlying camps and the key areas, but then, as Nye, the VCIGS, admitted, 'in the absence of a recent appreciation from the Military Authorities in S.E.A.C., it was very difficult to give a full picture of the situation.' The Chiefs of Staff recommended that SEAC mount a show of force against the Indonesians, although they admitted that there was always the danger that far from destroying nationalist opposition, it might provoke fighting on a much larger scale. Bevin agreed that military force had to be used, and pressed for additional troops, including light armour, to be sent to Java. Once again this raised the question of where the extra forces were to be found: the Secretary of State for India argued for the use of British or Dutch troops (i.e. of the 2nd British Division scheduled to be sent to Malaya or those Dutch units diverted away from Java at Christison's insistence); the Secretary of State for the Colonies was anxious that the British garrison in Malaya not be reduced lest the trouble in Java eventually spread there via the sizeable Malay population in Sumatra. All that Nye could offer was the possibility that the arrival in Saigon of the 9th DIC would enable the 20th Indian Division to be used in Java, but that would meet with the usual objections from India, while there were perhaps political reasons for keeping a British military presence in Indochina.[30]

These dilemmas had plagued SEAC's operations and the Defence Committee's considerations of them since the first landing of British troops in September. What was new about the discussion in early November was that for the first time the Committee was faced with pressure and criticism from sources in addition to the Dutch, whose stand was by now almost universally condemned in London and in SEAC. The Australian government protested to Attlee over Dening's statement to the nationalist leaders that the question of the return of the Dutch was essentially a matter to be settled between the Indonesians and the NEI government. The Australian External Affairs Department under Dr. H.V. Evatt had consistently maintained that Australia had a significant role to play in the post war southwest Pacific, and Evatt was not about to see what the Australian government described as a 'vital Australian interest in a satisfactory and enduring settlement guaranteeing political stability, social progress and ... [Australia's] military security' ignored or underestimated by Britain. He had no faith in the good intentions of the Dutch, having been rebuffed during the war in his attempts to discuss his proposals for some sort of shared sovereignty over the NEI. The Dutch rightly regarded these overtures as offensive and impertinent, while Evatt in turn saw the Dutch attitude as proof of their intransigence and unwillingness to accommodate the spirit of the United Nations.[31] But Britain was a different matter. With Evatt's strong backing, Prime Minister J.B. Chifley urged Attlee to maintain the ban on Dutch troops entering Java and to press the Dutch to issue a statement outlining significant reforms, 'with particular reference to a sponsor for national autonomy.' Furthermore, Chifley emphasised, it was essential that the responsibility for

solving the problem of the future of the NEI be made an international
one, for 'political decisions of [the] greatest importance to [the] nations
of [the] Pacific area should not have to be made by any one power.'[32]

In his reply Attlee referred to the difficulties facing the British
government. Britain's own colonies in Malaya and Borneo gave her
an obvious interest in a mutually acceptable outcome in the NEI,
but she was also anxious to preserve good relations with another
European power and was unwilling to interfere 'any further ...
than is strictly necessary' in Dutch internal affairs. Britain was loth
to put more pressure on the Dutch to widen their proposed
concession for fear that this would only encourage the Indonesians
to increase their demands. 'We should indeed be most reluctant', he
advised Chifley, 'to do anything to suggest that Sovereignty is a
factor which can be lightly set aside.' There could not have been a
more direct rebuff to Evatt's general position. Nor was Attlee any
more receptive to Evatt's specific recommendations. He made it
clear that the decision to allow more Dutch troops into Java was
one for Mountbatten and his military advisers to make, and that
the men on the spot had to be supported in their determination to
enforce law and order. Just as it would be counterproductive to
urge the Dutch to make greater concessions, so too any talk of
referring the problem to an international body would only encourage the nationalists to think that violence would bring them what
they had been unable to gain through negotiation. In direct contrast
to the Australian hopes for a much more open approach to the
whole question of the future of the NEI, Britain's position was that
she should 'do nothing which could be construed as an attempt to
impede resumption of Dutch control.'[33]*

Recent events, however, demonstrated that British forces were in
no position to facilitate the return of the Dutch without endangering their ability to fulfil the tasks laid down in the original
directive issued to Mountbatten by the Chiefs of Staff. There was a
growing conviction among the men on the spot in SEAC – the men
whose opinions Attlee had suggested to Chifley had to be the main
guide to policy-makers in London – that the problem required
outside intervention. In late October Pyman advised Slim that if
Dutch-Indonesian negotiations broke down, the United Nations
would have to become involved. He was not, however, optimistic

* See Chapter 10.

that the British government would adopt this course which would entail a major change in policy; rather, he thought that London would continue its policy of 'masterly inactivity' and urge the Dutch to negotiate while at the same time restricting SEAC's ability to take military action in the NEI. This, he thought, looked like the 'normal difficult course, which the soldier invariably has to follow'.[34] He was not alone in thinking along these lines. Two weeks later he discussed the situation in Java with Slim, who told him that unless there was a breakthrough in the negotiations and a settlement was reached, the United Nations, and especially the United States, would have to be brought in, since the task would by then be too big for Britain alone to handle.[35] This was also the view of SEAC's Joint Planning Staff, who advised that given the limited number of troops available in the NEI and in view of world opinion, which was firmly opposed to the forcible suppression of the nationalist movement, military operations did not provide a 'practicable solution'. Since it was preferable that the alternative, a political settlement, not be imposed unilaterally by Britain, it was essential that the United Nations become involved.[36]

The views of his closest military advisers undoubtedly weighed heavily with Mountbatten, who impressed upon his staff that it was imperative to spell out what a rejection of a UN role would mean.[37] In a signal to the Chiefs of Staff on 5 November, he provided a detailed appreciation of the prospects in Java. His conclusions were far from reassuring. He suggested that there were two likely alternative developments, each requiring a substantial British military commitment. In the event of an acceptable political settlement between the Dutch and the Indonesians SEAC would need to deploy three divisions [i.e. one more than allowed for in Java], one armoured brigade, and additional air forces so that Japanese troops could be rounded up and disarmed, p.o.w.s and internees protected and repatriated, and secure staging bases established for the landing of Dutch troops. If, however, negotiations broke down, the implications for Britain were far more serious. Mountbatten estimated that he would have to use two corps each of three divisions, together with full air and naval support 'to subjugate the country sufficiently for the Dutch to take over with a good chance of permanently re-establishing themselves.' Where were these extra forces to be found? There was some chance of moving the 20th Indian Division from Indochina when a replace-

ment French division arrived, and divisions slated to be sent to Hong
Kong and Japan could be switched to Java, but the objections to
these solutions, which anyway were only partial ones, had already
been registered. The only other division was the 11th East African
Division, but Slim had warned against its use on the grounds that its
troops were unreliable. In any case two months would elapse before
it could be re-equipped in India, and if the decision to deploy it was
taken the troops' repatriation under the PYTHON scheme would
have to be postponed indefinitely. Even if these divisions were
earmarked for Java, Mountbatten thought that his buildup would
not be completed before mid 1946 at the earliest, with alarming
consequences: 'I fear that in those areas which I could not soon
secure, all law and order will have ceased to exist and I shall be too
late to ensure the safety of those APWI not already in my protection.'
Not only would he be unable to carry out one of the main tasks
allotted to him by the Chiefs of Staff, but the cost of preparing the
way for the military and political return of Dutch control would be
horrifying. He warned that he would need to create a base in Malaya
on the scale of Montgomery's British occupation zone in Germany, a
massive undertaking that implied a long term commitment with all
the attendant dangers of antagonising world opinion, especially in
such countries as India and Australia which had already expressed
grave reservations over the course of events in the NEI.

This led Mountbatten to his most radical proposal. If negotiations
did break down, the military consequences for Britain would be
enormous. The costs and implications might be too great for the
British government to shoulder alone. Failing an American decision
to take an active role in military operations in Java, Mountbatten
urged that a political settlement be imposed on the Dutch and the
Indonesians by the two powers most closely involved – Britain and
Australia, with India being closely consulted. He emphasised that his
recommendation was based on military considerations alone – he
could hardly have said otherwise, but it was not a convincing claim.
Nor was his advice welcome. Of the alternatives he presented to
London one was so at odds with the government's thinking that it
was not a realistic possibility, and Mountbatten knew it.[38] The
other, itself scarcely attractive, was based on the assumption that
negotiations between the Dutch and the Indonesians would succeed.
It was at best a forlorn hope, for both sides, especially – it seemed to
the British – the Dutch, were becoming increasingly intransigent.

That left Britain, in Dening's words, as 'arbitrators with very little to arbitrate with.'[39]

The British government was anxious not to involve third parties in the NEI problem: they could offer nothing except unwanted complications to a thankless task. The one exception to this policy of exclusion was the United States, which London desperately wanted to enlist, at least politically and morally if not actively, on its side. Once US forces were withdrawn from an operational role of SEAC in August, and Mountbatten's American deputy left in September, there were fears that the Americans might seek to dismantle the inter-allied basis of SEAC. The Joint Planning Staff recommended in late October that the Joint Chiefs in Washington be pressed for an assurance that they intended to maintain SEAC as an allied command, and the request was duly made, but the response was disappointing: Marshall told Wilson that there was a 'very definite feeling that US participation in Mountbatten's area should be liquidated as rapidly as possible in accordance with the policy of this Government'.[40] The supply of equipment to SEAC under Lend-Lease had already stopped, and the US was concerned lest what equipment remained in SEAC's hands be used, and be seen to be used, in the suppression of nationalist movements. Pressure was applied on SEAC to remove all identifying US marks on such equipment – mainly trucks and jeeps – and Dutch requests for ninety day credit facilities to assist in the purchase of military equipment for their marine brigade training at Quantico were refused: cash only was the basis recommended by the Department of State in an attempt to turn the Dutch to other sources.[41]

The British accepted that once MacArthur had turned over Java to SEAC there was not the slightest chance of any American military involvement in the NEI, but they still hoped to be able to rely on US understanding of Britain's policy in the area even if Washington felt unable to identify itself publicly with the British stance. Efforts by the embassy in Washington to inform US officials of the dilemmas facing the British in southeast Asia were a continuation of a long-running campaign to bring to the attention of the Americans the role that Britain had played in defeating the Japanese and to disabuse them of the widespread notion that the war against Japan had been won solely by American arms.[42] But however much the British government tried to put their actions in southeast Asia in the best possible light, there was little likelihood

of persuading the US to identify itself publicly with western policies
there. The difficulties were too great, the dangers too obvious.
When in protest against Mountbatten's actions in attempting to
pressure the Dutch to enter into negotiations with Sukarno and his
supporters, Helfrich had written to MacArthur to urge that the
United Nations apply strong political pressure on Britain to take a
firm stand against the Indonesians, even MacArthur had more sense
than to get involved in that area.[43] True, he had been suspected by
the Foreign Office of not doing enough to stop pro-Indonesian
demonstrations in Tokyo in order to embarrass the British,[44] but it
was generally understood, if deprecated, that the US did not intend
to become an active participant, on whatever side.

Not surprisingly, Mountbatten's assessment of the situation in Java
was received with dismay in London. The Chiefs of Staff had
already complained of the paucity of information that SEAC was
sending: news of Mallaby's death in Surabaya had, for example,
been published in the British press well before any official reports
had arrived, but as Mountbatten replied, 'we are working under
war conditions here while the Press enjoy peacetime facilities.'[45]
The Chiefs of Staff in turn sympathised with SEAC's difficulties,
but insisted on 'full, frequent and timely information on all military
matters', and Nye, the VCIGS, sent his own man to Java to gather
first-hand information about conditions there.[46] Mountbatten's
request for a large increase in the number of troops in Java
suggested that he saw no hope of arriving at a political settlement.
That was Dening's interpretation, and his warning that the military
staff in SEAC thought that a military solution was the only
alternative to a breakdown in negotiations was taken up by the
Foreign Office, which advised the Chiefs of Staff to 'correct
Admiral Mountbatten's apparent lack of perspective.'[47]

Dening was right, but with some important qualifications.
Mountbatten and his commanders in SEAC had long argued for a
political settlement, and had been at a loss to understand why
London had not put far stronger pressure on the Dutch to open
serious negotiations with the Indonesians. But in the absence of
talks between the two main parties, what options were open to
Mountbatten if he was to fulfil the tasks set down in the as-yet
unchanged directive that was the basis of all SEAC operations in
the NEI? While the Dutch in particular argued among themselves

about whether or not Sukarno could be included in any talks with the nationalists, the military situation continued to deteriorate. It was SEAC's appreciation of the political impact of military developments on world opinion that made Mountbatten determined to force the issue, for the fighting in Surabaya had merely highlighted disturbing trends. There had been mounting criticism in the British press, especially in the reports from Java of the *Daily Mail's* Noel Monks, about Mountbatten's failure to round up and disarm Japanese troops. Lacking sufficient forces himself to maintain law and order, and most notably to protect p.o.w. and internee camps, SEAC had been forced to rely on the Japanese to carry out policing duties. In some areas Japanese troops performed well, but there was considerable ill-feeling aroused over incidents wherein British soldiers were apprehended by Japanese military police.

More important, there were growing indications that in other areas the Japanese had not only failed to follow the surrender instructions and maintain law and order pending the arrival of allied troops but had actually handed over their weapons to the Indonesians. Some of the Japanese officers had done little to conceal their support for the nationalists,[48] and in the fighting at Surabaya there was strong evidence that Japanese troops were playing an active role in operations against British troops: Japanese soldiers were found among the killed, and the long range artillery employed by the nationalists seemed to be manned by Japanese gunners, since fire patterns corresponded to those used by the Japanese army.[49] By early December, however, when fighting had reached the mopping-up stage, the emphasis on Japanese involvement was much less. The Weekly Intelligence Review for 1 December referred to the 'small number' of Japanese who had fought with the Indonesians, but dismissed the rumours that they had had any part in planning or directing the operation.[50] The Political Warfare Division advised all commands in SEAC that the 'line plugging Japanese participation in and instigation of Indonesian extremists should be modified forthwith'. Henceforth, it was to be emphasised that the few Japanese who had participated were traitors, and that there was no evidence of any specific Japanese plot behind the outbreak of violence; rather what had happened in Surabaya was in accord with 'long term and purely general Japanese plans for Asia [which have] encouraged such situations as have now arisen in NEI and FIC.'[51]

The military, especially in SEAC, were very much alive to the question of public opinion. The Chiefs of Staff, removed from the immediate problems of Java, were perhaps more concerned with image when they agreed that Mountbatten should be empowered to use tear gas to disperse rioters, but emphasised that it was to be called 'tear smoke'.[52] Christison was permitted to employ air power in Surabaya but only in such a way – advance warning, essential targets, and guaranteed accuracy were required – that would be 'acceptable to world opinion' as an 'appropriate' weapon against extremists.[53] The results, however, were unsatisfactory: the enormous damage to key public buildings in no way diminished the determination of the nationalist forces, who charged British tanks with rifles, knives and in some cases bare hands. Mountbatten and his staff agreed that the effect on world opinion had been out of all proportion to the military gains and urged Christison (and Gracey in Indochina) to use air attacks much more sparingly.[54]

Christison felt that he had been virtually forced to employ air strikes and naval artillery to overcome the numerical inferiority of the forces available to him at Surabaya. From the point of view of military operations, this was the greatest handicap under which SEAC laboured. With the determination of the British government to proceed with the PYTHON repatriation and demobilisation pro- gramme, additional troops could only be found outside the United Kingdom. The Viceroy, the Indian government and the C-in-C, India, all opposed any increase in the number of Indian troops dep- loyed in the NEI, and predicted sharp political reactions if India was drawn on for SEAC reinforcements. These arguments did not carry equal weight with everyone: Christison was appalled to hear that on approving his plan to clear Batavia of armed nationalists, which involved military operations that were bound to result in casualties, Mountbatten had insisted that Indian rather than British troops be used – 'he did not want British troops widowed at this time so long after the war' – but to his credit Christison's representative at the meeting, Lt Colonel W. Ridley, had answered his Supreme Commander with the comment, 'Sir do you really think it is different if Mrs Poop Singh is made a widow?'[55]

In October Mountbatten had warned the Chiefs of Staff that the troops, both Indian and British, must not get the idea that they were engaged in putting down a local independence movement (which, in the absence of any substantive Dutch political concessions is precisely what they were doing), but these fears, especially where

Indian troops were concerned, were largely dismissed by Ministers and their military advisers in London. They were not without foundation however, as is shown by a report from Colonel Pugh (Mallaby's successor in 49th Brigade) on operations in November. Pugh noted that although morale was high among his Indian troops, there was a growing undercurrent of dissatisfaction arising out of a feeling that the fighting in Surabaya could have been avoided had the powers in Batavia been more in touch with local conditions and had not, through the dropping of the hardline leaflet, caused the 'arbitrary precipitation of hostilities' when local negotiations had been proceeding satisfactorily. Pugh requested that a 'pronouncement on the highest level' [i.e. presumably Mountbatten] be made to 'define the object, scope and duration' of the Surabaya operations, and to explain the circumstances that led to the outbreak of fighting on 28 October. Pugh clearly agreed with his troops on the latter question, for he noted that he had already sent a report to Mansergh at 23rd Division 'refuting the opinion in ALFNEI W[eekly] I[ntelligence] S[urvey] No. 2 [i.e. a report from Christison's headquarters in Batavia] that the hostilities were the unpremeditated and spontaneous action of the mob.'[56]

Despite the urgings of Helfrich and Van Oyen in particular, Dutch forces did not constitute a viable alternative to the use of Indian units. There was unanimous agreement that Dutch troops were unreliable and likely to make the situation worse by their lack of discipline. Terms such as 'trigger-happy', 'neurotic' and 'provocative' figured regularly in reports from SEAC, and there had been no British opposition to Christison's decision to prevent any Dutch forces from landing in Java until conditions were under control. The only non-British division available for use in Java, other than Dutch or Indian, was the 11th East African Division, but here again political considerations had to be taken into account. Apart from its lack of appropriate training and equipment, and the difficulties of supplying the special diet its troops required, it was felt in SEAC that not only would its deployment in Java have an 'adverse effect on world opinion' but that a British decision to use black troops against the Indonesians would go down badly both in the NEI and in Malaya, just as – falsely, as it turned out – the French had been criticised for moving African units into Indochina.[57]

These constraints made SEAC's primary humanitarian task – to rescue all p.o.w.s and internees – all the more difficult. As British troops pushed further into Java, more camps were discovered, with the result that the numbers originally thought to fall within the RAPWI programme were soon proved to have been wildly underestimated. The population of the camps was far greater than scanty intelligence reports had indicated, but in addition RAPWI efforts were threatened by a huge influx of people who sought to identify themselves with the eventual return of Dutch rule. As extremist groups resorted to armed attacks on British units, particularly as suspicions grew that the British were merely creating bridgeheads for the infiltration of the hated Dutch, large numbers of Indonesians, by no means all of them Eurasians, sought refuge in various camps from the violence of the streets. These IFTUs [Inhabitants Friendly To Us], as they became known in military circles, numbered thousands, and it was not always possible to distinguish between true wartime prisoners and internees and those who wanted to be protected from the fury of the nationalist armed bands. For example, in early November, Mountbatten told the Chiefs of Staff that the numbers of internees in Surabaya alone had grown from an estimated 1400 to more than 10,500, not all of whom were thought to be genuine internees; a month later, he reported that there were some 147,000 IFTUs who might well be at risk if British forces withdrew without having crushed nationalist opposition, with serious implications for Britain's standing in the court of world opinion.[58] Even where numbers themselves were not a problem, there still remained the question of providing protection for the camps and especially of safeguarding convoys to embarkation areas which had to run through territory nominally under the control of the Indonesian government but all too often patrolled by extremist groups who attacked, tortured and murdered the former internees and those small detachments of troops who were all that the main commands could spare for escort duty.

Despite advice from the Foreign Office to correct Mountbatten's perspective, there was little that the Chiefs of Staff could offer as an alternative. The forces that he had argued would be needed in the event of a breakdown of negotiations were judged to be 'excessive' (as Mountbatten undoubtedly knew them to be). Instead the Chiefs of Staff urged Mountbatten not to think that a failure in the forthcoming negotiations necessarily meant that the full scale military option was all that was left. Rather, they emphasised, London was continuing to put pressure on the Dutch to adopt a reasonable position and that, in conjunction with the military actions planned in Surabaya and in central Java, would probably bring both parties to the negotiating table. In the meantime, Mountbatten was instructed to prepare to ship a third division to Java, though the Chiefs of Staff warned that if shipping from outside the SEAC's resources was required (as Mountbatten had made very clear would be the case) it would have 'serious repercussions' on the PYTHON repatriation programme. Where was the third division to be found? Hardly surprisingly, the Chiefs of Staff could find no acceptable alternative to the further use of Indian troops. However, they did admit that there was a limit to the impositions that could be made on India, and reluctantly suggested that Dutch troops might have to be used in Java before Mountbatten, Slim and Christison thought they were ready to assume an active role.[59]

If to his critics in London – mainly in the Foreign Office but also in the War Office – Mountbatten seemed to be losing his grip on developments in Java, there was little evidence that London had any better course to advise. Their attempts to pressure the Dutch had borne little fruit except to stiffen Dutch resistance and had done nothing to dampen Indonesian suspicions that Britain was merely acting as the stalking horse for the resumption of Dutch rule. In the confused conditions of Java in October and early November it was difficult to make a distinction beween the humanitarian role of SEAC's forces and those acts which had clear political implications. Mountbatten's attempts to bring the British government to clarify its own position so that the limits on Britain's involvement could be spelled out got nowhere. Neither the government nor SEAC appreciated that the control of the situation in Java was in the hands of three groups, the British, the Dutch and the Indonesians. The end to the political stalemate came not when London was able to force the Dutch to change, nor when British troops crushed the nationalists, but when internal Indonesian political developments created a climate in which concessions on all sides were clearly possible. None of the experts in London or in SEAC had foreseen that.

Chapter seven

A British policy for Java?

Whatever military pressure the British and the Dutch applied in Java, it was clear, at least to the British, that some form of negotiations would eventually have to be held with the Indonesians. The Dutch baulked at this. The sticking point was Sukarno and his collaborationist followers. As long as he led the Republican movement, the Dutch government refused to enter into discussions with the nationalists. Not only was Sukarno damned by his 'quisling' past, but his statements on the future of Indonesia seemed to leave the Dutch with little room to manoeuvre, certainly none within the terms of the 1942 declaration. Despite some sympathy with the Dutch view of those who had identified themselves with the Japanese, for whatever reason, during the war, there was growing irritation and concern in British official circles that the Dutch rejection of all contacts with the nationalist leaders was creating a dangerous stalemate in which all moderation on the Indonesian side might eventually be destroyed, with disastrous consequences for British forces in the NEI and for the British position in southeast Asia.

By late October, when he had seen the nationalist revolution at first hand and had talked with the republican leaders, Dening's assessment had changed from his initial dismissiveness. Support for the Republic, he told the Foreign Office, 'is very widespread and of a nature to be almost frightening.'[1] Clearly pressure on the nationalists alone would not bring about a peaceful settlement of the problem. Soon afterwards, he warned London that 'Having now bullied the Indonesians as far as my conscience will allow I now propose to devote my attention to the Dutch.' He had tried to persuade Sukarno to accept something less than full independence, but when Sukarno rejected a version of Dominion status with the comment, 'you see, we know the Dutch too well', Dening was forced to admit that 'I am afraid that when I consider the general Dutch attitude Indonesian suspicion may not be entirely unfounded.' The problem with the Dutch in Java, he advised the Foreign Office, was that they 'cannot be persuaded of the truth that the East has changed and changed radically as a result of the war. . . . The day of a master race is over.'[2] Most of the Dutch in Java he described as both 'atrophied' and 'dangerously neurotic and "trigger happy" '.[3] The one exception was Van Mook. Although he had originally showed that he completely identified with The Hague's position on talks with the nationalists, he gradually accepted that it was unrealistic to exclude Sukarno. After Mountbatten undertook to make it clear that Britain, and its forces, recognised Dutch sovereignty alone, and followed this up by successively occupying Buitenzorg, Bandung, Semarang and Surabaya in the second half of October, Van Mook agreed to have discussions with Sukarno and his followers. The Hague government objected strongly to any meeting with Sukarno, but under pressure from the British to help defuse the critical situation in Surabaya, arrangements were made for 31 October. Little of substance was achieved – feelings in Surabaya were running too high for that – but at least the two sides had met and exchanged views, however guardedly. For the British – for Dening and for Mountbatten and his subordinates – it was a major advance. For the Dutch government it was hardly less than treason on Van Mook's part. The Dutch Prime Minister denied that Van Mook had ever been authorised to meet Sukarno, and his possible dismissal was discussed by the cabinet.[4] Dening's reaction was unusually sharp and pointed:

I do hope at this late and very delicate stage the Netherlands government are not going to intervene in a manner likely to wreck our negotiations. . . . If at what is probably the most crucial moment in the history of the NEI they are nevertheless disposed to give public vent to their spite against one individual they may have serious cause to regret their action. They may be entitled to jeopardise their own position but they are not entitled to jeopardise ours.[5]

The Dutch insistence on distinguishing between moderate and extremist elements within the nationalist movement had tended to be interpreted by the British as little more than a device to avoid *any* negotiations in that it was unrealistic to talk of separating Sukarno from the nationalists who were acceptable to the Dutch.

Although the political advisers in SEAC, Dening and Walsh, clearly
recognised that there were factions within the broad spectrum of
Indonesian activism, they did nothing to explore, let alone exploit,
them. The shifting alignments within the republican movement had
little impact on them until the events of early November made them
aware of new opportunities to break the political deadlock. Those
oppportunities arose out of a political revolution within the
nationalist ranks.

At the end of October the nationalists split and power was seized
by a group whose policy was decidedly more 'moderate' (in British
eyes) than that espoused by Sukarno and his followers. Most
important in the context of relations with the Dutch, the new
leaders symbolised opposition to the previous identification of the
nationalist cause with Japanese sponsorship. Although Sukarno
retained his position as president of the republic, the cabinet was
now headed by Sutan Sjahrir, who had retired from public and
political life during the period of the Japanese occupation and who
consequently could not be charged with the slightest degree of
collaboration, which the Dutch had insisted was the immovable
stumbling block to any negotiation with Sukarno. Prior to the war
Sjahrir had spent years in political exile, a badge of honour that
helped to offset the nationalist suspicion of his receptiveness to
western ideas. In the 1930s he had broken away from Sukarno's
Partai Indonesia to found, with Muhammed Hatta, the (new)
Partai Nasional Indonesia and to establish the contrast of
approach that became so important in late 1945: Sukarno basing
his authority on his powers of oratory and mass mobilisation, less
concerned with details than with consensus, Sjahrir stressing tight
organisation, analysis and discussion. In the months leading up to
the proclamation of the Republic in August 1945 Sukarno had
been indispensable to the nationalist movement. His personal
qualities of magnetism and compelling oratory and his constant
exhortation to sacrifice and struggle as much as his willingness to
work closely with the Japanese to further the republican cause gave
hin unchallenged authority. By October, however, Sukarno's hold
was weakening. The fighting at Surabaya showed the power of the
revolutionary *permuda* (youth) which he was unable to control.
Fighting between Japanese troops and *permuda* forces in Bandung
and Semarang cast Sukarno's wartime collaboration in a new and
less favourable light, if only for tactical reasons: the Japanese were

by then 'yesterday's men' and a spent political force. To those who looked to negotiation (*diplomasi*) to produce a settlement with the Dutch it was clear that Sukarno was a major obstacle to Dutch/ Indonesian talks. In Batavia, general if incomplete allied control denied the *permuda* the scope for the violent methods they employed elsewhere and strengthened the hand of the educated elite among them who disliked the authoritarianism of Sukarno's style and the narrowness of his cabinet in which their representatives had no place.

Sjahrir was well equipped to capitalise on this discontent. His war-time record was impeccable in that he was not tainted by collaboration with the Japanese, which had by October become a liability; he was relatively young (36) and compared with Sukarno and his closest advisers could pass as the same age group as the *permuda*; and he spoke in terms that appealed to them but which also opened the door to negotiation. Internationalism rather than narrow nationalism was his creed, democratic change rather than violent upheaval his model. If the reality of the political changes of early November reflected less the triumph of ideals than the manoeuvrings for power within a relatively small group (from which the communist Tan Malaka was excluded) the formation of Sjahrir's first cabinet on 14 November marked a new and hopeful phase: here at last was a leader whose language could be understood by the western powers. Sukarno remained as president, symbol of the August revolution, but Sjahrir was the man with whom the Dutch and the British henceforth had to deal. Sjahrir's rise to power was undoubtedly welcomed by the British: compared with the mercurial Sukarno, he was calm, patient, and methodical. But his control of the nationalist movement was no more secure, as was illustrated by the virtual monopoly of portfolios in his cabinet by himself and Amir Sjarifuddin, and just as Sukarno on occasion had broken off talks with the British to consolidate his standing with the masses away from Batavia, so Sjahrir could move no faster than he could take the power brokers and their followers within the nationalist movement with him. In particular his authority over the extremist *permuda* waned as it became clear that while he owed his rise in part to their support, he did not on that account espouse their more radical policies. He opposed physical attacks on real or imagined opponents but was increasingly unable to prevent them.[6]

In the short term the political changes within the republican government added to the confusion of early November. Van Mook's planned meeting with Sukarno, at which the latest Dutch proposals were to be discussed, had to be postponed when the fighting in Surabaya forced Sukarno to leave Batavia in order to attend political rallies in other towns. Sukarno's absence deprived the allies of their hope of scoring a decisive dual victory over the nationalists: politically the Dutch had hoped that their new plan for the future of the NEI would drive a wedge between the extremists and the moderates, while Christison intended to take simultaneous military action to round up extremists in the Batavia area and to seize all essential utilities so that control of them could not be used either to stall further negotiations or to put pressure on the military government.[7] Christison's headquarters anticipated a possible pre-emptive action from the nationalists, and intended to reinforce the British garrison with Dutch troops, but hurriedly changed its plans once the meeting between Van Mook and Sukarno was postponed. 'The landing of Dutch troops before some form of settlement is reached', Christison advised Slim, 'is the one act which will nullify all past efforts for peaceful solution and it will without shadow of doubt cause a general uprising in which we must inevitably all become involved.'[8] Mountbatten's subsequent decision to divert Dutch troop ships to Malaya – to allow them to disembark in Java would be 'provocative', he told the Chiefs of Staff[9] – produced a furious response from Helfrich. The 'humiliation' arising out of SEAC's continuing refusal to admit Dutch troops to Java, he complained to Mountbatten, was 'almost unbearable'. There was a growing bitterness among former Dutch p.o.w.s and internees that lives were being lost unnecessarily because of a policy of surrender to the demands of the nationalists, who used the postponement of promised meetings to strengthen their position in the countryside surrounding allied military strongholds and the many camps scattered throughout Java. If nothing else, Helfrich urged, those Dutch troops diverted to Malaya could be used for internal security duties within British-held areas, thus freeing more highly trained forces for an active role against nationalist armed bands.[10]

Helfrich's protests were to no avail. The same day that he reproached Mountbatten for keeping Dutch forces out of Java, an incident occurred that confirmed Christison's view that Dutch native troops were 'trigger happy'. Shooting broke out in a section of Batavia, and among the wounded was one of the nationalist leaders. Was this merely another example of the deplorable discipline of the Dutch troops, or had they been engaged on an assassination mission? Rumour fed counter-rumour, and the situation in Batavia quickly deteriorated as nationalist groups fired back at allied troops, British and Indian as well as Dutch. Christison's local commander in Batavia, Major General D.C. Hawthorn, put the blame squarely on Van Oyen, accusing him of 'either deliberately disobeying . . . orders' or of being 'incapable of controlling' his troops.[11] When Christison told Van Mook that Van Oyen had shown himself 'nervous and incompetent' and would have to be dismissed, Van Mook replied wearily that his own position was becoming 'impossible', squeezed as he was between the uncompromising positions of his own government in The Hague and of the Indonesians: if Van Oyen was summarily dismissed, it might prove to be the last straw.[12] Two days later, Christison informed Helfrich officially of his decision to relieve Van Oyen of his command:

I have regretfully come to the conclusion that he is under such strain that his actions and reactions are no longer balanced and reliable. As a result of this mental strain, no doubt, he has frequently not carried out my orders, and has created alarm and despondency in Batavia which is inimical to Netherlands interests.[13]

Christison's attack on Van Oyen caused great anger in Dutch circles: not only in their eyes had Christison exceeded his authority in seeking to influence Dutch appointments but his impartiality was brought into question, not least when in early December he withdrew his complaints and apologised to Van Oyen. Van Mook, who otherwise admitted that he had considerable sympathy with Christison's problems in handling the Dutch military leaders (they were, he said, 'apt to get excited and ignore the realities of the situation'), was taken aback by Christison's demand.[14] Under attack from his own government for meeting the Indonesian leaders, he became increasingly isolated from his military commanders through his acquiescence in Christison's action. Within narrow limits Van Mook was anxious to pursue a moderate policy; Helfrich and his senior subordinates sought a military solution. For the means to implement that solution of arms, however, they had to look to the British. The first Dutch European battalion did not arrive in Java until January 1946, and already by mid November

1945 Christison and Hawthorn had reached the conclusion that the native Dutch troops, together with units raised from Dutch p.o.w.s, were totally unreliable. Christison ordered them moved out of Batavia and concentrated in special camps on the city's outskirts, a decision that further enraged Helfrich who fumed that he had not been consulted over the earlier decision to divert Dutch troops to Malaya and that any order to relocate the Dutch garrisons in Batavia would be 'unacceptable' to him.[15] Christison ignored Helfrich's protests and – in Helfrich's eyes, at least – added insult to injury by vetting appointments to Helfrich's staff on the basis of their willingness to work within the guidelines that Christison had developed.[16]

The British made little attempt to conceal their disdain for their Dutch counterparts: they considered the Dutch staff bloated and inefficient (the Dutch had two lieutenant generals and four major generals for a force barely the equivalent of two battalions), and incapable of providing the control and restraint that the British thought essential for the successful deployment of Dutch troops. With 'such a surfeit of Generals', the Foreign Office remarked, Van Oyen was 'easily replaceable'.[17] Nor were Dutch military sensitivities soothed by Christison's attempt to create better understanding among British troops of the Dutch plight. Constant criticism, Christison suggested, was 'un British'. It was not the fault of the Dutch troops, he insisted, that they were 'slovenly and badly dressed'. The British had to remind themselves constantly that 'the majority of these unfortunate Dutch people are temporarily mentally sick.' 'We British criticise the Dutch, and rightly so', he went on, 'for wanton attacks on Indonesians, but men in an unstable state of mind, thirsting for revenge, cannot or will not discriminate between moderates and terrorists.'[18] As a public message that was bound to come to the attention of his Dutch subordinates, it was a peculiarly clumsy intervention in the sphere of worsening Anglo-Dutch military relations.

With its military resources stretched to the limit, and with little prospect of external reinforcements, SEAC naturally looked to a political settlement that would enable it to fulfil the limited British objectives while allowing it to claim that Britain had been faithful to the spirit, if not the letter, of its agreements with the Dutch. The emergence of Sjahrir as the leader of and spokesman for the republican government signalled an end to the pre-eminence of the collaborationist elements in the nationalist movement, and offered the clearest possible opportunity of arriving at a moderate settlement, one that would at least be acceptable to the British if still rejected by the Dutch. Sadly, the chance was missed. When the first meeting between Van Mook and the new Indonesian leaders took place on 17 November, Sjahrir asked that the British act as arbiters between the two sides. But Dening, who only a short time before had railed against the obstinacy of the Dutch, tried to pressure Sjahrir into undertakings that he felt he was in no position to give. Not unreasonably, Sjahrir replied that he needed more time to consider his position, even though Dening complained that during the month he had been in Batavia no progress had been made. Christison suggested that quite apart from political discussions, there had to be an urgent meeting of experts to tackle the growing economic problems arising out of a breakdown in transport and power services, which was having a serious effect on food supplies. This was a useful way of bringing both sides together on a practical basis, but the more Dening insisted on immediate undertakings on the part of the Indonesians, the more he dissipated the goodwill and expectancy that the announcement of the meeting had created. Even a Dutch observer remarked on Dening's high-handed manner. It was not a promising start to the new round of negotiations.[19]

Mountbatten's hopes of containing the British involvement in Java were undermined from two directions. In an attempt to prevent Christison from taking military action against the Indonesians, Mountbatten had warned him not to make any statements that in any way departed from the official British policy, namely that British troops were in Java to maintain law and order, disarm the Japanese, and repatriate p.o.w.s and internees. Christison was permitted to tell the Indonesians that force might be used to keep order, but Mountbatten clearly intended that Christison should minimise his intrusion into the political situation.[20] That was becoming more and more difficult, not least because there were growing signs of unrest among Christison's troops. Walsh complained that at Surabaya, eight Australian journalists had spoken to British troops 'in a way that can only be interpreted as tampering with their loyalty.'[21] Mountbatten was sufficiently concerned by these and other reports – which seemed to give credence to the fears long expressed by Wavell and Auchinleck – to ask for an investigation: what did British and Indian other ranks think of the tasks they had been called upon to carry out in Java, and had their general views affected morale? He also wanted to know whether Christison or Dening thought that SEAC was no longer able to stand by the limited interpretation of the Chiefs of Staff original directive, and if so, what they suggested should be the proper course to follow.[22] The possibility of an early withdrawal seemed to be fading rapidly. Christison's difficulties with Dutch troops in Batavia had shown that it was impractical to suggest that the Dutch would be in any position to assume control in the near future, and the reports on Dutch European forces being prepared for service in the NEI – it was estimated that 70,000 would be available by September 1946 – were not encouraging: Montgomery, who was responsible for training Dutch troops in Europe, described their morale and discipline as low, and estimated that they might not be fit even for occupation duties in the NEI.[23]

Added to these problems was a hardening in the attitude of the Foreign Office, which advised Dening to 'continue to avoid using terms which suggest that the Indonesians themselves have an organized Government capable of controlling warring elements.' Dening was urged to stress that since the Dutch had made considerable concessions, any failure of negotiations would arise out of the Indonesians' inability to make decisions and carry them out. This inability, in turn, was a legacy of the Japanese-inspired hatred and distrust which, according to the Foreign Office, prevented the Indonesians from realising that 'their own real aspirations . . . can develop peacefully and in an orderly manner inside the Dutch Empire.'[24] The nationalist leaders' inability or failure to control the extremists was seen by Dening as the major stumbling block to any progress in negotiations. In the atmosphere of terrorism and intimidation that prevailed in parts of Batavia and the surrounding countryside, it was impossible to discuss political developments calmly. That was a view which Christison and his military staff shared, just as they agreed with Dening's solution, namely that a military 'cleanup' operation was needed 'to create the necessary degree of security'. The drawback, of course, was that only British forces were available to carry out such an operation.[25]

Dening's view that the onus for progress in further talks now lay with the Indonesians was rudely shattered by a broadcast on the BBC by the former war correspondent, Chester Wilmot, who gave details of an interview he had held with the Dutch Minister for

Overseas Territories, Professor Logemann, some days earlier. According to Wilmot, Logemann had spoken disparagingly of the Indonesian Republic and had stated unequivocally that the Dutch were prepared to use force to retain the NEI as part of the Kingdom.[26] The broadcast created an uproar. Christison was furious that on the eve of talks between the Dutch and the Indonesians, with himself in the chair, the Dutch government had apparently seen fit – yet again – to disavow its local representatives and to take an impossibly intransigent stance, one moreover, that had serious military implications not so much for the Dutch as for the British. 'Unless categorical denial issued and Logemann resigns', he insisted, 'the military consequences here may be more than I can deal with. No other course possible. . . . Request your immediate action before things go too far.'[27] Mountbatten supported Christison's demand for Logemann's resignation, while Dening, protesting about the 'peculiar lunacy' of the Dutch position, called for 'drastic action' against Logemann to prevent his endangering both British troops and Dutch civilians in the NEI.[28]

The Foreign Office agreed that Logemann's statement had 'gravely prejudiced' the situation.[29] Its earlier advice to Dening to press the new Indonesian leaders to fall in with the Dutch proposals and to accept the 'considerable concessions' that the Dutch had made now looked decidedly shaky. It had been based on the assumption that between them the Dutch and the British could construct a combined diplomatic and military front in the face of which the nationalists would have little alternative but to negotiate and enforce on their supporters decisions that were made around the conference table. That combined approach was in danger of crumbling. The Hague had again apparently abrogated both the tenor and the substance of Van Mook's dealings with Sjahrir, while Christison's dismissal of Van Oyen further strained military relations between the British and the Dutch in Java. Both in London and in Java, British patience was running out as the chance of a peaceful solution, or at least the chance of minimising the British involvement, seemed to be slipping away. In those circumstances, London began to look at ways of extricating itself from its commitment. When the Defence Committee asked for a legal opinion on the precise extent of British obligations in the NEI under the Civil Affairs agreement with the Netherlands, it was told that beyond action against the Japanese, it was required only to recognise Dutch sovereignty and to do nothing that might impede the resumption of Dutch control.[30] Its obligation did not extend to pulling Dutch chestnuts out of Indonesian fires.

The need to limit British commitments to the NEI was reinforced by several signals that Mountbatten sent to the Chiefs of Staff in early December. At the end of November, when there seemed to be reasonable hope that the Dutch and Indonesians might begin serious negotiations, Mountbatten had assured Bevin that he was following the British government's policy while trying, as far as possible, to avoid irreparably antagonising either side in Java.[31] The reassertion of the Dutch hardline policy put paid to that shortlived optimism which in any case had been slight: Mountbatten told Bevin that the probable result of his following a strict middle line had been to get both parties offside. The situation in Java, he advised the Chiefs of Staff in December, was even more serious than his previous reports had indicated, and was likely to become even more as a result of Logemann's statements, which had been interpreted by the extremists as a 'virtual declaration of war'. The fighting in Surabaya had not only demonstrated the strength and determination of the republican forces, but had drawn attention to a new factor – the IFTUs. Their numbers in Surabaya were estimated to be 147,000, including some 90,000 Chinese, a figure far beyond SEAC's evacuation capability. (Pyman had already insisted that they all had to be abandoned to whatever fate might await them, which would depend largely 'on the temper of the extremists at the time and the state of political settlement.'[32]) Much smaller numbers – about 19,000 – were at Semarang, and these could be evacuated. It was Surabaya, the scene of so much fierce and bloody fighting, that convinced Mountbatten that a decision on future British policy had to be made urgently, and made on 'mainly political' grounds.

He suggested that there were three courses of action open to him, and requested a speedy approval of one of them. Course A involved the 'very early' withdrawal from Surabaya, which would allow those troops thus released to be used in the reinforcement of Batavia and the surrounding countryside. Under Course B, Surabaya would be held for some time and only evacuated either when peaceful conditions had been restored or when Dutch troops were available to replace British and Indian troops. Course C called for British and Indian forces, 'presumably' assisted by the Dutch, to impose law and order throughout the whole of Java.

As with his previous alternatives, Mountbatten outlined the advantages and drawbacks of each option. Course A would mean the abandonment of thousands of IFTUs and consequent charges that the British had deserted those who had supported the western cause. Without Surabaya the repatriation of the Japanese from east Java would be severely hampered, and the Dutch would react strongly to the loss of their major naval base in Java, through which it had always been intended they would pass their troops for the pacification of east Java. (Helfrich, Mountbatten said, had already sent him a 'violent protest' about the possibility of losing Surabaya, but this was untrue: Helfrich's letter was, in fact, a reasonable, restrained and non-alarmist statement of the probable consequences of the loss of Surabaya.[33]) The wider result might well be increased disturbances in other parts of the NEI and general unrest throughout southeast Asia, with both friend and foe interpreting the withdrawal as a sign of Britain's unwillingness or inability to carry out the directive under which it had originally moved into Java. The adverse effects of a precipitate withdrawal from Surabaya would be avoided under Course B, but at the cost of an immediate increase in the commitment, for the only way that Surabaya could be held for a longer period while Batavia was reinforced was to move the 7th Indian Division from Siam to Batavia. That, of course, raised the whole problem of the use of Indian troops, which both Auchinleck and Wavell continued to stress threatened to become a major political issue within India. However, as long as there were no signs of overt disaffection among Indian troops deployed in Java, it was possible to continue to use them, since Wavell had emphasised that the critical point would come in early 1946, when the Indian Congress was expected to make a public call for their withdrawal from the NEI. The third course was hardly a practical proposition. Against the sole advantage of enabling Britain to offer the maximum assistance to the Dutch, with whatever political benefits might flow from that, it would involve British forces – as many as six divisions – in a 'full-scale war, with the unrestricted use of modern weapons against hostile forces in the field, and then the attempt to establish security in a situation analogous to Ireland after the last war, but on a much larger scale.' This was a daunting prospect, and one that Mountbatten knew was unlikely to be accepted by London.[34]

Mountbatten followed this outline of the possible options with another signal to the Chiefs of Staff, one that was restricted to British eyes only. As a result of his enquiries of Christison and Dempsey in Batavia, he reported on the 'delicate' matter of troop morale:

Both by the Press and by letters from home the British troops are being made to believe that the imposition of Dutch authority by force of British arms is a wrong cause. They do not like fighting for this, though they are quite ready to fight to secure the safety of European and Eurasian women and children. The Indian troops are subject to Indonesian propaganda which is insidious and well directed. Neither British nor Indian troops like the Dutch and they despise the lack of discipline, and the irresponsible behaviour of the Dutch troops with whom they have come into contact. . . . Although all troops are still behaving magnificently, I must warn you that the longer we remain in Java and Sumatra the more the morale will deteriorate.[35]

The only solution, Mountbatten told Wavell, lay with the British government, who had 'to make up their minds firmly once and for all'.[36]

For his part Mountbatten tried to keep a tight rein on activities in Java, but it was difficult to restrain local commanders from reacting to attacks with tactics that exceeded the firm but moderate approach Mountbatten wanted to adopt. When it was discovered that the survivors of a Dakota aircraft that had crashed on a flight between Bandung and Batavia and the search party that had originally gone to look for them – 22 in men in all – had been tortured and murdered, Christison ordered stiff measures to be taken against the 'Black Buffaloes', the extremist group known to be responsible for the massacre. Most fled into the jungle when British troops approached but about 60 made a stand outside Bekasi and in the ensuring fight were all killed. On Christison's instructions Bekasi (a town of some ten thousand rather than the 'village' as it was usually described) was then burned to the ground as a deterrent. This retaliatory action dismayed Mountbatten, who had had previously reprimanded Gracey in Saigon for using British troops to set fire to suspected terrorist villages. As he subsequently told the Chiefs of Staff, 'although reprisals will no doubt take place as the immediate result of understandable human reactions to gross cases of brutality or murder they must not be taken in cold blood as a matter of principle.'[37] Christison later claimed to Wash that the raid on Bekasi was not a reprisal but had been an 'operational necessity'. 'If this is indeed true', noted Mountbatten, 'it is a thousand pities they could not have told us this in the first instance.' He was also angered by Christison's subsequent apparent disregard of strict instructions that air strikes against nationalist positions were only to be called in after warning leaflets had been dropped. When Dempsey tried to justify Christison's action in retaliation for attacks on RAPWI convoys near Bandung on the grounds that local commanders often had to make quick decisions, Mountbatten ordered that in future all aircraft liable to be used in air strikes carry appropriate leaflets.[38] Nor was Mountbatten pleased by reports of politically sensitive comments emanating from AFNEI headquarters in Batavia. It was 'intolerable', he told a staff meeting in Singapore, that one of his subordinates should make statements on British policy when even he was unable to do so – and would not consider doing so.[39] The blame for this unfortunate incident was not immediately fixed on Christison, but his stock seemed to be declining rapidly.

When Mountbatten's three options were considered in London, it quickly became apparent that none was attractive. The third course, an increased British commitment to enable the Dutch to conquer the whole of Java, was not even seriously considered. That left a choice between an immediate or a phased withdrawal from Surabaya and east Java in order to concentrate British and Indian troops around Batavia. The Chiefs of Staff leaned towards an early evacuation of east Java, even though they recognised that the 'political repercussions throughout the area will be tremendous.' Not least would be the reaction arising from a British abandonment of friendly people, but whichever course of action was adopted there was little that could be done for these people. (Colonel Nangle, who had been sent out to Java from the War Office after the Chiefs of Staff had complained of the paucity of information coming from SEAC, went even further: not only were the IFTUs beyond rescue, but so were the thousands of ex-prisoners and internees not yet within the allied safety net. Even if their camps could be located quickly, 'they would probably be murdered before they could be reached. . . . This is inevitable.'[40]) The Chiefs of Staff were inclined to accept that penalty, for the alternative course, they thought, would have a serious effect on India.[41] The Far Eastern Department of the Foreign Office, on the other hand, favoured the second course, on the grounds that while Britain's strictly legal obligations did not go so far as to require British troops to instal the

Dutch against the opposition of the local population, Britain had a strong moral responsibility to stand by its wartime ally. While a phased withdrawal from Surabaya had its drawbacks, it would enable Britain to claim, with some justification, that it was pursuing a policy that was basically consistent with its original public aims. Moreover, it would not entail the abandonment of the friendly population in Surabaya for whom Britain also had some responsibility. However, if Surabaya was handed over to the Dutch, the nationalists might interpret this as a pre-emptive move by the allies and break off all negotiations. Far better, therefore, to delay the arrival of the Dutch in force in the hope that another round of negotiations under a British chairman might produce a peaceful settlement.[42]

The Defence Committee's discussion was inconclusive, for the difficulties inherent in either of the options before it were so great that no quick decision was possible. Rather than incur the political or military consequences of either course, it was decided to accept Bevin's suggestion that a final effort should be made to negotiate a settlement, not through the men on the spot but by means of a top level commission. Mountbatten was ordered to hold Surabaya but was empowered to evacuate Semarang, where the number of IFTUs was within the capability of SEAC to protect and move. No additional Indian troops were to be sent to Java, a concession to the growing unrest in India where, the Committee was told, there was some justification for the belief that Indian troops were being used as 'mercenaries' to carry out a policy that the British, intent on not disrupting their repatriation programme, found distasteful. Nor were Dutch troops allowed to land in Java, for the evidence before the Committee – from Mountbatten, Dening and Colonel Nangle – was overwhelmingly of the opinion that the introduction of Dutch forces was likely to irreparably damage the situation in Java.[43]

Bevin's suggestion reflected a mounting unease in London that SEAC was unable to handle the problem confronting it. Although he sympathised that 'our Commanders and representatives on the spot were being placed in a most unfortunate and invidious position in having to act both in their capacity as Commanders in the field and as statesmen adjudicating in a problem outside their immediate concern', he was in fact expressing a widespread concern that military considerations and solutions had predominated too long.[44] When the Defence Committee's refusal to allow additional Indian troops to be moved to Java – Mountbatten had proposed shifting the 7th Indian Division from Siam – was relayed to SEAC, Dening thought it yet another example of London's lack of understanding of the problems that SEAC faced.[45] Mountbatten and Dening agreed that only an approach that combined both military action and a willingness to negotiate would succeed, for without measures to control the armed violence that had become endemic in parts of Java in particular, neither Mountbatten's original tasks nor a political settlement could be achieved. More than a month before, Mountbatten had warned London that because of the unforeseen difficulties that had arisen in the NEI, the disposition of his limited forces throughout SEAC had become unbalanced.[46] By December he had concluded that not-withstanding the worsening imbalance, an additional temporary commitment to Java would be necessary if Britain was to be able to claim that it had carried out its allotted tasks, let alone that it had brought about an acceptable political end to the strife.

The mounting distrust of the few Dutch troops in Java had already led Christison to urge the removal of Van Oyen and the concentration of Dutch troops in special camps outside Batavia, but the problem still remained of the circumstances in which European Dutch forces would eventually be admitted into Java. Helfrich's statements were far from reassuring. Rejecting Mountbatten and Dening's distinction between moderates and extremists among the nationalists, Helfrich insisted that 'when dealing with native rabbles the most profitable way was to hit immediately and hit hard.' In answer to the criticism that the anticipated forces from Europe would not be fully trained, he replied that since they would not be opposed by a 'modern army', full training was not essential: 'Every man equipped with a rifle or machine gun could shoot. . . . They were young fanatical boys. . . . and were well-suited to the task in hand.'[47] This merely confirmed the worst fears of Christison and others, and moved the liaison officer appointed by the Netherlands government, Count Van Bylandt, to describe Helfrich's assessment as 'painfully unbusinesslike and unmilitary' and to press for his removal.[48] J.C.R. Proud, the Australian Political Representative, commented on the 'violence' with which Helfrich spoke of suppressing the nationalists, and noted that 'Helfrich does not enjoy the confidence of any British Commanders in the theatre, who consider his ideas in strategy outmoded and reminiscent of the pre-Crimean days.'[49] By December there could be no

5 Admiral C.E.L. Helfrich. Dutch Commander-in-Chief, Netherlands
East Indies

question but that the extremists in Dutch circles in SEAC had discredited themselves and destroyed any possibility of SEAC attempting a military solution, even had one been possible, while the inability of the new moderate nationalist leaders to curb the violence of the extremists made a limited military action the necessary precursor to a negotiated settlement.

Dening's criticism that London seemed collectively unable to appreciate the delicate balance in Mountbatten's approach was well-founded. Individuals, however, were aware of the possible repercussions on wider issues. Bevin's comment to Mountbatten, for example, that he was spending more time than he wanted on the NEI problem was more than just an expression of irritation.[50] It reflected the growing concern in London that the apparent stalemate in the NEI was having a souring effect on Britain's relations with a number of countries, notably, of course, with the Netherlands, but also with the United States and Australia. If Bevin had little concern for or interest in imperial relations, he could still not ignore the warnings from the Dominions Secretary that any move to follow up the suggestion from the Chiefs of Staff to request Australian military assistance in the NEI might well produce a 'peremptory refusal' and might in the long run do more harm than good.[51] From August on, some thought had been given to the postwar defence structure in southeast Asia, and there was growing interest from the Chiefs of Staff in the proposal to make Australia one of the main centres of that system, but the increasing divergence between the positions of the British and Australian governments over developments in the NEI threatened to make the plan stillborn. The alternative to Australia was the United States, but that possibility seemed to be ruled out by the mounting American hostility to Britain's perceived intention of restoring Dutch rule. Bevin's statement in the House of Commons on 23 November was open to varying interpretations, and American suspicions of British intentions in southeast Asia obstructed Bevin's desire for close cooperation in western Europe between the two countries. Both Mountbatten and Bevin realised that Java was consuming a disproportionate share of British diplomatic and military effort, but it was Mountbatten and his subordinates in SEAC who first understood that the only way out of the commitment was to increase it in the short term. The result of London's failure to develop a long term policy, the secretary of the cabinet

General Ismay commented, was to place Mountbatten in an 'unfair' position.[52]

Much as Bevin and others wanted a political settlement, developments in Java forced London to approve a greater military involvement. By mid December conditions in western Java, both within Batavia itself and in the surrounding areas, had become so critical that Mountbatten proposed a series of actions designed, as he advised the Chiefs of Staff, to 'put our house in order militarily'. Sniping in the streets of Batavia, attacks on RAPWI camps and convoys, and the imminent breakdown in food production had created a situation which gave free rein to the extremists – on both sides. If early negotiations failed and if Sjahrir was unable to curtail the Indonesian terrorists, SEAC's forces would have to assume local control by detaining known or suspected extremists, disarming and detaining the republican police force, members of which were suspected of joining the night sniping forays, and confiscating trucks controlled by Indonesians, since it was thought that the road transport system was used as an intelligence network to keep nationalist armed bands informed of British troop and RAPWI movements. The disadvantages of this proposal, Mountbatten cautioned, were that it would undoubtedly cause a 'great flare up in the Press of the World' and might well in the short term unite the moderates and the extremists in a common opposition to SEAC. However, the deteriorating position in Java, especially in the western end of the island, not only made negotiations virtually impossible but raised the spectre of significant increases in British (as opposed to Indian) casualties as the first British brigade was landing in Batavia. On purely military grounds early action against the Indonesian extremists was essential, but Mountbatten sought specific Cabinet approval in view of the 'grave political implications'.[53]

Before any decision could be made, a furor erupted over comments made by Christison to the press. After Christison had spoken 'off the record' to members of the press in Batavia on 9 December, the BBC broadcast an interpretation of his remarks which suggested that the clean up operations in western Java had the long term aim of restoring Dutch rule. The reaction was immediate. Sjahrir responded with a uncharacteristically violent denunciation of the British role in the NEI, and immediately left Batavia for the interior of Java, thus breaking off talks and effectively tying Christison's hands, since attempts to separate the extremists from the moderates had been based on the understanding that Sjahrir would be kept informed of any new military operations against Indonesian terrorists. Mountbatten was furious that yet again Christison had apparently been drawn into political discussions:

If you had carried out my instructions and refrained from entering the political arena, none of this would have happened. . . . I must once more make my orders quite clear to you that you are not, at any time, to get involved in discussions concerning H.M.G. policy. This, you will realise, is to protect you from the consequences which have twice followed from political discussions, and to enable you to concentrate on your military tasks without repeatedly having to answer charges from London. You will naturally draw the attention of C-in-C ALFSEA [Dempsey] to any military repercussions of any political telegramme which Walsh has sent. . . . I can foresee no other occasion on which you will require to refer to political matters.[54]

This was hardly realistic. All military operations in Java had political implications, and short of refusing to speak to the press Christison could not avoid making statements that carried political overtones. Indeed, the Chiefs of Staff had made it clear to Mountbatten that they wanted senior officers in SEAC to give 'off the record' briefings to the press, but the guidelines they laid down for such briefings were not passed on by Mountbatten in time to prevent Christison from trespassing on ground that more properly belonged to his political adviser, Walsh. Had Mountbatten acted more quickly, the Chiefs of Staff noted, 'the uproar would never have arisen.'[55]

That was a dubious assertion, for there was widespread agreement that any statements made by official spokesmen in SEAC were liable to be distorted by the press. Mountbatten complained bitterly about the 'deplorably low' standard of press representatives who were reporting on developments in southeast Asia (there were said to be 65 correspondents in Java alone) and said that in the wake of the latest incident, his policy would henceforth be to 'provide the minimum necessary to prevent a spiteful outcry against SE Asia Command. . . . the less said about the N.E.I. the better. . . . [for the] soldiers were not proud of what they were now having to do in Southeast Asia; they did not want publicity.'[56] There was little, however, that Mountbatten could do. Censorship had been lifted immediately after the end of the war against Japan, and short of reimposing it, which was politically impossible, Mountbatten and the British government were powerless to control the press. They could try to persuade newspapers to adopt a more 'responsible' approach, as was done following complaints from the British ambassador at The Hague about reporting of *The Times'* southeast Asia correspondent, Ian Morrison,[57] or they could register official protests about critical radio programmes, for example in the case of the news commentaries broadcast over Radio Australia,* but as the Foreign Office advised Walsh, any attempt to withdraw accreditation and remove correspondents 'would cause the newspapers, including those not directly affected, to put the worse possible construction on such a decision'.[58] The position was at best an uneasy one, and gradually developed into outright distrust of the press. Thus in late December Walsh could write of various correspondents: 'Sharpe [BBC] has again disgraced himself . . . his alcoholic intemperance is now pronounced'; 'Steen [*Daily Herald*] also tends to alcoholism and spends most of his time in bed'; 'Thompson [Australian Broadcasting Commission] . . . a rabid Communist.'[59] Walsh's solution was to accredit those correspondents approved by Christison and himself and to expel the rest, which brought from the Foreign Office the comment: 'the value of Consul General Walsh's estimate of the correspondents named as a bunch of unreliable drunks is . . . seriously diminished by the unwisdom of his suggestion for dealing with the situation.'[60] There was other evidence that Walsh's judgement was unsound. He complained to the Australian Political Representative, Macmahon Ball, of the 'dreadful and provocative' slogans painted by the 'natives' on the walls of buildings in Batavia and said they had to be removed; a cursory examination showed that most were quotations from the speeches of Abraham Lincoln, no doubt chosen in the expectation that American troops would liberate the city.[61]

Mountbatten himself recognised, however, that the British role in the NEI was at best controversial and open to misinterpretation. The lack of clear policy directives from London, despite Mountbatten's repeated attempts to get the Cabinet to issue firm guidelines, made it virtually inevitable that local commanders would be drawn into politically sensitive areas of discussion. It could not have been

* See chapter 10.

otherwise. At SEAC headquarters Mountbatten insisted on making any statements on political matters himself; his political adviser, Dening, had no authority to speak publicly on questions of political importance. In Batavia, Mountbatten demanded that Christison defer to his political adviser, Walsh, but with military operations, large and small, as the basis of Britain's involvement in Java, Christison could not avoid being drawn on political questions whenever he briefed the press on what SEAC was doing and why. Mountbatten explained to the Chiefs of Staff that the news agencies showed no compunction in inventing stories if necessary, and he added that Christison could not be blamed entirely for the incident since he had not received the guidelines before talking to the press.[62] But it made little difference: Christison's days were numbered.

Despite the steadily deteriorating situation in western Java, Mountbatten prevented Christison from taking any extraordinary action to curb attacks on allied servicemen or internees until a clear ruling had been obtained from the Chiefs of Staff. Christison's optimistic assessment that there would be minimal political repercussions from striking hard against the extremists was not shared by Mountbatten or by most of his advisers, although so hopeful was Dening that negotiations might prove fruitful that he changed his mind and urged a postponement of immediate military steps.[63] When the Chiefs of Staff replied to Mountbatten's request for instructions, they did not give him quite the firm ruling that he had sought: he was permitted to take immediate steps against the extremists in western Java, or to delay such action if he felt that the absent Indonesian leaders should have a 'reasonable' time to return and to resume negotiations. However, in allowing Mountbatten to move against the extremists when he saw fit, the Chiefs of Staff did not approve his plan to move the Dutch Marine Brigade to Surabaya, which would have enabled him to withdraw the 5th Indian Division there in order to strengthen his forces in western Java.[64] The Chiefs of Staff's objections to allowing the Dutch Marines to land in Surabaya were in part a reflection of their sense of confusion over what appeared to be the inconsistency of the advice they were getting from Mountbatten: at the beginning of December he had argued against the deployment of additional Dutch forces in Java and had endorsed Christison's refusal to allow those troops already en route to land, while at the same time he claimed that he had insufficient strength to control the major centres in all of Java; three weeks later, he was seeking to use Dutch Marines in Surabaya in eastern Java while undertaking major operations in western Java.

Furthermore it appeared to the Chiefs of Staff, and to the Foreign Office, that the press statement which Mountbatten proposed to issue to explain the operations in western Java had struck the 'wrong note, in that it gives the impression of over-anxiety on our part to justify our action'.[65] Dening had earlier made much the same point, when he wrote to Sterndale Bennett that 'it is we who should call upon them [the Indonesian leaders in Batavia] to explain their conduct and not vice versa.'[66] When operations to restore a measure of law and order to western Java began on 27 December, Mountbatten's public statement simply referred to the need to suppress attacks against British troops and to protect civilians. Political considerations were not mentioned. Yet in preparing to launch these operations, Christison took action that had deep political overtones. In an attempt to protect the convoys of internees moving from outlying camps to repatriation ports and to speed up the concentration of disarmed Japanese troops at points on the coast, Christison agreed that units of the *Tentara Keamanan Rakjat* (the TKR – People's Security Army) would provide armed escorts. When the Dutch learned of this, they were outraged. It seemed to them to promote the TKR as a responsible organisation, and to come dangerously close to a *de facto* recognition of the Republican government and its legitimate role in two of the main tasks imposed on SEAC by the Combined Chiefs of Staff.[67]

The fragmentation of advice that was coming from SEAC, and the apparent willingness of the men on the spot to seek a military solution, or at least to use military means to create the conditions in which a political solution could be arrived at, made it all the more necessary for the British government to initiate fresh moves to break the stalemate. At two levels London sought to take more direct control of developments in the NEI. The first was by calling a meeting between the leaders of the British and Dutch governments, so that in face-to-face talks there could be agreement on a common approach; the second was by appointing a special commissioner who would in effect outrank the Supreme Commander and bring a new perspective to bear on the situation in Java. Both had been proposed by Bevin, who had earlier told the Dutch ambassador that while 'Christison had done valuable work in bringing the parties together . . . the conduct of political discussions was an unfair burden to place upon a military commander faced with an anxious military situation.' What was needed, Bevin suggested, was to lift discussions 'on to a higher plane, and, so to speak, above the battle.'[68]

The Chequers conference at the end of December was the first time that Attlee and his Dutch counterpart, Professor Schermerhorn, and their senior political and military advisers, had met to discuss the situation in the NEI. Nothing was resolved, and the meeting was little more than a rehearsal of the positions, and grievances, of both parties. The communiqué that was issued at the end of the talks spoke of the need to arrive at a political solution, and the British government acknowledged its obligation to 'establish without delay conditions of security in which it would be possible for the Government of the Netherlands East Indies to continue negotiations with representative Indonesians.' In the course of the discussions, however, Attlee had given a much more restrictive interpretation of the British responsibility, emphasising that it was limited to the restoration of law and order in western Java while rejecting Dutch requests to allow Dutch troops to be landed in the eastern part of the island. To that specific grievance was added the complaint that the Dutch in Java were consistently ignored by the local British commanders, who preferred to reach understandings with the Indonesians rather than use those Dutch troops who were at hand. Again, Christison was singled out for criticism, for Van Mook made it clear that the bypassing of Dutch authority and manpower in Java had become noticeably worse once Dening left Batavia and returned to Singapore. Unless the Dutch were brought fully into developments in Java, there was a danger that the Dutch government might fall, and be replaced by a Conservative government which would withdraw the proposals, subsequently described by the communiqué as 'consistent and liberal', and pursue an intransigent and hardline policy.[69]

Although the British representatives defended Christison's individual actions, privately there had been some criticism of his tendency to cut the Dutch out of day-to-day discussions in Batavia while having close contact with Sjahrir and his supporters. There was no escaping the fact that Christison had become an obstacle to a wider Anglo-Dutch agreement and a danger to the political survival of the only Dutch government capable of and willing to accept the necessity of substantial political concessions in the NEI. His replacement was only a matter of time, as was the appointment of a top level commissioner to take charge of political developments on the spot. To that extent, Dutch charges that British policies espoused in London were not reflected in British actions in Java struck home. Equally, however, little progress had been made towards answering Mountbatten's plea a month earlier to 'state unequivocally what H.M. Government's policy is in the NEI, so that we who have to carry out that policy will no longer be left in any doubt as to what our instructions are.'[70]

Chapter eight

The British withdrawal from southern Indochina

The marked lack of a sense of urgency that characterised the British government's approach to the military problems of southern Indochina had no parallel in France. De Gaulle had been taken aback when he discovered that by late September Leclerc had still not gone to Saigon, and promptly ordered him to move there at once. Leclerc had always insisted that the French could not assume responsibility until they had sufficient forces in Indochina, and on those grounds he had decided to remain in Kandy rather than become a general without troops in Saigon, completely under Gracey's control and unable to bring any pressure to bear on developments. De Gaulle accepted that the French military buildup was important but emphasised that it was even more important for Leclerc simply to be on the spot in Saigon. 'Every delay reinforces the appearance of French impotence', he wrote, 'and leaves the field free to British authority.' The British did not necessarily have any ill-will, he added, but they were poorly motivated.[1] Leclerc was inclined to agree that the British lacked the sense of urgency that the French felt was necessary to contain the spread of anti-French violence. The sharp exchange between Leclerc and Mountbatten over SEAC's failure to press for the accelerated arrival of the 9th DIC raised doubts in Leclerc's mind over Mountbatten's forthrightness. Mountbatten, he told his staff, was 'too political', whereas Slim, 'an old soldier', was 'much better', assuring Leclerc that on matters affecting French interests he took him fully into his confidence and kept 'no secrets' from him.[2] Despite de Gaulle's instructions, Leclerc was still reluctant to go to Saigon before a sizeable number of French troops were there, fearing with good reason that the British (or at least Mountbatten's staff) would try to draw on his political authority without allowing him any voice in the control of military operations.[3]

Leclerc's arrival in Saigon on 5 October came two days after the remainder of the 5th RIC landed from the French battleship *Richelieu*. Despite this increase in the number of French troops at his disposal, Leclerc still lacked the forces to act independently, and the weakness of French power was symbolised by the fact that when he drove from the airport to the centre of the city, his route was lined with Japanese and Gurkha troops, acting as guards in both the ceremonial and practical sense. Nevertheless, Leclerc was both impressed and relieved on meeting Gracey: impressed by him personally, and relieved to find that they agreed on the measures that had to be taken. It was a meeting of military minds, their common outlook reinforced by Leclerc's discovery that Gracey 'does not like Mountbatten but admires Slim'. 'We share that view', Leclerc's staff recorded.[4] The ceasefire had been in effect since 2 October, but there was little prospect of a political settlement that would make further military action unnecessary. De Gaulle's emphatic rejection of a broadening of the March statement blocked any further political initiative, and Leclerc went empty-handed to Saigon. When Cédile broadcast on Radio Saigon on 1 October – the first time he had spoken publicly about France's plans for the future of Indochina – he claimed that the March declaration proved that French policy was true to the principles of the Atlantic Charter, but went on to stress that those who had collaborated with the enemy (that is, Vietnamese who had worked with the Japanese since the March *coup*) would suffer the same punishment as traitors in France. Before the political developments promised in the March statement could be implemented, order had to be restored and maintained. The French, he insisted, had to set an example, not least so that the great majority of the Vietnamese could see that they had nothing to fear by cooperating with the French authorities.[5] It was a tough and unyielding speech, designed to prop up support among the French community rather than to convince the Vietnamese of France's good intentions, and followed as it was by military reinforcements and the arrival of Leclerc who was known to favour strong military action, it signalled that the French were prepared to seek a military solution if negotiations on their terms, and on their terms alone, did not succeed.

In SEAC headquarters there was a mounting sense of unease over Indochina but no agreement on what the British role should be. Dening urged Bevin to speed up the despatch of the 9th DIC 'if we are to avoid accusations both from the United States and the East of supporting French imperialistic designs', but otherwise had nothing to recommend.[6] Pyman, who visited Saigon soon after Leclerc's arrival, came to the conclusion that if the Vietnamese refused to negotiate with the French and were unable to curb the violence within their own ranks, then the British and French would have to use all the military force at their disposal to bring the situation under control. That possibility was made all the more likely by the fact that though the French negotiators displayed a generally conciliatory tone and had promised a liberal policy with no reprisals against the Vietnamese, 'nobody will believe a French guarantee'.[7] If the ceasefire did not hold and fighting was renewed, what role should British forces play? Slim complained to Brooke, the CIGS, that 'the directions we have been receiving from various sources seem to me to have been somewhat involved and at times contradictory'. The Secretary of State for War, Lawson, had emphasised when visiting Singapore that SEAC's forces were not to become involved in nationalist struggles in non-British territories but were to disarm and evacuate the Japanese. Even if British troops did not provide active assistance to the French, French forces would still be operating under his, Slim's, overall command and ultimately under Mountbatten's command. 'As long as we retain this command', he noted, 'we cannot divorce ourselves from the responsibility for their actions.'[8]

That responsibility appeared all the heavier in the second week of October, following the breakdown in talks between the French and the Viet Minh on 6 October. The French representatives refused to go beyond their original offer to bring selected Vietnamese into the public administration, and simply stated that questions of sovereignty – the only subject the Viet Minh were really interested in discussing – were outside their competence and would have to be referred to Paris. Continuation of the ceasefire was clearly dependent on progress in the Franco-Vietnamese discussions, and once the latter had stalled because of the local French representatives' inability to move beyond the very limited concessions outlined in the March declaration, it became very doubtful that the truce would be maintained. On 9 October, Brigadier J.E. Hirst (who was effectively in command of 20th Division while Gracey was preoccupied with the affairs of the Control Commission) met the Viet

Minh delegates and demanded their formal acceptance of the truce
and their compliance with its terms – that the requirements of
Gracey's original proclamation be met; that no arms be carried;
that all attacks on allied soldiers should cease; that there should be
no interference in the movement of allied forces; and that normal
trade and public services should be allowed to resume. If the
Vietnamese agreed to abide by these conditions, Hirst guaranteed
that only British forces, rather than French, would be used to
disarm, concentrate and evacuate the Japanese. It was a small but
important concession, and was warmly welcomed by the Viet Minh
representatives, who promised not only every assistance in moving
the Japanese out of Indochina but civic receptions for British troops
on the completion of their task. However, Hirst made it clear that
his guarantee did not preclude the deployment of French forces,
even in the areas where the majority of the Japanese were camped,
although privately Repiton agreed that the use of French troops in
those areas would be provocative. The alternative to the Viet Minh
acceptance of the terms of the truce, Hirst stressed, was military
confrontation:

I have sufficient force at my disposal and I shall make use of all the
weapons which I have – armed cars, guns, mortars, aircraft and so on. I am
determined to carry out the terms of this proclamation, and those people of
whatever nationality who oppose my forces, must take the consequences.
The British forces here are the finest trained troops in the world today –
what chance have your half trained levies against them? You are fools if
you think your troops can oppose them successfully. The only result will be
a lot of needless and useless bloodshed – the outcome of the struggle will
not be in doubt.

It was an uncompromising stand, especially given Hirst's private
admission that the Viet Minh had some justification in claiming
that 'although we say we have no political interest in this country
and are impartial, we are in fact being used to cover the concentration of large French forces'.[9] Mountbatten was gloomy about
the prospects of further talks, not least since any undertakings given
by the Viet Minh had to be set against their demonstrated inability
to control some of their followers, and at talks in Rangoon with
Gracey, Leclerc and Cédile his only attempt to limit Gracey's use of
military force was to insist that prior warning through leaflets and
radio announcements had to be given each time Gracey proposed
action, and to emphasise to Gracey, who clearly expected a

breakdown in the ceasefire, that the British role was a 'preventive' one and that political considerations had to be borne in mind. The French were understandably pleased with the outcome of the meeting,[10] for there had always been the possibility that Mountbatten would insist on a very narrow interpretation of Gracey's task, but at the time the problems of Indochina seemed comparatively straightforward compared with the worsening situation in the NEI, where Christison was confronted by far larger nationalist armed forces, much more scattered Japanese, and the prospect of an indefinite delay before Dutch troops could relieve the British. Further, Christison's relations with his Dutch military counterparts and the Dutch political representatives were icy at best, in contrast to the warm cooperation and harmony that marked Gracey's involvement with the French.

In fact neither Mountbatten nor Leclerc could be totally satisfied with developments in Indochina. Leclerc still felt keenly the absence of French troops, which made him dependent on Gracey's willingness to intervene on his behalf, while Gracey's guarantee that only British troops would carry out the disarming and concentration of Japanese forces was a humiliating reminder of France's record in the war against Japan. Mountbatten could do little other than appprove Gracey's plans to use force if the truce broke down, but as he advised the Chiefs of Staff, the case for accelerating the arrival of the 9th DIC was 'more urgent than ever', not on the basis of the revised date of late December but measured against the original mid-November schedule.[11]

Mountbatten's fears of a deepening British involvement in Indochina were quickly confirmed. Even while Hirst was meeting the Viet Minh representatives, news came of further violations of the ceasefire. At the Rangoon conference Gracey had told Mountbatten that he was 'not prepared to accept indefinite casualties to his soldiers' from sniping in the vicinity of Saigon. The breaking point came on 10 October, when a British Indian Engineering Reconnaissance Party was ambushed outside Saigon. In the ensuing fight one British Officer, one NCO, and two Indian other ranks were killed, and a further seven wounded; many more of the Vietnamese attackers were left dead. Other incidents in the general Saigon area confirmed that the ceasefire had irrevocably broken down, and the following day 32nd Brigade began clearing the residential areas in the northern suburbs of Saigon. For Gracey the attacks of 10 October were irrefutable proof that the Viet Minh were either unwilling or unable to control their followers, and that there was no choice open to the allies but to deploy all the force at their command, as Hirst had threatened only two days before. Gracey was convinced that drastic measures were required to stem the rising tide of violence. As he told Slim, the attacks on the Engineering Party amounted to murder, but the only recourse open to the British was to hand the offenders to French courts which were already overloaded with cases, with the result that punishment was slow to be meted out and therefore had little immediate deterrent effect. In place of that unsatisfactory procedure, he suggested a system of summary justice: it was 'most essential for [the] morale of [our] own troops and of [the] French for me to be able in flagrant cases to authorise subordinate commanders to try these criminals and if necessary bump them off'. Individual cases could be heard by a lieutenant-colonel and two other officers, and if the Brigade commander confirmed the death sentence, it should be carried out 'on the spot'. Alternatively culprits could be tried as war criminals, and Gracey be allowed to impose the death penalty without reference to higher authority. This would have involved a dramatic heightening of the conflict, and hardly surprisingly Gracey was turned down. 'War crimes can only be committed by those engaged [in the] prosecution of war', he was reminded. 'Present situation not war but civil disturbance', and for Mountbatten to impose British Military Administration, which would make Gracey's suggested course possible, would involve a major departure from the British government's policy, which had always been to limit the involvement of British forces to those tasks arising out of the end of the war against Japan.[12]

Within three days, Gracey was able to report that operations to clear the northern and north-eastern suburbs were going smoothly. French troops were of variable quality: the 5th RIC had fought 'well and correctly', but the 11th RIC, released from confinement to barracks after its rampage through the centre of Saigon following the *coup*, had displayed the same weaknesses that had caused it to be removed from an active role a month earlier. It was poorly trained and led, and its troops lacked discipline, but when Gracey raised the matter Leclerc was inclined to shrug it off, clearly feeling that any French troops were worth having to redress the British/French imbalance. Leclerc's indifference did not prevent Gracey from allying himself even more closely with French policy for, as he told Mountbatten, the Viet Minh's new aim was obviously to try to drive a wedge between the British and the French by stressing that the result of British involvement was to provide a cover behind which French control could be reinstalled. Gracey was determined that no split would develop between himself and Leclerc, but rather that their cooperation would become even closer. 'In fact', he advised Mountbatten, 'it has now become inevitable for the proper execution of key tasks that I should act hand in hand with Leclerc policy as to key areas only. By doing so I inevitably provide considerable assistance to political aims of French in this area.' He dismissed the Viet Minh's four-point basis for negotiation – the re-establishment of the Viet Minh government ousted in the September *coup*, the disarming of all French forces and the confinement of French nationals to specific areas, and the cessation of all British military assistance to the French – as nothing more than a 'rehash of all the old demands'. There could be only one conclusion to draw, he told Mountbatten: '[The] Viet Minh will not repetition not consider or discuss any terms other than those stated. In view hopelessness this attitude I do not intend to reply.'[13]

The contrast with Christison could hardly have been more marked. In Java Christison used his military power in parallel with a continuing political initiative, originally set in motion by his own decision to open negotiations with the nationalists despite strenuous objections by the Dutch and disquiet on Mountbatten's part. Even during the worst fighting at Surabaya, Christison never shut off negotiations with the nationalists, and continued to urge the Dutch to adopt a more realistic and generous policy. Gracey, on the other hand, defined his own role extremely narrowly (measured against either of his directives), and took no political initiative of even the most basic kind – such as meeting the Viet Minh representatives on or shortly after his arrival – until ordered by Mountbatten to arrange talks between the French and Viet Minh. Even then, his own remarks to the Viet Minh delegates were always couched in stark military terms: either obey the terms of the proclamation, which entailed a surrender to the hated and despised French of all the gains they had made since the heady days of the August revolution, or 'face the consequences'. Yet despite his determination not to become involved in the internal affairs of Indochina, Gracey eventually admitted that his expanded military role had precisely that effect, namely that British forces were creating a shield behind which the French could progressively reoccupy the country. There is no evidence to suggest that Gracey was ever troubled by the irony of his position, nor that he considered bringing pressure to bear on the French. His action against the 11th RIC following the *coup* had been only temporary, and in any case they were not the only offenders. American sources in October reported intermittent firing at night in various parts of Saigon, most of it attributed to French troops, 'many of whom are frequently drunk on duty'.[14]

Whereas Christison continually pressed the Dutch to expand their 1942 statement on the future of the NEI, there is no indication that Gracey ever questioned the French position that there could be no discussion beyond the terms of the March declaration until order – and French law – had been restored, even though the only means by which that could be achieved, at least within the key area of Saigon-Cholon, was by the extended use of British military power. Again, in the purely military sphere, Christison used his position to control Dutch excesses, as far as possible, to the extent of refusing to allow insufficiently trained Dutch troops to land in Java and confining those already there – those recently released from imprisonment at the hands of the Japanese – to camps outside Batavia. Gracey made several feeble protests to Cédile and Leclerc, but otherwise did nothing in the face of Leclerc's inclination to be more 'lenient'. The strongest criticism of French military conduct came from within French circles: American intelligence sources reported that by early January 1946 social relations between d'Argenlieu and Leclerc had broken down partly as a result of revelations of French troops torturing Vietnamese prisoners. D'Argenlieu had been shocked and had ordered the officers involved to be court-martialled. Leclerc agreed in principle but, according to the American informant, 'finds many excuses for his men to whom he shows a fanatical loyalty which is returned.'[15] Christison combined conciliation with firmness towards both sides; Gracey upheld the French at every turn and used his strength to crush the Viet Minh. Cédile wrote to Leclerc shortly after the *coup* that 'Gracey understands perfectly and backs me up with all his forces', and in mid October the Service des Renseignements in Calcutta spoke of the 'true collaboration' between Gracey and the French.[16] From the moment he arrived in Saigon, Leclerc – convinced that a military solution was necessary – saw in Gracey a staunch ally who could be relied on to back the French cause, as opposed to Mountbatten whom Leclerc increasingly mistrusted even while admiring many of his qualities. By October Gracey seemed incapable of distinguishing between operations that were necessary to fulfil his major role of disarming and removing the Japanese and those that not only directly assisted the French in their political and military struggle with the Vietnamese but had the effect of postponing completion of the very task that had brought him to Indochina in the first place.

Throughout the second half of October French and British drives against the Viet Minh and their supporters intensified. Having urged the early despatch of the 9th DIC, the French sought to delay its arrival if it could not be sent fully equipped, for that, it was claimed, would damage the prestige of French troops in the eyes of the Vietnamese.[17] Any shortcomings in French military capability were made good by the British. Gracey informed Mountbatten on 19 October that he had ordered air action against Dalat, where there was 'very strong evidence' that the Vietnamese intended attacking the Japanese garrison and the French population. This was 'absolutely essential', Gracey claimed, to prevent a 'possible disaster'.[18] Mountbatten made no immediate comment, no doubt because Gracey complied with the general requirement that leaflets be dropped before air strikes were made, but when he eventually saw the text of Gracey's leaflet he protested mildly:

I must say that it would be most indiscreet for a British Commander to put on record that 'tanks, ships, aircraft and guns' are massed against virtually unarmed people, and that 'useless misery' might ensue. Any leaflet, worded in such a way, must be signed by the French Authorities for we must not further embarrass H.M. Government or the French Government by making it appear that we are strongly threatening the Independence Movement.[19]

Threatening the independence movement, of course, was precisely what Gracey was doing, and doing with forces that were almost completely Indian, a fact which Auchinleck continued to stress to Mountbatten had grave political implications, for, he wrote, 'I am quite sure that if we were to use Indian troops on a large scale for this purpose there would be serious trouble in this country'. Auchinleck and Wavell had urged the speedy withdrawal of Indian troops from Indochina and the NEI once SEAC's primary tasks had been completed, and had opposed the transfer of Indian units to those areas when a strengthening of the British presence seemed necessary: political opinion in India, they argued, would resent the use of Indian troops in operations designed to reinstate European colonial rule. By October, when the Indian National Army trials were about to begin, Auchinleck feared that political resentment might spill over and 'affect the stability of the Army itself'.[20] Some relief came in mid-October when eight trooping ships supplied by the United States enabled the Chiefs of Staff to reschedule the movement of the 9th DIC to Indochina without disturbing either the PYTHON programme or the return of Indian divisions from the Mediterranean. Mountbatten's refusal to consider using the mainly black Madagascar Brigade (or alternatively of using a small all-white portion of the Brigade) had forced the Chiefs of Staff to press the United States to make extra shipping available. As a result of the earlier arrival of the 9th DIC, troops of the 20th Indian Division in Indochina could be withdrawn correspondingly earlier.[21]

With the 9th DIC now due to arrive at the end of November, rather than December as had appeared to be the prospect only several weeks before, Mountbatten and Gracey were under greater pressure to prepare for the final concentration, disarming and evacuation of Japanese troops from southern Indochina. Until preliminary moves had been made to begin the process, Mountbatten felt unable to go through with the important ceremony wherein Terauchi would surrender his sword, thus marking the absolute acceptance of Japan's defeat by its forces within the boundaries of SEAC. Terauchi's declining health had delayed the ceremony, originally planned to be held in Singapore in September, but so too had the fact that with British forces having to rely on the Japanese for the maintenance of law and order both in parts of Saigon and in most of southern Indochina, a public and ritual insistence on Britain's supremacy would have appeared somewhat hollow. Mountbatten was convinced that a ceremony was essential to emphasise Japan's defeat and to enable British forces to be withdrawn on the basis that their primary tasks had been completed. Gracey's apparent willingness, amounting almost to gusto, to use airpower against Vietnamese roadblocks and minor fortifications seemed to Mountbatten an unnecessary involvement of British forces in what was soon to become an almost entirely

French campaign to which there was no early end in sight. Mountbatten was particularly sensitive to political and press criticism, and the British, American and Australian press had fixed on air strikes as an example of the use of unwarranted and disproportionate force in both Indochina and the NEI. He was even more horrified when he learned that British troops had been destroying houses in villages and towns. 'Cannot you give such unsavoury jobs (if they really are military necessities) to the French in future', he asked Gracey.[22]

Gracey vigorously defended his actions. The Vietnamese, he told Mountbatten, had demonstrated that they had no intention of trying to differentiate between the roles and operational activities of British and French forces (which he also admitted they would have difficulty in doing), with the result that they were 'actively hostile' to the British. In those circumstances, both to protect his own troops and to carry out his primary tasks, Gracey had no option but to take offensive action against the forces of the Viet Minh. There was a third reason: it was necessary 'to maintain a proper standard of British prestige in the eyes of the French and Chinese, two very susceptible communities, with active uncensored press'.[23] It was an extraordinary statement, for when Gracey drew Slim's attention to the 'unnecessary brutality' with which the French had carried out their operations, he added that the French 'are leaving a pretty good trail of destruction behind them, which will result in such resentment that it will become progressively more difficult for them to implement their new policy, and, I am convinced, will result in guerilla warfare, increased sabotage and arson as soon as we leave the country.'[24] That 'new policy' was simply a restatement of the very limited promises made in the March declaration, and Leclerc had never concealed his belief that at least in the short term a military solution was the only course that could be followed. Massu, in charge of the Combat Command of the 2nd Armoured Division which had preceded the 9th DIC into Indochina, was brutally frank in dismissing resistance to the return of French rule as 'merely a surface phenomenon' which had to be smashed by all available means. 'Indochina', he told a press correspondent, 'forms part of the French Union and any other attitude is unacceptable to France.'[25] French policy in Indochina was characterised by a combination of an unyielding political position and unrestrained use of available military power: far from seeking to moderate the latter (the former he consistently felt was not his concern), Gracey virtually endorsed it and sought to deploy maximum British power to maintain British 'prestige'. It was, to say the least, an odd sense of prestige and a completely blinkered approach.

Gracey then defended his action in dropping leaflets that Mountbatten judged to be poorly worded. They were, he argued, 'dropped from aircraft in order to persuade the vacillating elements of the population why peace could be the only sensible policy to adopt', and far from the Vietnamese being 'virtually unarmed', as Mountbatten described them, they were in fact 'well equipped with rifles, L.M.G.s, medium machine guns (in small quantities), grenades and grenade dischargers'. Mountbatten had suggested that the French rather than the British should have signed the leaflets, but Gracey rejected this on the grounds that at the time the leaflets were dropped, the French had no means of their own to implement their warnings in the event of non-compliance except to rely on British troops. 'Surely such signature would have put H.M.G. in an invidious position', Gracey questioned, 'as we should have laid ourselves open to the charge of openly promising to aid and abet French domination?'[26]

The third major criticism Mountbatten raised was the burning of houses by British troops. Gracey explained that house searches rarely produced any results, and were almost invariably followed by renewed sniping and grenade attacks, whereas burning the houses – 'or, as they really are, basha huts' – 'has inevitably produced a series of resounding detonations giving ample proof of the presence of ammunition'. Since British forces were responsible for the maintenance of law and order within key areas, the French could not be given the responsibility for conducting house searches or for carrying out what Gracey thought was the operationally necessary task of burning down houses to locate arms caches. 'The actual effect of obtaining French assistance would result in the complete destruction of not 20 but 2,000 houses, and probably without warning to the occupants!' he told Mountbatten. 'In the area for which I am responsible I do not honestly feel I can risk such a travisty [sic] of justice: You may doubt the veracity of this statement, but I can assure you that French measures in such cases know no such thing as minimum force.'[27] There is no record of any direct response on Mountbatten's part to this exercise in twisted logic, but a week later instructions were issued to commanders in both the NEI and Indochina that aircraft were to be used 'only as an emergency measure and to the minimum extent', and in December even more strongly worded orders went out forbidding reprisal raids under any circumstances.[28]

The news that the 9th DIC would arrive by the end of November established a clearer time for the transition from British to French control of operations in Indochina and led the French to assert themselves more forcefully than had been the case when their military strength was much less than that of the British. Leclerc pressed Gracey to accelerate the concentration of Japanese troops prior to their disarming and eventual repatriation to Japan, preferably in areas where they could be closely guarded and prevented either from influencing the local population or assisting the anti-French elements by passing over arms, as had been much in evidence in September and October. The stronger the French military presence became, the more Leclerc sought to take over key areas from Gracey, much to the latter's annoyance, for he felt that while the British task of restoring law and order had not been completed, his forces were more than adequate to the task. Leclerc also asked for Spitfires to be equipped for bombing operations, and continued to make transport demands on the British that Gracey described as 'extravagant'.[29]

Leclerc's growing assertiveness was partly the result of his increasing military strength which almost daily made him less reliant on British forces and thereby gave him a freer hand to pursue the military solution that he sought; it was also a response to the fact that he was no longer the sole senior French authority in southern Indochina. With d'Argenlieu's arrival in Saigon at the end of October Leclerc had to contend with another equally powerful voice in the formulation of French policy. Like Leclerc, d'Argenlieu had de Gaulle's support (indeed in October and November, Leclerc was worried that his own delayed move to Saigon had cost him de Gaulle's favour), and seemed equally committed to the maintenance of French control in Indochina. His first act on landing in Saigon was to dismiss all but a handful of the old French administrators, whom he regarded as collaborators, and to replace them with inexperienced Gaullist appointees, which removed the taint of the Vichy regime from public life but did nothing to endear him to the local French population. If in public he showed himself as an uncompromising adherent to de Gaulle's concept of the French colonial mission, and supported Leclerc's attempts to tie the gradual diminution of the British military involvement to the rate of arrival of French troops, in private he indicated some disquiet over Leclerc's single-minded pursuit of a short term military solution, and for his willingness to accept that the Japanese had an indispensable role to play in the maintenance of order he was likened by the French civil population to the head of the wartime Vichy government in Indo-china, Admiral Decoux.[30] Within months their positions were reversed, Leclerc arguing that a military solution was no longer attainable, d'Argenlieu opposing negotiations when French military power in Indochina was at its height; but in late 1945 Leclerc was apprehensive that d'Argenlieu's arrival would undermine his own authority and possibly interfere with his military plans.

Those fears proved unfounded and Leclerc's troops moved through southern Indochina with all the force and speed at their command so that by mid-December the French weekly operational report could note with satisfaction that conditions in Saigon-Cholon were returning to normal, with a resumption of work and commerce, and that once the French had demonstrated their determination to restore order, a large number of Vietnamese who originally had feared reprisals had now rallied to the French cause.[31] Mountbatten accepted Terauchi's formal surrender at a private ceremony in Saigon on 30 November (Terauchi was ill, and had been diagnosed as senile by British doctors) and at a meeting with Gracey, Leclerc and d'Argenlieu the same day confirmed that the withdrawal of the 20th Division would begin in late December and rejected Leclerc's attempt to link the final departure of British forces to the arrival of the 9th DIC together with all its equipment.[32] A week later in Singapore Leclerc again tried to argue that the French forces lacked necessary equipment, especially landing craft, and that until it arrived from Europe the final British departure should be delayed, but neither Mountbatten nor the visiting CIGS, Brooke, were prepared to see Gracey's mission extended beyond January, pointing out that on the withdrawal of the 20th Division, some 1300 trucks would be turned over to the French in addition to the 600 already supplied and the 1900 in India due to be made available for the 3rd DIC.[33]

Gracey had earlier reported on the aggressive conduct of French troops, but had done nothing to try to curb it apart from making a mild protest to Leclerc. By December, as the French prepared to assume control in southern Indochina, he felt obliged to protect his own troops from the excesses of Leclerc's forces. Problems arose in particular from the attitude of the newly-arrived 9th DIC, whose treatment of Gracey's Indian and Gurkha troops led Gracey to protest to Leclerc:

The camaraderie which exists between Officers of the Indian Army and their Gurkha and Indian soldiers must be explained to them. Our men, of whatever colour, are our friends and must not be considered 'black' men. They expect and deserve to be treated in every way as first class soldiers, and their treatment should be, and is, exactly the same as that of white troops.

There is no more fruitful source of friction between Indian Army Officers and their men on the one side, and French troops on the other, than when our Indian and Gurkha troops are regarded and treated as 'black' by French officers and men. I mention this point particularly as cases have occurred in which it is obvious that our Indian Army traditions have not been understood.[34]

Leclerc, who initially had regarded the behaviour of his troops with a certain indulgence, tried to raise the standard of discipline, but there were still many instances of rape and looting (although it must be added that complaints were also made by the Vietnamese against Gurkha troops, who were accused on several occasions of looting business premises).[35] His staff were less sympathetic to Gracey's concern, arguing that while Leclerc was fully aware of the problem, the British had to understand that the new French troops were very young and knew next to nothing about conditions in Indochina; in that sense they were like the first British troops who fought the Japanese when their only previous experience had been in the western desert. As well as lacking knowledge, they also lacked equipment, and the solution would take time, the implication being that if the British had heeded Leclerc's earlier pleas for an acceleration in the movement of equipment, the problem would not have arisen.[36] In fact the problem was far more basic than a question of equipment. British observers noted that many of the troops of the 9th DIC (and subsequently of the 3rd DIC) were recruited from the ranks of Maquis, and were, in the words of one critic, 'entirely unamenable to regular Army routine'. More important, many complained that 'they – themselves representatives of the Maquis of France – came to FIC [French Indochina] to fight the Japanese not the Maquis of the Annamites.'[37]

6 'Citoyen d'honneur': Gracey and Leclerc take the salute at the Hôtel de Ville, Saigon. Between them in a light suit is Jean Cédile.

Fortunately for the British their role was all but over and it remained only to transfer control to the French. On 1 January 1946 Mountbatten and d'Argenlieu announced in a joint statement that the French had taken over responsibility for all military operations in southern Indochina, with the exception of a small area around Cap St. Jacques where Japanese forces were being concentrated prior to their evacuation. January 28 was fixed as the date when the command of all French military forces would pass from Gracey to Leclerc, at which time Gracey would withdraw from Indochina, leaving two battalions to protect a reduced Inter-Service Mission and the Japanese awaiting repatriation. Mountbatten suggested that once the headquarters and the bulk of the 20th Division were withdrawn, southern Indochina (with the temporary exception of Cap St. Jacques) should be removed from SEAC, but the Joint Chiefs in Washington oppposed giving the French co-equal status in the post surrender period in the Pacific, and it was not until 1 March, by which time the British military involvement had been liquidated, that the Americans accepted the reality of the situation and the Combined Chiefs approved the change of boundaries.[38]

On the day he left Saigon, Gracey was honoured at a ceremony at the Hôtel de Ville, where he was presented with a scroll and made a *Citoyen d'Honneur*, the first time in its history under French rule that the city had bestowed the honour. It was a fitting tribute to the man whom the French regarded as responsible for preserving the hope that metropolitan rule might be restored. Almost exactly two months later, on 26 March, the last forces of Gracey's command left Indochina. The 2nd battalion, 8th Punjab Regiment, which had been the first British Indian troops to arrive in Saigon, staged a farewell march past. Leclerc took the salute, and with that final display, the British involvement in southern Indochina had effectively come to an end. Japanese evacuations began in earnest in May, and on 12/13 May, Mountbatten relinquished formal responsibility to act in Indochina as MacArthur's agent. A little over two weeks later, Mountbatten himself left SEAC, secure in the knowledge that at whatever cost, Britain had fulfilled the primary tasks allotted to it under the terms of the post surrender settlement.

Chapter nine
Breakthrough in Java?

By January 1946 it appeared that the situation in Java had become stalemated. Both British and Dutch patience was running out, though for quite different reasons. The British complained that the Dutch political leaders were unwilling to move beyond their very restricted offers to the Indonesians, while their local military commanders were incapable of controlling the 'trigger happy' elements in the Dutch forces whose wild excesses threatened to destroy the very continuation of discussions between the various parties. The Dutch felt aggrieved at the British tendency to bypass local Dutch authorities and to deal directly with the Indonesians on matters affecting the RAPWI programme (thus undermining the Dutch claim to be the sole legitimate civil power), while the apparent reluctance of British commanders to curb outbreaks of extremist violence – usually, though not always, directed against Dutch civilians and Indonesian sympathisers – smacked at the very least of double standards. It is hardly surprising that in these circumstances the clash of personalities was an added, and complicating, factor. Mountbatten's undoubted sympathy for the general aims of the nationalists made him impatient with the stolid Dutch approach, especially given that as the lack of political progress drew British forces deeper and deeper into the situation, the politically – and personally – critical question of added British casualties weighed more heavily in his deliberations. Increasingly, and especially in light of the lack of clear political direction from London, Mountbatten's aim became one of limiting the damage to British interests and to British forces, and to his own reputation. Several key figures fell victim to this end.

The first was Helfrich. Already marked for replacement, Helfrich was summarily removed on Christison's insistence with Mountbatten's approval when a series of violent incidents showed that he was incapable of imposing discipline on his own troops. The suspicion was, of course, that he was unwilling to demand restraint and that he had consistently turned a blind eye to the assaults of his forces on the Indonesian positions and leadership. Christison had long complained about the aggressive patrolling of the Dutch, their propensity for shooting first, and abnormally high ratio of Indonesian deaths to injuries that resulted from Dutch military actions, all of which suggested that the Dutch troops had taken to heart the 'fire-breathing' sentiments for which Helfrich was notorious in allied circles in Batavia. The breaking point came in early January when Dutch native troops burned two kampongs near Batavia, a clear violatioñ of Mountbatten's prohibition of reprisal actions. More important were the two incidents on 2 January in which Dutch troops fired into Sjahrir's house. Mountbatten was furious and demanded of Helfrich the strongest possible repudiation:

I wish to know what steps you propose to take to disavow publicly the irresponsible action of this element of the Dutch forces. If the news of these actions appears in the press, I am reserving the right to cause a statement to be made disavowing their action, if you yourself should fail to do so. In this connection I should like to suggest that you should issue an Order of the Day in your own name to the troops, making it clear that you will not tolerate any form of indiscipline or any disloyalty to your Government's policy.

I require to know from you what steps you have taken to ensure that there shall be NO repeat NO repetition NO repeat NO recurrence of such incidents.[1]

Helfrich's reply to this stinging rebuke was subdued, although he disputed the accuracy of Mountbatten's information and argued to Christison that he could not be held responsible for the behaviour of Dutch forces since they were not under his operational control.[2] His Order of the Day was a strongly-worded but dignified demand that Dutch troops show 'the utmost self-control and discipline, even though the fault should lie with others.'[3]

For Helfrich this was merely another in a long line of humiliations. As he later wrote to Mountbatten when leaving the East Indies for The Netherlands, he had been slighted by Christison in Java from the very beginning: his advice had never been sought, nor had his cooperation in any active sense been canvassed. Instead he had been subjected to 'violent criticism' from Christison, who had added insult to injury by failing to observe normal social courtesies. Christison's attitude, Helfrich complained, was one of 'unusual aloofness': 'I have always been to see him and also his Chief of Staff; he has never come to me. . . . I must observe that the Commander-in-Chief, A.F.N.E.I. has never found it necessary to pay his respects to me and did not even pay a return-call when immediately after my arrival in Java I went to make his acquaintance.'4 Mountbatten's directive to Helfrich provoked a strong protest from the Dutch government, which bitterly criticised its language and tone as 'not the way to treat "an old admiral" who was anyway already under orders to withdraw.'5 Mountbatten, however, was unrepentant, and although he denied that he had been motivated by personal antipathy, he had done little in the previous months to conceal his impatience with the die-hard attitudes of Helfrich and his senior Dutch commanders. Under duress, Helfrich had issued an Order of the Day which Mountbatten described as 'excellent', but Helfrich's private attempts to explain Dutch actions, especially in the incidents involving attacks on Sjahrir's house, were dismissed by Mountbatten as 'an unconvincing apologia.'6 At the end of January Helfrich returned to The Netherlands, together with the Dutch army commander, Van Oyen. Helfrich's post as Commander of Dutch Forces in the East Indies was abolished, and henceforth the senior Dutch commander was General S.H. Spoor, who was thought to be less rigid in his approach than his predecessors had been, with their constant harping on Dutch honour. In the event, Spoor proved a disappointment, but at the time it seemed that the removal of Helfrich and Van Oyen had opened the way to a more realistic, and responsible, Dutch military policy.

British pressure to replace Helfrich was matched by Dutch efforts to have Christison moved. In the absence of any directive that acknowledged the real situation in Java, Christison had on several occasions strayed from the narrow interpretation that Mountbatten had wished him to apply. No matter that by these actions he had forced a reappraisal of the British role, and had opened negotiations with the Indonesians at a time when the official policy was to deal only with those whom the Dutch considered acceptable: by late December he had become a liability in Mountbatten's eyes. Both the Dutch and the Foreign Office complained that he ignored local Dutch authorities in Java, and that he took too much upon himself, while his briefings to the press and his public statements were, by their very bluntness, inimical to the smoothing over of differences between the various parties.[7] His willingness to cut through the preconditions with which both the Dutch and the Indonesians surrounded their negotiating positions horrified and alarmed the Foreign Office, disturbed Mountbatten, and angered the Dutch, but his no-nonsense approach undoubtedly injected a very necessary note of realism into the situation in Java.

This achievement, however, was not without risk to his own position. Browning noted in early January that 'Christie hovers between being on top line for a Peerage and being reduced to the rank of corporal',[8] but action was already in train to secure his removal. Mountbatten told the CIGS that it would be an 'advantage' if Christison could be given another appointment, and Bevin agreed with the Dutch that a change of command in Java was desirable. The difficulty was that Christison could not be moved until a suitably senior position was available, since the impression had to be avoided that his departure from Java implied any criticism of his conduct there in general, and of his role in persuading the Dutch and the Indonesians to resume talks in particular. When Alanbrooke informed Mountbatten that Christison could be given Northern Command in Britain, Mountbatten leapt at the chance, even though he was forced to accept Lt General Sir Montagu Stopford from Burma Command as Christison's successor, a choice Mountbatten had originally opposed. On 25 January, Mountbatten informed Christison that the 'CIGS, with the approval of the King, wants you for GOC-in-C, Northern Command', and added: 'I am afraid that I have no option but to comply.'[9] Christison had indeed 'carried the can' for Mountbatten, as Browning had originally made clear was to be his role, but by early 1946 he was perceived as an obstacle and had to go. The following day, as a matter of urgency to quash rumours that Christison had in effect been sacked, the press was informed of his promotion to Northern Command and his replacement by Stopford. Nevertheless Mountbatten held over the announcement until the new Dutch-Indonesian talks were well under way, lest the news of Christison's departure signal to the Indonesians that the Dutch had successfully pressed a much harder line on the British.[10]

Christison's replacement was ostensibly a military matter – he had served throughout the war in southeast Asia and was long overdue for another appointment – but its political motivation could hardly be concealed. Indeed, Dening was asked for his opinion, and he advised Dempsey that 'politically . . . the advantages . . . would outweigh the disadvantages.'[11] Dening had on a number of occasions been at loggerheads with Christison, complaining to Mountbatten that Christison was prone to barging into sensitive areas which he was neither competent nor authorised to handle, and he was not unhappy to see him go. Barely had Dening spoken approvingly on Christison's 'removal' (Dening's own word) than he was himself involved in a bitter row with Mountbatten over lines of authority. The dispute arose quickly, but its roots went back several years to the establishment of SEAC in 1943. As Supreme Allied Commander in SEAC, Mountbatten had exercised absolute control in his theatre. As long as it was in practice an active war zone, there could be no question but that all communications with London went through him. Once the Japanese had surrendered, however, the situation changed. Political considerations assumed a far greater, even an overriding, importance. The relationship between Mountbatten and Dening, between the Supreme Commander and his Political Adviser, was no longer what it had been during the campaign against Japan. The political situation in southeast Asia was confused, and the British government, at least on the question of the East Indies, was slow to formulate a clear and firm policy to guide Mountbatten's activities. Increasingly, Dening claimed that while he continued to give political advice to Mountbatten, he also had the right to give independent political advice to the Foreign Office rather than, as had been the practice during the war, to tender all advice through Mountbatten.

Matters came to a head in January 1946. As the Dutch and the Indonesians moved closer towards opening new negotiations, Dening asked that he be sent to Batavia on the specific instructions of either the Prime Minister or the Foreign Secretary so he could be sure that his 'advice' on political matters would prevail. The Chiefs of Staff baulked, claiming that such a procedure would imply a 'derogation' of Mountbatten's position as Supreme Commander.[12] Blocked on this avenue, Dening then attacked SEAC's Far Eastern Publicity and Political Warfare Department for being one-sided in its approach, favouring the Indonesians at every opportunity. It had become, he advised the Foreign Office, a 'political menace', and if it could not be placed under the absolute control and supervision of the local Foreign Office representatives – i.e. Dening and Walsh – it should be closed down.[13] Since at Mountbatten's insistence all political matters ultimately rested in his hands, this was a barely concealed attack on the Supreme Commander, which Dening reinforced by demanding that all political directives be cleared by him or Walsh. Mountbatten was furious, and signalled to Bevin that he could no longer keep Dening on his staff after such an act of outright disloyalty.[14] Far from being cowed by these threats, Dening in turn told Bevin that Mountbatten's charges were a 'mixture of fiction and malice.' The difficulties which now confronted the British in Java, Dening claimed, were largely of Mountbatten's own making, lacking as he was in first hand knowledge of the situation and consistently prone to failing to consult his political advisers or to ignoring their advice when it was tendered. 'It is perhaps worth recording', he noted, 'that [with the exception of the Cairo Conference] of all the outside journeys Supreme Commander has taken where political questions have been involved, on not one single occasion did he take me with him, while on many occasions I only learned of the circumstances after the event.' In requesting that he himself be withdrawn from SEAC, Dening proposed that if it was thought necessary to continue with a system of Political Advisers, the appointment should be at a much higher level than he had enjoyed, preferably at ambassadorial rank. 'I am not satisfied', he wrote to Bevin, 'to leave my staff at the tender mercies of the Supreme Commander and his H.Q. which has now attained a standard of inefficiency which makes it a byword. . . . My experience during nearly two and half years convinces me . . . that the Supreme Commander is impressed only by superior rank.'[15]

Bevin could hardly do other than back Mountbatten. Fortunately, as he told Dening, Dening had not repeated his 'unwise' telegram to Mountbatten, for had he done so the incident might have developed into the 'first class row' that Bevin feared and wanted to avoid. Arguing that Dening had placed himself in the wrong by sending unilateral advice on the reorganisation of a branch of SEAC, i.e. the Political Warfare Department, Bevin pressed him to take the 'difficult and distasteful' step of healing the breach with Mountbatten:

. . . we are under fire in regard to our conduct in South East Asia. We are working under the eyes of the United Nations and the World and I look to you and the Supreme Allied Commander to settle this incident and to continue to work together as a team. . . . I am telling Admiral Mountbatten what I have asked you to do and have urged him on his side to do what is necessary to settle this incident amicably. It is your duty in the national interest.[16]

Dening had no choice but to comply. After he had unreservedly apologised for trespassing on Mountbatten's prerogatives, Mountbatten agreed to keep him on his staff until a replacement could be found, but that was the limit of Mountbatten's magnanimity. Dening had performed well in the negotiations over Siam, Mountbatten told Bevin, and he had intended to recommend him for a knighthood in the Victory Honours List. But that was no longer possible, and in the event Dening had to wait several years before he was knighted – and then on the recommendation of others.[17]

The fourth significant change in personnel coincided with Dening's demise. It may have sharpened his sense of being excluded from the inner circle of policy advisers to Mountbatten, who more and more appeared to lean towards military solutions that had the effect, intentional or otherwise, of undermining the long-term position of the Dutch. The military commanders in SEAC could barely disguise their impatience with and increasingly their contempt for the Dutch, and though they criticised the 'unreliability' of the nationalist leaders, it was to the Indonesians that they looked for a short term settlement that would enable them to withdraw British forces. In Java Christison developed increasingly close ties with the nationalists, while bypassing Helfrich and restricting the entry of Dutch troops. At SEAC headquarters Browning spoke for many when he talked in terms of the 'continued stupidity' of the Dutch.[18] 'It is amazing', he later wrote to Mountbatten, 'how true to form the Dutch have remained during the last 130 years, i.e. dense, stupid, obstinate and not overtrustworthy.'[19] He continued:

As you know, my view has always been that the Dutch are a defeated nation, that in this world it is a matter of the survival of the fittest, and that as they lost their colonies and did nothing, unlike us, to get them back, the sooner we are absolved of any activities on their behalf the better.[20]

It was hardly surprising in the face of such sentiments that Dening felt that his efforts to promote a balanced settlement had little support within SEAC, and that as a result he felt he had to compensate for the pro-Indonesian bias by swinging violently the other way in what Christison thought was 'an attempt to balance the scales again'.[21] In allied headquarters in Batavia, Christison reported, there was a general belief that Dening's attitude sprang partly from his jealousy of Browning's knighthood, and Mountbatten thought that Dening had always been ill at ease in the military dominated SEAC.[22]

Dening's feelings could not have been improved by Bevin's decision in mid January to appoint a top-level diplomat to chair the proposed meetings between the Dutch and the Indonesians. Even though Dening himself suggested that a political adviser had to be of sufficiently senior rank to impress Mountbatten, the announcement that the former ambassador to Moscow, Sir Archibald Clark Kerr, would fly to Batavia to take charge of the talks would have done little to convince him of London's support for his own efforts, notwithstanding Bevin's assurances that Clark Kerr's appointment was no reflection on the way Dening had handled negotiations up to that point.[23] Attlee wrote personally to Mountbatten, impressing on him the urgency which the government attached to a settlement, especially because of the implications that the continued employment of Indian troops would have on the political situation in India, where the Congress Party had foreshadowed a much stronger campaign against the involvement of Indian forces in the NEI. Clark Kerr's advice on political questions, Attlee told Mountbatten, was to be followed by the Force Commander in the NEI unless there were overriding military grounds for referring the matter to Mountbatten.[24] Dening had requested similar powers but had been refused, and the fact that they had been granted to Clark Kerr was a clear indication of London's determination to bring about a political solution if at all possible.

Barely had Clark Kerr arrived in Batavia on 1 February than the British government appointed yet another political adviser. From the British Embassy in Cairo, Lord Killearn (formerly Sir Miles Lampson) was made Special Commissioner for South East Asia. His first reaction was to refuse, suspecting an intrigue inspired by the Egyptian palace to have him removed before negotiations over Egypt's future began, but on hearing from the Foreign Office that it was either southeast Asia or retirement, he chose to accept the appointment.[25] Bevin had been considering such a position for several months, and both the fact and circumstances of Dening's departure crystallised his intention. Originally it was planned that Killearn should have overall responsibility for political questions in the whole of southeast Asia, but within days of his appointment, Bevin was forced to narrow his immediate task. The food situation throughout the world was serious, and in south and southeast Asia it was critical. 'Not a moment must be lost', he impressed on Killearn, 'if we are to prevent a major catastrophe. . . . [It] is essential that you should proceed with the utmost speed.'[26] Killearn arrived in Singapore on 16 March and within ten days had convened a Food Conference which pointed up the difficulties in coordinating supplies and distribution. Siam was not delivering rice on the required scale, and on Java significant rice-growing areas were controlled by the nationalists, who thereby had another bargaining tool to use in the prolonged negotiations with the Dutch. Access to food therefore became an additional and complicating factor, affecting not only the broader question of British control in India, Ceylon and Burma, where shortages were the most severe, but also the role of British forces in the NEI.

In late December Mountbatten had launched military operations designed to clear the main centres in western Java of 'terrorists' (the term Mountbatten preferred to 'extremists', which he thought implied the existence of an organised political party).[27] Those operations had in the main been successful, though not without cost. Mountbatten's use of Indian troops had given rise, yet again, to protests from politicians in India and from the Indian government itself. This created special difficulties for the British government, which was unwilling to be seen as overriding the objections of the Indian government, but the demands of the military situation in Java left it no choice but to insist that the employment of Indian forces in Java was an allied responsibility, the fulfilment of which by India would confirm its 'rightful status' in international affairs.[28] It was a feeble argument, and the Indian dimension to the problem added to London's anxiety to find a way out of the whole Indonesian situation. The British garrison in Batavia was reinforced by the 5th Parachute Brigade, whose exemplary conduct in systematically clearing the kampongs around Batavia was spectacularly offset by their drunken rampages through the city over the Christmas period which terrorised the local population, resulted in widespread looting and destruction, and caused one victim, a restaurant owner whose premises had twice been attacked, to compare the Red Berets unfavourably with the Japanese: 'at least they had more discipline'.[29] Isolated though these incidents may have been, they undermined British criticisms of Dutch troops, a double standard that Helfrich was not slow to point out to Mountbatten.[30]

When the operations around Batavia had been completed the 5th Parachute Brigade was redeployed to Semarang in central Java, where in the previous months attacks by nationalist forces had reduced the area controlled by the allies to the town itself and its immediate surroundings. It was essential to expand that sphere of control, because Semarang was an important embarkation point for large numbers of APWI in the interior, whose rescue was one of Mountbatten's main priorities. Equally important was the fact that as long as they remained in territory controlled by potentially hostile forces they provided a means by which both the Dutch and the nationalists could exert pressure on the British. In the course of the operations around Semarang, a situation developed which the Brigade itself later described as 'gilbertian', and which illustrated the complexity of the British involvement in Java, a complexity which seemed to grow as the British commitment deepened.

Following the Japanese surrender in Java, the Kido Butai battalion around Semarang had handed its weapons over to the nationalists who in turn put a large number of the Japanese in goal. Not content with this move, however, extremists subsequently murdered many of the Japanese, which sparked off a prolonged attempt by the rest of the battalion to recover their weapons, in which they were ultimately successful even though they had only their bare hands and stones to use against the extremists. The rearmed Japanese then proceeded to re-establish control over the whole of the town, an operation that began on the very day that the 5th Parachute Brigade landed at the docks at Semarang. Working from opposite ends of the town, the Japanese and British troops converged, completely ignorant of the existence of the other until they met, fought briefly, and then realised that they were in fact clearing out a common enemy. They joined forces and for the rest of January and February the Japanese operated under British command, both as fighting troops and in protecting convoys of APWI moving to Semarang for repatriation. 'There is no doubt', the Brigade reported, 'that it would not have been possible to operate without these Japanese forces .... [who] did sterling work'.[31] Mountbatten's first task under the terms of the directive of the Chiefs of Staff was to round up and disarm the Japanese but by early 1946 they had become indispensable to British attempts to impose control. The potential for embarrassment was obvious, and at the beginning of February orders were issued forbidding the use of Japanese war materiel for operational purposes lest 'serious political repercussions' follow on the grounds that Britain had not properly discharged its duty in disarming the Japanese.[32] Such were the confused circumstances in Java.

Mountbatten had consistently argued that as long as British and Indian troops bore the brunt of the military tasks in the NEI, he was entitled to make whatever arrangements he thought necessary to complete the tasks allotted to him, notwithstanding the provisions of the Civil Affairs agreement which required him to act on the political advice of the Dutch in the person of Van Mook. Thus in December he approved Christison's enlistment of the cooperation of the TRI (successor to the TKR) in the evacuation of APWI from the interior of Java on the grounds that peaceful means of rescuing those casualties of the war against Japan were preferable to a military confrontation with the nationalists that would prolong the suffering of the internees and prisoners and almost certainly result in further deaths among their number. The Dutch, however, regarded this working agreement as tantamount to recognition of the Republic, and demanded that all contact with the TRI cease. Mountbatten rejected this, insisting that since the rescue of APWI was among the tasks laid down by the Chiefs of Staff the military problems associated with it had to take first priority.[33] The Dutch were doubly offended because while Christison was seeking the cooperation of Indonesian military forces he refused to allow Dutch troops to be landed in Java. Even when he relented in early January to the extent of replacing Dutch Ambonese troops in Batavia with some 800 Dutch European troops who had been trained in Malaya, he had restricted them to police duties, and had sent back to Singapore the other 1600 troops who had arrived at the same time. The Dutch protested bitterly and pressed for a more active military approach that would involve Dutch as well as British and Indian forces, arguing that the compromising British policy had only stiffened the Indonesians' resolve not to negotiate.[34]

That was not Mountbatten's view. By the middle of January he was pressing Van Mook to return to the NEI. Conditions for a negotiated settlement, he argued, were 'as good as they are going to be'. Only Van Mook had the authority to speak on the Dutch side: in his absence Helfrich was the senior Dutch representative, while Van Mook's political subordinates complained that he had neither left them instructions nor kept them informed of any developments at The Hague.[35] After visiting Batavia and conferring with Christison Dempsey reinforced Mountbatten's assessment: 'I am more than ever convinced', he wrote, 'that the situation is now ripe for the opening of negotiations [and] . . . that there is little more that we can do to improve it.'[36] In London, Bevin was similarly convinced that there was no time to be lost, and bemoaned the fact that the Dutch government seemed to be delaying Van Mook's return in a deliberate attempt to postpone the reopening of talks.[37] Dening, however, disagreed, and urged that Christison not make any move to bring the parties together – at least not until he, Dening, was there to guide Christison. In this cautious approach he was supported by the Foreign Office,[38] but his request to be granted the power to direct Christison on political matters was denied, and he was soon embroiled in a bitter confrontation with Mountbatten over his right to give independent, not to say binding, political advice.

When Clark Kerr arrived in Batavia at the beginning of February, he came with the knowledge that the British government regarded the general Dutch position as set out in the Queen's 1942 speech, Van Mook's statement in November 1945 and the Chequers communiqué, as 'very liberal . . . and . . . a fair and reasonable basis of settlement'. He was confident that an agreement could be reached within weeks, especially since the military situation was under control, with the worst excesses of both the Dutch and the Indonesians apparently curbed. If the Indonesians failed to respond to the constructive Dutch approach, he advised the Foreign Office, 'I shall despair of their wisdom.'[39] That optimism failed to take account of the divisions within the nationalist movement, divisions which simplistic categories of 'moderates' and 'extremists' barely recognised. Since early January, when the Republican capital was shifted from Batavia to Jogjakarta in central Java, those divisions had deepened. In Batavia Sjahrir and his cabinet moved in an environment that was more or less controlled by the allies. Daily they were forced to confront the reality of British and Dutch power (such as it was) which could set the terms on which negotiations could proceed. But in Jogjakarta there was no allied military presence. There independence seemed a reality. Displaced from the cabinet in the November revolution, Sukarno found in central Java a natural and receptive audience that had little interest in the details of discussions in Batavia. Increasingly the careful negotiations of Sjahrir appeared as little more than the diplomacy of accommodattion, a pale substitute for the oratory of resistance that emanated from Jogjakarta.

When discussions reopened between the Dutch and the Indonesians in early February, Sjahrir's position was much weaker than it had been even a month before. From Mountbatten's and Clark Kerr's point of view, the time was ripe for negotiations; for Sjahrir it could hardly have been worse. The Dutch proposals that were finally unveiled on 10 February were, despite Clark Kerr's endorsement, limited and unimaginative in nationalist eyes. The Dutch plan to create a 'Commonwealth of Indonesia', with varying degrees of self-rule for the constituent parts, avoided the fundamental question of independence and, consistent with the Dutch line, made no mention of the Republic.[40] Sjahrir's office was swamped with letters and telegrams from all over Java and the Outer Islands, urging on him an outright rejection and a commitment to complete independence as the basis for future negotiations. He was in a difficult position. Clearly he could not ignore these overwhelming expressions of nationalist opposition, yet he had to accept, as Clark Kerr told him when explaining the nature of his directive from Bevin, that Britain supported Dutch sovereignty and would not recognise the Republic. Van Mook was equally adamant: although in his subsequent elucidation of the February proposals he went further than the Dutch government had agreed, he nevertheless accused Sjahrir of living in a 'dream world of independence'.[41]

Within days the discussions had bogged down. Sjahrir had little room to manoeuvre, since his own position was increasingly under threat from the more radical groups in Jogjakarta, who urged a break with the legalistic Dutch policy of gradualism. Under pressure to broaden the composition of his cabinet and to create a genuinely representative national government, Sjahrir sent a secret letter of resignation to Sukarno on 23 February. By the time the letter was made public on 28 February, the government had already fallen. Internal rivalries and fundamental disagreements over the policy to be adopted prevented a new cabinet from being announced until 12 March, by which time any sense of momentum in the Dutch-Indonesian talks had completely dissipated. Even before Sjahrir left Batavia for Jogjakarta on 25 February to confront his critics, Clark Kerr confessed that 'I begin to bite my thumbs a little when I remember that three weeks have passed and little or nothing has been achieved.' But his stricture to Sjahrir – 'I made it clear to Dr. Sjahrir that I could not go on indefinitely watching the political antics of his people at Jogjakarta' – showed how little he understood the complexities of nationalist politics.[42] Van Mook, on the other hand, seemed to Clark Kerr insufficiently aware of the need to respond to Sjahrir's dilemma with something more than the familiar and by now well-rehearsed arguments. The bottom line for Van Mook, Clark Kerr suspected, was 'the thought that in the last resort he will be able sooner or later to shoot his way to peace.'[43]

That possibility became distinctly stronger at the beginning of March. Dutch pressures for the landing of Dutch European troops in Java were irresistible, and by late February the only question to be settled was that of timing. Browning recommended that if Sjahrir could win the political support of Sukarno and the radical groups in Jogjakarta, the landing of Dutch forces should be delayed until about 9 March in the hope that this might enable talks to reopen in a relatively unthreatening atmosphere. Van Mook, however, insisted, and Browning agreed, that if Sjahrir failed to gain the necessary backing landings would have to begin on 4 March lest the displacement of the moderates lead to turmoil that would in turn require 'immediate military steps'.[44] Pyman feared that faced with a political collapse of the Indonesians, which was his interpretation of the conflicting reports of the difficulties in which Sjahrir was embroiled, the Dutch might take advantage of the situation to impose a military settlement and to be 'needlessly brutal' with the Indonesians.[45] Evidence that he was right was suggested by several incidents that occurred soon after Dutch forces began landing on 8 March. Clark Kerr complained that despite Helfrich's departure, his 'whiff of grapeshot' policy had stuck, and that 'many allegations [of Dutch 'atrocities'] have been proved substantially correct', but Sterndale Bennett, with Orme Sargent's approval, replied that 'now is a very bad time to bring this up with the Dutch'.[46]

Sjahrir's new cabinet, which was announced on 12 March, in no way fulfilled Sukarno's prescription for a truly national coalition. It was still heavily dominated by western-educated members of the professional class, and the key positions of Foreign Affairs and Defence were held respectively by Sjahrir and his close political associate, Amir Sjarifuddin, with Sjahrir continuing as Prime Minister. This was hardly a stark rupture with the moderate stance that Sjahrir had demonstrated in earlier discussions with the Dutch, but Van Mook insisted that since a complete breakdown in the talks was likely, he was entitled to know how far he could rely on British military support in the event of a showdown with the Indonesians.[47] In particular he wanted to know whether British forces would continue their operations to clear west Java, and, if negotiations collapsed, whether the British would persist militarily until Dutch control had been restored completely. Mountbatten accepted that Britain's obligation to evacuate all Japanese surrendered personnel and to maintain and supply Dutch forces was unquestioned, but he asked the Chiefs of Staff for a 'clear statement of policy immediately' on the British commitment to operations in west Java.[48]

Mountbatten's request pointed again to the ill-defined nature of Britain's involvement in the NEI. The Chiefs of Staff were anxious to minimise British responsibilities, arguing, for example, that though Britain had undertaken to release APWI from Japanese captivity, it had never made any promises about those APWI who had subsequently fallen into Indonesian hands. Even if a moral responsibility for their fate was acknowledged, their rescue 'might well involve reconquering the whole island and this we have no intention of doing however long we retain responsibility.' Similarly, the Chiefs of Staff insisted that Britain's responsibility for the evacuation of surrendered Japanese extended only to those already under British control or who could be brought under British control without involving any extension of British zones of operation: any others were properly the responsibility of the Dutch. This was a much narrower interpretation than Mountbatten had accepted, but the Chiefs of Staff feared that any prolongation of the British role in Java, for whatever ostensible purpose, would convince the Dutch that they could rely on British arms, and that as a result 'their interest in obtaining a settlement may tend to diminish.' They therefore recommended that while Britain should continue to carry out operations against terrorists in the limited areas that it sought to control, it should commit itself to a firm policy of withdrawal as soon as the Dutch were strong enough to assume British responsibilities and refuse to be drawn into any further involvement.[49]

Not for the first time, the Foreign Office demurred. Wilson Young wrote that 'the situation is far from clear even to the War Office and ourselves',[59] but Sterndale Bennett was more blunt. 'There is something rather odd', he suggested, 'about fixing a programme for the withdrawal of troops and then asking for guidance as to policy. One would expect that policy would be decided first and a withdrawal fixed in the light of it.' Instead, the Chiefs of Staff had let their anxiety to get British troops out of Java dictate the broader lines of British policy, and their recommendations, if implemented, might thereby contribute to the breakdown of negotiations, thus bringing on the very situation they wished to avoid. If British troops were precipitately withdrawn, or if Britain made it clear by its actions that its commitment was a strictly limited one, even on such fundamental questions as the evacuation of surrendered Japanese and the rescue of APWI, the Indonesians might become even more intransigent in their demands and extremists might seek to sabotage the talks.[51] Orme Sargent agreed, and added that since the Dutch were already suspicious of British intentions, the whole question would have to be referred to the Defence Committee and subsequently communicated to the Dutch personally in another top-level meeting.[52]

The Chiefs of Staff tried to dampen speculation that the British had firm plans for withdrawal by directing Mountbatten and Auchinleck to instruct their commanders to avoid making public statements, but Bevin was still worried that the Dutch might get the impression that even if negotiations broke down through no fault of theirs, the British would nevertheless 'contemplate leaving them in the lurch and abandoning . . . [their] military responsibilities'.[53] He was anxious, he told the Defence Committee, not to lock Britain into a timetable that allowed no flexibility, and he shared the Dutch fear that the progressive withdrawal of British forces might prompt the Indonesians to drag out negotiations in the belief that time was on their side. Attlee, however, pointed out that it had always been

Britain's intention, even if negotiations failed, to withdraw from Java, leaving the Dutch a foothold from which they could undertake a reconquest of the island. That foothold had already been established, and it would not be possible for Britain to continue to hold the key areas indefinitely while the Dutch marshalled their forces: Indian opinion alone, and the political problems associated with the continued use of Indian troops in Java, made such a policy untenable. As for the suggestion that a British withdrawal might encourage the nationalists to play for time, Attlee was inclined to think that it was the other way round. The Dutch, he said, 'seemed to be conducting negotiations in a very leisurely manner', and he reminded the Committee that it had already been agreed that the Dutch should be warned not to go on relying on the support of British military power.[54]

These discussions in Britain were based on the assumption that negotiations were likely as not to fail. But the talks were continuing, and though there were some outbreaks of violence in central Java, there were some reasons for guarded optimism. When, for example, British troops decided to clear the southern part of Bandung of armed nationalists, who had been launching mortar attacks on APWI camps in the northern half of the town, Sjahrir undertook to organise a withdrawal of Indonesian forces to avoid a potentially bloody confrontation. He and the TRI, in Browning's words, 'kept faith' to the extent that the two British brigades had to fire only six shots between them.[55] These hopeful signs in the military sphere were matched by encouraging developments in the talks, where the sticking point had been the nationalist demand for recognition of the Republic, on which Van Mook, in accordance with the policy of the Dutch government, was adamant. The impasse was broken when, on 25 March, Van Mook produced a draft treaty that had been inspired by the Franco-Vietnamese agreement. The key was Van Mook's proposal that the Republic be granted *de facto* recognition in Java, excluding areas that lay within the allied secure zones, and that it cooperate with the Dutch to establish a Federal Indonesian Free State. Together with Van Mook's statement that Dutch troops landing in Java had not come with any 'aggressive intent', the draft, which Van Mook had deliberately couched in conservative terms to allow him subsequent room for manoeuvre, could not fail to signal to Sjahrir that the way was open for constructive negotiations.[56] Sjahrir's counter-proposals had much in common with Van Mook's draft, and even his insistence on naming Sukarno as President in the document was not seen by Van Mook as an insuperable obstacle to winning the acceptance of the Dutch government. Clark Kerr reported on Van Mook's 'buoyant' mood, but admitted that it was only a beginning.[57] Nevertheless, together with a delegation from the Republic, Van Mook prepared to return to The Netherlands and Clark Kerr flew back to London to brief the cabinet.[58]

The discussions between Van Mook and the Dutch cabinet showed that Clark Kerr's caution was well founded. In his talks with Sjahrir, Van Mook had accepted the nationalist demand to include Sumatra in the Republic, but he reneged on this undertaking once back in The Netherlands, apparently fearing that if he persisted in it, any chance that the agreement might be acceptable to the Dutch as a whole would be lost.[59] Thus a fundamental point in the Indonesian programme was unilaterally jettisoned, making the Dutch claim that the changes they were proposing were 'purely a matter of form and not of substance' wildly misleading. Yet that was exactly the claim the Dutch Prime Minister made in London, when a Dutch cabinet delegation met Attlee, Bevin, the CIGS (Alanbrooke), Sargent and Clark Kerr (now Lord Inverchapel). Constitutional and political objections – a general election was to be held in The Netherlands in May – made it impossible for the Dutch government to sign a treaty with the Republic, but it was prepared, simultaneously with the Republic, to issue unilateral declarations to the effect that the Dutch government would submit to parliament a new constitution based on the proposals that had been worked out with the Indonesians. Nothing was said about Sumatra, on which the Dutch and Indonesian positions were now completely at odds. The British had no reason to suspect that such a major point had been rejected by the Dutch, and were more concerned to ensure that the Dutch propensity for legalistic interpretation would not throw up some last minute obstacle. When Attlee asked whether the form of the agreements would find favour with the Indonesians, the Dutch Prime Minister replied that the Dutch government 'did accept the word "republic".' Since this had always been the point which the Dutch had hitherto refused to concede, their new willingness to grant *de facto* recognition to the Republic was seen as a clear sign that negotiations could proceed with reasonable expectations of success.

Reassured on the political front, the British gave way on military matters. Previously Attlee had opposed any suggestion that the commitment of British forces might be prolonged beyond the fulfilment of a strictly limited interpretation of their tasks, but when Alanbrooke and Bevin promised that some 19,000 troops would be kept in Java until the end of the year, when Dutch replacements would become available, he raised no objection. Bevin went even further, undertaking to maintain the British zones in west Java as a 'firm base from which Dutch troops could operate' and stressing that British control of those areas 'would free many Dutch troops for further operations against the extremists.' The Dutch could hardly have asked for anything more. Far from adopting a conciliatory stance towards negotiations with the Indonesians, they had, unbeknown to the British, virtually scuppered any talks before they had begun. In return for what by then was a meaningless gesture, they had obtained an extended military commitment from Britain. It was a cheap but very important victory.[60]

Two days later Dutch-Indonesian talks opened at the Hoge Veluwe, a holiday resort east of Amsterdam. Armed with assurances of British military support and mindful of the approaching election, the Dutch took a hard line. Schermerhorn, the prime minister, rejected the suggestion that a treaty be signed between the Dutch government and the Republic, preferring instead an exchange of protocols, which – Dutch concerns for constitutional and legal niceties notwithstanding – the Indonesians properly interpreted as a much lower level of political recognition than they sought. When Van Mook was tackled on this change of policy, he replied that his proposals in Batavia had been made only to break the deadlock and that they should not have been taken as a draft that had been endorsed by the Dutch government. This uncompromising attitude was followed by an equally blunt pronouncement on the future of Sumatra: despite the claims of the nationalists, it would not form part of any Republic of Indonesia. The Dutch stand on these two fundamental issues killed the talks. They dragged on until 24 April, when the disillusioned Republican delegation left for Java.[61]

The failure of the Hoge Veluwe conference, and the success (from the Dutch point of view) of the London talks that preceded it, left the way open for a much more aggressive Dutch policy in the NEI. Even before the negotiations had proved fruitless, there was evidence that General Spoor's reported comment to the effect that the Dutch intended to seek a military solution was no idle threat. On 17 April, Dutch troops attacked Pesing, a kampong several miles outside Batavia. A preliminary mortar bombardment was followed by an infantry assault, which resulted in some thirty Indonesians being killed. Aware that the British commander in Batavia had specifically forbidden any offensive action against the Indonesians without prior approval, the Dutch commander attempted to conceal the fact that fighting had occurred and in his original report had stated that in the course of a normal patrol Pesing had been entered by Dutch troops and found to be unoc-cupied.[62] The British Consul-General at Batavia, MacKereth (who had succeeded Walsh in February) held Spoor directly responsible – 'it is difficult to believe that he could not have prevented recent excesses' – and warned of the emergence into the foreground of the 'reactionary elements' in Dutch official circles[63] Ten days later, the Dutch asked for British military support in an operation ostensibly designed to take control of the rice-growing area around Batavia, but it was refused on political grounds. By now aware of the Dutch role in undermining negotiations with the Indonesians, Bevin insisted that the Dutch be told in unmistakeable terms that they could expect no military assistance from the British, while Mountbatten advised rejection of the Dutch request on the grounds that the proposed operation would take place around Bekasi, which would be 'provocative' in view of the British reprisals there the previous November. In any case, Mountbatten warned, the ability of the Dutch troops to carry out the operation without calling on British land and air support was 'so doubtful as to be tantamount to certain embroilment of our forces.'[64] Another incident in early May seemed to confirm British fears that the proponents of a military solution were in the ascendant. The Dutch reported that one of their patrols had been ambushed in a kampong twelve miles west of Surabaya, and that hand-to-hand fighting had broken out. According to the Dutch, the Indonesians had been armed only with swords and grenades, yet Indonesian casualties had amounted to 60 killed and 40 wounded, for the loss of only two Dutch soldiers and three wounded. Browning noted that this disproportionate ratio clearly indicated that 'the Dutch must have gone on shooting much longer than was necessary, without apparently making any attempt to take prisoners.'[65] Attlee reacted angrily, telling the Chiefs of

Staff that a 'strong line must be taken with the Dutch. Their conduct is intolerable.'[66]

Other developments lent weight to Killearn's suggestion that the Dutch were intent on prolonging British involvement in the NEI. In late April, the Dutch asked for permission to retain in Java, Dutch New Guinea and Bali some 22,500 surrendered Japanese, whom they intended to use on the docks and in food growing projects. For several months Mountbatten had urged Van Mook to establish labour units using either European or Indonesian personnel, but little had been done. The suspicion was that Europeans were considered too valuable for military purposes to be diverted into support categories, while Dutch attitudes made any attempts to recruit local labour virtually doomed to failure. Since the first task Mountbatten had been given was to disarm and repatriate all surrendered Japanese from the territories of SEAC, compliance with the Dutch request would have postponed the day on which he could claim that he had fulfilled the first part of his directive, and would therefore have delayed the withdrawal of British forces. As long as those troops remained in Java and Sumatra, they performed duties that would otherwise have fallen to the Dutch, who were thereby enabled to concentrate more directly on confronting the military forces of the Republic. Secondly, Dutch claims that their military buildup in the NEI would be much slower than Mountbatten had predicted reinforced the belief that they were intent on persuading or pressuring the British to stay in force, even above the division that had been promised at the April talks in London.

The British commitment had been made in the belief that a political settlement was imminent. Once the collapse of the Hoge Veluwe talks showed than an early agreement was unlikely, the internal contradictions in the British position became stronger. Britain's promise to retain a division in Java until late 1946 conflicted with its anxiety to liquidate its involvement in the NEI as quickly as possible, especially once its main responsibilities – the evacuation of Japanese and the repatriation of APWI – had been fulfilled. The hardening of the local Dutch attitude, which manifested itself in an increasingly aggressive military policy, made it all the more necessary for the British position to be clarified. What were Britain's priorities? How far should it be dragged into supporting the Dutch? Certainly Killearn, who had succeeded Clark Kerr as Mountbatten's political adviser, did not know. 'I don't think any of us here rightly know what . . . [British policy] is', he wrote in his diary, 'and I gravely doubt whether H.M.G. do either.'[67] He told Mountbatten and his senior staff in Singapore that while he 'was definitely in some doubt as to what our aims . . . were', he felt that Britain should 'get out of . . . [its] extremely embarrassing commitment in Java just as soon as . . . [it] decently could.'[68] This was a theme to which Killearn returned in early May, when the full extent of the political deadlock between the Dutch and Indonesians was apparent. The 'best and really only right line', he decided, 'is to get out of that embarrassing commitment just as soon as we decently can.'[69] The sticking point was the British undertaking to maintain a division in Java until the end of 1946, which would enable the Dutch to mount operations outside the British-controlled secure zones. Mountbatten was openly critical of the results of the April meeting in London, and told his staff that on reading its minutes he had been 'disturbed' to find that the British government had 'promised more than was wise'. In particular he regarded Bevin's suggestion that the retention of a British division would give the Dutch a much freer hand in Java as 'ill advised'.[70]

Like Killearn, Mountbatten was determined to wind up British involvement in the NEI as quickly as possible. In light of the conflicting aims of British policy, he was convinced that the only way to achieve the primary goal of withdrawal was to present the British government with a series of options on the main issues, and to emphasise that far from delaying an overall political settlement, the withdrawal of British forces would pressure both sides to arrive at a satisfactory agreement.[71] As he had done on several previous occasions when trying to force a definition of policy out of London, Mountbatten cast the alternatives in such a light that his preferred option was bound to be accepted. Following a visit to Sumatra, he suggested to the Chiefs of Staff that it was now possible to set a date for the total withdrawal of British troops. Compared with Java, little attention had been paid to the situation in Sumatra, where the British commander, Dempsey, had thought that the anticipated Dutch-Indonesian settlement would provide the framework within which British forces could complete their primary tasks. Once that hope proved groundless, Mountbatten felt both obliged and free to make a firm proposal to which London would have to respond.

Under his recommended plan, all Japanese on Sumatra would be removed by the end of June, and the 19,000 APWI would be evacuated by the end of August. On a restricted interpretation of his directive, Mountbatten would be able to claim that he had fulfilled his responsibilities and British forces could be withdrawn entirely. That was Mountbatten's preference, and in it he was strongly backed by Killearn. There were, however, wider political considerations. It was doubtful whether Sjahrir's writ ran to effective control in Sumatra, and there was the possibility that if the British garrison was precipitately withdrawn, anarchy would prevail, and Britain might well come in for severe criticism. If the British government was unwilling to face that eventuality, it would have to retain troops in Sumatra in sufficient strength to prevent a total breakdown of law and order. The existing garrisons in Medang and Palembang would have to be reinforced by a total of five British and Indian battalions from Padang, where the prevailing stability made the removal of British forces acceptable, and from the 5th Parachute Brigade in Java. If political pressures from India ruled out the continuing deployment of Indian battalions in Sumatra, those units of the 2nd British Division in Malaya, on standby call for India should the civil power require assistance to quell popular unrest, could be sent in their place. In this way, the British involvement, while extended beyond levels which Mountbatten and Killearn thought desirable, could still be relatively contained. Other plans canvassed the possibility of guarding either or both of the Anglo-Dutch and American oil refineries at Palembang, as well as the coal fields at Padang, but the additional military resources that Mountbatten said would be needed for those extensions of British responsibility – up to two extra brigades from outside SEAC plus the retention of some 20,000 armed Japanese – ruled them out from the start.[72]

Clearly Mountbatten intended to leave the Chiefs of Staff no option but to agree to his preferred plan for an early and total British withdrawal from Sumatra. Bevin had already concluded that Dutch proposals to carry out extensive military operations in Java and their requests to retain large numbers of surrendered Japanese showed that they were not inclined to make the compromises necessary to reach a political settlement, but his growing disillusionment had not yet brought him to consider reneging on the April undertaking to keep a British division in Java.[73] If carried out, Mountbatten's recommendations on Sumatra would have brought into question the British commitment to Java, thereby relinquishing any hope that by its presence Britain might have been able to moderate the extremes in Dutch policy and avert an outright Dutch-Indonesian military confrontation which inevitably, it was thought, would involve British forces if they were still engaged in their primary roles of evacuating Japanese and rescuing APWI. Mountbatten's preferred option was therefore rejected in favour of a continuing British garrison role in Sumatra, even though the Chiefs of Staff had urged acceptance of the early withdrawal plan as the 'only sound military course'.[74] Notwithstanding Killearn's endorsement of Mountbatten's recommendation,[75] the political perspectives of the Foreign Office prevailed, while Bevin's suspicions of the Dutch were effectively muted by his absence in Paris. From the beginning of his mission, Killearn had urged a swift withdrawal on the grounds that the British involvement in what he considered an internal Dutch matter was 'intrinsically unsound and, moreover, opposed to the usual standards of our foreign policy', but by mid-May he had almost become resigned to the lack of understanding of the Indonesian situation that seemed to permeate the Foreign Office:

We here become daily more conscious of what a difference it makes, and is going to make, not having Beneto [Sir Alexander Cadogan] in charge of our destinies at home. With him there we could feel assured that the point would be grasped and at least properly presented. Moley Sargent is a delightful person, but hardly sufficiently interested or of the right calibre to make much of an effort; and we are none of us particularly happy at the apparent prospect of having Dening, late of this Mission, in charge of the Dept.[76]

Those misgivings were well-founded, for when Killearn raised the question of whether Britain's involvement in the NEI should be prolonged after the completion of its primary tasks, and repeated Mountbatten's argument that a continued British presence was impeding rather than assisting a settlement, he was told that 'in view of . . . [the 12 April] firm undertaking we are precluded from advancing the date of our withdrawal for the sole reason that our military commitments will have been fulfilled much earlier than was expected.'[77]

Mountbatten himself had no illusions about the dangers of retaining a British presence in the NEI. Each contact he had with the Indonesian leaders provoked accusations from the Dutch that he was undermining their position, even when, for example, the cooperation of the TRI had proved essential in repatriating APWI and in bringing rice supplies from the interior to Batavia. MacKereth's advice to Van Mook to adopt a less legalistic approach – 'We were little impressed by constitutional objections, we had often in our history had to waive them' – had not gone down well, and the Dutch continued to complain about every action which in their eyes suggested that the British accepted the legitimacy of the Republic, even though at the April talks in London their willingness to use the term had implied that they also were prepared to extend recognition.[78] By late May, when no resumption of Dutch-Indonesian talks was in sight, Mountbatten was more determined than ever to force at least a partial divestment of British responsibility. A meeting with Van Mook and their respective staffs proved unexpectedly fruitful. Mountbatten made two proposals, both of which were accepted by Van Mook. The first laid down that responsibility for all the NEI except Java and Sumatra should be transferred to the Dutch at the end of June, the second that after that date the Dutch should be free to conduct whatever military operations they saw fit outside the British zones in Java and Sumatra, on the strict understanding that they could expect no British assistance if things went wrong. The only British military activity beyond their secure perimeters would be carried out by the Royal Navy and Royal Air Force in the APWI programme, and a press statement to this effect would be published so that there could be no misunderstanding of the British position or subsequent Dutch appeals to go to their aid. At a stroke Britain's involvement in the NEI would be dramatically curtailed. To offset any sense that this was a premature withdrawal, Mountbatten offered to allow the Dutch to retain a number of Japanese in Java for labour purposes, notwithstanding the Chiefs of Staff rejection of an earlier Dutch request and clear evidence that the Dutch had some difficulty in controlling Japanese labour forces at Surabaya.[79]

This was yet another example of Mountbatten's willingness to seize the issue and to force, if possible, a resolution in place of hesitation. There had been no discussions with London on the question of setting an early date for transferring responsibility, and the April commitment to maintain a British division in Java until late 1946 had always been tied to a British prohibition on Dutch military operations that had not first been approved by the British command. Why had Mountbatten acted so decisively, and risked a humiliating rejection at what he privately thought would be a 'terribly stormy' meeting? Undoubtedly, he thought that the best time for a settlement had passed when it had proved impossible to bring both sides together in January: since then the prospects for a peaceful solution had steadily receded. As they did so, the Dutch seemed more and more set on pursuing a military end, to the extent that Van Mook remarked that even if there was a negotiated settlement, 'a certain amount of military action would be necessary.'[80] The prospect that British forces would be dragged into that action, however unwillingly, had always been an alarming one, and had become even more likely when after the May conference, Van Mook did little to avoid the impression that in their anxiety to launch military operations against the Indonesians before the end of 1946, the Dutch military command might 'push this desire to the point of insubordination.'[81]

A pragmatic assessment based on first hand knowledge led Mountbatten to urge an early end to Britain's involvement in the NEI. Everything that he heard and saw convinced him that British forces had accomplished as much as they ever would, and that in every realistic sense the tasks set down by the Chiefs of Staff in their original directive had been fulfilled. There was also a personal reason for Mountbatten's haste. His request to leave SEAC had been granted, and he was to fly to London on 31 May for the Victory Parade in June. What better note on which to depart?

Chapter ten
From the sidelines

The distrust, suspicion and at times outright antagonism that marked relations between Britain and her allies in the war against Japan did not diminish once the war was over. Britain's reluctance to extend its military involvement in the Pacific war, its protestations to the contrary notwithstanding, was transformed after the surrender into an anxiety to retain at least a symbolic American presence in southeast Asia and if possible to involve the United States actively in supporting the difficult role that had been thrust on SEAC as a result of the boundary changes agreed to at the Potsdam conference. By the time of Roosevelt's death, American policy towards the return of the colonial powers had considerably softened, not least under the pressure of military reality, but the suspicion remained, and the United States sought to distance itself from direct involvement in or responsibility for the problems that confronted Mountbatten. The American position was an uneasy one, for having urged on the colonial powers during the war a commitment to political change once Japan had been defeated, the United States held back from directly participating in the immediate post surrender activities in southeast Asia when the practical questions of control and future political direction were at the very heart of the conflict between the western allies and the various nationalist forces.

In September 1944 Cordell Hull sent to Roosevelt several memoranda on the importance of southeast Asia to the United States that had been written by the new head of the Division of Southwest Pacific Affairs, Abbot Low Moffat, a long standing critic of western imperialism and a firm advocate of a system of trusteeship to replace imperial control. 'It would seem of substantial military importance to secure for the United Nations the goodwill of the native peoples of southeast Asia', Moffat wrote. 'It is suggested that early, dramatic and concerted announcements by the nations concerned making definite commitments as to the future of the regions of southeast Asia would save many American and Allied lives and facilitate military operations.' Furthermore, while arguing that southeast Asia was of prime importance to America's post war strategic and economic interests, in another simultaneous memorandum on British attitudes he urged that the United States avoid involvement for fear that it would become identified with British activities in southeast Asia:

All reports indicate that the military operations of SEAC are aimed primarily at the resurgence of British political and economic ascendancy in Southeastern Asia and the restoration of British prestige. To minimize American association in the public eye with restoration of British imperialism which is admittedly highly unpopular in Asia, no American civil affairs officer is to serve in any area in the SEAC theater unless under independent American command, and no American officer may collaborate in SEAC political warfare.[1]

Two months later, despite this self-imposed policy of non-participation, Roosevelt made it clear to the American ambassador in London that he expected 'to be consulted on any arrangements as to the future of Southeast Asia'.[2]

Those arrangements could only be implemented in the wake of the military defeat of Japan, and on the question of French participation in that defeat Roosevelt was at best equivocal. When the British overrode American objections and accepted a French Military Mission at SEAC headquarters, the subsequent publicity in the American press was criticised by Mountbatten and his staff, and their concern conveyed by the Foreign Office to the British embassy in Washington, on the grounds that although the Mission had been established with some degree of secrecy the Japanese had now been warned of the possibility of increased allied activity in Indochina, thus putting the proposed clandestine role of the CLI at risk and perhaps precipitating pre-emptive Japanese action that would add to the purely military problem of reconquering Indochina.[3] Shortly before his death Roosevelt agreed to allow American air forces to assist French operations in Indochina if this could be done without detracting from the main drive against Japan, and dropped his opposition to French post war control if the French government undertook to make independence its eventual political aim.[4] By the time the war in Europe had come to an end American policy towards French participation in the war against Japan had been considerably relaxed from the virtual ban imposed by Roosevelt. Henceforth, although there was no question of using American troops in Indochina, French offers of assistance were to be considered on their military merits in relation to the defeat of Japan, and American materiel assistance could be provided if it did not divert resources from areas of higher priority.[5] The enlargement of SEAC's boundaries at the Potsdam conference, however, removed the key areas of Indochina and the major part of the NEI from American theatres, and the conclusion of hostilities against Japan a month later meant that the question of French participation in the Pacific war was no longer an issue. Already in the areas of the NEI within MacArthur's theatre, a Civil Affairs agreement gave the Dutch complete political jurisdiction without any of the qualifications formerly expressed by Hull, whose successor at the State Department, Stettinius, gave much less weight to the opinions of those pushing the trusteeship proposal and relied instead on the Europeanists who were unwilling to endanger relations with the European powers for the sake of what they saw as secondary American interests in southeast Asia.[6] American influence on the post surrender settlement in southeast Asia could now be at best indirect.

At the beginning of September 1945 the American consul at Colombo, who had regular and close contacts with officials at SEAC headquarters in Kandy, urged the State Department to make a public declaration on American policy in southeast Asia. In Indochina, he reported, the British were preparing to give 'complete support' to the French, who in their efforts to reassert French control would be 'extremely harsh'. In despatching Indian troops to back the French the British would undoubtedly emphasise the allied nature of the command authority under which Mountbatten was operating. Similarly in the NEI, if a show of force became necessary, the British would stress that Mountbatten was acting under the control of the Combined Chiefs of Staff. British motives remained suspect, and there was a danger that however distant its association with British activities, the United States might attract strong criticism:

Evidence indicates British are becoming increasingly determined to seize every opportunity [in] SEA to prove British strength and mastery of European over Asiatic. In view forgoing and apparent inclination for unilateral decision and action, while emphasizing responsibilities in manner to purport US concurrence, and in view questionable wisdom British methods, it appears most important that US attitude [in] this area, now Japanese resistance has ceased, be understood, and that British be convinced that actions undertaken in name of Allies must have US approval.[7]

Dean Acheson, Assistant Secretary of State, replied that while 'strictly military US interests in SEAC [were] rapidly diminishing, political responsibility on US military [was] correspondingly increasing', and that responsibility, particularly for acts carried out in the name of the Combined Chiefs of Staff, could not be avoided simply by not taking part in discussions.[8] Several weeks later Acheson asked how far the United States was prepared to go in implementing in southeast Asia the principles to which it was committed under the Atlantic Charter, but it was only a rhetorical question, for when John Carter Vincent, Director of the State Department's Office of Far Eastern Affairs, proposed an American initiative on Indochina in the form of the establishment of a US-British-French-Chinese 'joint Allied investigating commission', the report of which would provide the basis for an international discussion with Vietnamese representatives on the future of Indochina, Acheson agreed with H.T. Matthews, Director of the Office of European Affairs, who rejected the suggestion on the grounds that it would inevitably lead to the end of French rule. 'In addition to this being bad for the French and for the Western powers generally', Matthews wrote, 'I think this would also be bad for the Indo-Chinese themselves.'[9] Eighteen months earlier Mountbatten's request to have American civil affairs officers attached to SEAC had been rejected by the State Department, which in terms of Acheson's argument on joint Anglo-American responsibility made a continuing American military participation in SEAC's affairs, at least at the highest levels of policy formulation, essential, but that came to an end in October 1945 when American military personnel were withdrawn from SEAC and American military participation in SEAC's activities ceased.

Thereafter the United States played little part in the affairs of southeast Asia during the remainder of Mountbatten's period as Supreme Allied Commander. In the first weeks after the surrender ceremony in Tokyo Bay, the Dutch regretted that Java had been transferred from American military jurisdiction to SEAC, apparently thinking that they would have been much better placed to regain control of the NEI under a combination of the Civil Affairs agreement concluded with the United States and access to American military largesse, rather than from the position in which they found themselves as a result of the Potsdam boundary rearrangements, namely dependent on a parlous Britain whose public statements raised doubts about her commitment to the restoration of Dutch rule.[10] Dutch regrets ignored the fact that it had been the American decision to prevent reinforcement of the Dutch Marine Brigade training at the Quantico base in Virginia and the early provision of transport to the NEI that as much as anything had prevented the Dutch from having their own troops readily available for use in the NEI rather than being forced to depend on British forces. The United States protested about trucks originally supplied under Lend-Lease being used by Dutch troops in the NEI and asked for the removal of the 'US' stencilled on their sides, and the State Department rejected a Dutch request to pay for the equipment and training of the Marine Brigade on a 90 day credit basis, arguing that the question should be dealt with as a purely military matter for if, as seemed likely, the deteriorating situation in the NEI led to the Dutch using force to restore their rule, 'it is very probable that a considerable clamor might arise from many circles, both Right and Left in this country'. It was a meaningless gesture and rightly drew the scorn of American critics of Washington's position. When coupled with an official reluctance to endorse the claims of Sukarno's nationalist government, it pointed up the shallowness of the American position of 'strict neutrality'.[11] American policy makers had no clearer ideas on how to handle the political problems of the NEI than did Mountbatten or the British government, while on the immediately pressing problems of removing the Japanese and protecting former prisoners and internees from nationalist attacks they had nothing to offer, if indeed they were even aware of the magnitude of the difficulties facing SEAC. For his part Dening tried to keep the local American political representative, Charles Yost, fully briefed on what SEAC's forces were doing, and both the Joint Staff Mission and the British Embassy in Washington were urged to keep American military and political leaders apprised of developments.[12]

Dutch criticisms of the British for their lack of firmness (in Dutch eyes) in meeting the situation in the NEI were slightly muted by the growing realization of the magnitude of the task and of the fact that the British inability to respond with greater force was to some extent as much a function of the inadequacy of the military means at their disposal as it was an expression of their unwillingness to become further embroiled. While the Dutch never stopped urging Britain to do more, it was to the United States that they looked for materiel support when it became clear that British resources were stretched to breaking point. Notwithstanding the policy of strict neutrality, the American insistence that proposals for mediation to bring about changes in the political status of the NEI had to come from the sovereign power, i.e. The Netherlands, reassured the Dutch of American support, which made the American decision in early November to embargo the sale of surplus weapons and equipment to the Dutch in the NEI all the more of a shock.[13] Some 65,000 tons of equipment had been sold to the Dutch in October, but it did not include combat materiel and a request to purchase 29,000 carbines and pistols together with ammunition had been rejected. The Chiefs of Staff supported the Dutch in trying to have the November decision reversed but to no avail, for the Joint Chiefs argued that since American security interests were not involved the matter was one for the State Department to settle.[14] The British suffered as well: when Mountbatten complained that the Joint Chiefs of Staff had vetoed the use of American ships for SEAC activities, including even the repatriation of ex-prisoners of war and internees, the Chiefs of Staff advised him that despite the strength of his case they did not intend to pursue the matter at the Combined Chiefs level 'since such action would probably resurrect [the] whole question of U.S. responsibilities in S.E.A.C. and your status as an Allied Commander and might well be ultimately to our disadvantage.'[15]

American military assistance, even in the primary task assigned to Mountbatten, was out of the question, but American political support was still a possibility, and every effort was made in Washington and London to enlist it. In June, shortly after the capture of Rangoon, Mountbatten had entertained members of the world press, including 17 American editors, and afterwards had recorded in his diary: 'It is horrifying to think that the American and Indian press evidently still regard us as merely Imperial monsters, little better than Fascists or Nazis.'[16] Much of the press criticism, especially in the United States, derived from the belief that British activities were directed towards the recovery of colonial territories rather than against Japan, and once Japan had been defeated it focused even more clearly on what were seen as Britain's military activities in support of the discredited colonial powers. Specific criticisms were made of the slowness in rounding up Japanese troops and their employment in support of British operations, the native casualties arising out of the battle of Surabaya and other actions, and the excesses of French and Dutch troops which the British had failed to restrain. The Joint Staff Mission in Washington appealed to Mountbatten for detailed information on which to base its rebuttals, noting somewhat plaintively that the charges had to be viewed 'in the light of the American belief . . . that any colonial people at war with their masters necessarily have a just case.'[17] Halifax stressed to Secretary of State James F. Byrnes that since Britain was acting in a joint allied role it was entitled to 'all the moral support' that the United States could give, but he warned the Foreign Office that although Byrnes had acccepted his arguments, his agreement 'does not make me feel to confident that, if the issues are blurred here, the United States government will take steps to clarify them.'[18]

In fact American policy was moving significantly closer to the British position. In reply to hints that Britain would welcome American support in its efforts to bring about a negotiated settlement in the NEI, Byrnes suggested that the United States could informally urge the Dutch to hold out more liberal concessions to the nationalists and to move beyond the restrictions of the 1942 declaration.[19] The initial British reaction was to accept the American offer, but eventually it was decided to ask the State Department to adopt a more even handed approach directed at both the Dutch and the Indonesians and stressing by means of a public statement that negotiation rather than confrontation or a refusal to embark on discussions was the only way to arrive at a satisfactory settlement.[20] The suggestion was agreed to, and on 19 December the State Department issued an official public statement in which it called on both sides to be flexible and to work towards a peaceful resolution of their differences. The statement has been described by one historian as a 'diplomatic triumph for the United States'.[21] It was, in that it marked the beginning of the emergence of an American policy based on a realistic assessment of existing conditions rather than simply reflecting the American assumption of moral superiority in matters of colonialism. In every other respect, however, it merely reinforced and followed what had already been said by the British, months before by Christison, Mountbatten and even Dening in SEAC, more recently by the government in London. But given the previous American record, perhaps even a statement of the obvious could be termed a triumph.

British involvement in southern Indochina attracted much less official American attention, which was directed far more to events north of the 16° parallel, where the Chinese occupation was already wreaking havoc. OSS reports from Saigon acknowledged Gracey's difficulties, not least with the French, but ultimately concluded that Gracey 'had acted with much less circumspection at Saigon than General Christison had demonstrated at Batavia.'[22] That was a charge that could have been made equally well against the OSS in Saigon in the early days of the allied reoccupation. The small OSS team of twelve men sent there was headed by Lt Colonel Peter Dewey, who on his own authority magnified his limited tasks of protecting American interests including property belonging to former prisoners of war, and collecting information for use in war crimes trials, to developing contacts with a range of political groups, including the Viet Minh. Within days of Gracey's arrival, he complained of Dewey's activities, which he regarded as subversive of the work of the Control Commission and of British forces in trying to maintain law and order. Dewey ignored all warnings that he was endangering himself and others, and on 26 September was ambushed and killed at a Viet Minh roadblock in the north of Saigon.[23] Thereafter the OSS team in Saigon confined itelf to reporting on the situation rather than involving itself directly in it, in contrast to the north, where several OSS members, including Captain Archimedes Patti, sought to identify American policy with the claims of the Viet Minh. Like Dewey, Patti had no previous experience of Indochina: his reports were largely discounted and Patti himself was dismissed by another American operative as 'an egotist of almost psychopathic degree'.[24] Nevertheless the impression was created in Hanoi that the United States actively sympathised with anti-French forces.

Whatever the private misgivings of the American government over developments in southern Indochina, in practice it increasingly aided the French. The key issue in late 1945 was Leclerc's request for American equipment (mainly transport) and weapons. The imminent withdrawal of the British threatened to deprive the

French of their main source of materiel and that at a time when Leclerc was anticipating an expansion of the military effort against the Viet Minh. The French therefore approached the United States to release supplies, which required a reversal of Washington's long standing opposition to the use of American equipment in colonial conflicts. As in the NEI, pressure had been brought to bear on the British and the French to disguise the American origin of trucks, light tanks, automatic weapons and small arms, but American correspondents in Saigon, who were unanimously critical of the suppression of the Viet Minh, reported that many American trucks still bore a poorly blocked out white US Army star and that most French officers carried American .45 calibre automatic pistols.[25] American suspicion of French policy towards Indochina was reciprocated by the French, who saw Washington's backing of the Chinese occupation of the north and its insistence on the rights of colonial peoples as little more than a disguise for American economic penetration of Indochina at the expense of France.[26] It was by no means certain, therefore, that Leclerc's request for American assistance would be granted, and American intelligence reported that 'Saigon is anxiously awaiting the decision'.[27] The specific request came from the British who sought American approval to hand over to the French some 800 jeeps and trucks originally supplied to British forces under Lend-Lease for use in the war against Japan. The Joint Chiefs of Staff supported the transfer but admitted that the use of American equipment by the French for the express purpose of maintaining order in southern Indochina might attract considerable criticism. Pragmatism won out over principle, and in mid January 1946 the request was approved, Truman arguing that there would be no new injection of American equipment into the theatre and that the removal of the Lend-Lease equipment already there would be impracticable.[28]

The American decision recognised that without an American presence, the influence that the United States could exert was limited. In the immediate post surrender period political influence was closely tied to military involvement, and by withdrawing from active participation in the affairs of SEAC, the United States imposed severe restrictions on its ability to shape the course of events in southeast Asia. At first critical, then avowedly neutral, it finally came to support the British position that only bilateral negotiations between the Dutch and the Indonesians could avert a major military confrontation. The pity was that the combination of America's political stance on post war developments and its undoubted ability to pressure its western allies was by its own designs withdrawn from southeast Asia as soon as Japan surrendered. Had it not done so, its own future involvement there might well have been less blighted.

Much closer to southeast Asia, but at the other end of the scale of western political influence and military power, was Australia. During the war it had been home to both the NEI government-in-exile and to MacArthur's South West Pacific Area command, and the Australian government had taken a close interest in the future of those territories immediately to the north and northwest of Australia. With the end of the war against Germany, however, questions of post war domestic reconstruction assumed first priority, and the Australian military participation in the war against Japan, which had been declining since 1944, was even more severely limited, and a provisional offer to the Dutch government to train Dutch troops in Australia was withdrawn in June 1945. Two weeks after the surrender of Japan, Prime Minister J.B. Chifley made it clear that Australia looked to the respective sovereign powers, i.e. the European colonial powers, to take over control as soon as possible.[29] Australian troops were responsible for Borneo, Sulawesi, and the eastern islands with the exception of Bali and Lombok, but the government declined any further involvement in the reoccupation of the NEI. Unlike the forces of SEAC, Australian troops were already on the spot when hostilities ceased, and quickly occupied the main cities. They were accompanied by units of NICA, and were able to instal the Dutch administration before the republicans had time to organise in any strength. The commander-in-chief, Blamey, had warned that the Japanese would be dealt with fairly but severely by the Australian occupying forces; the same severity was displayed towards those nationalists who sought to oppose the return of the Dutch, despite the Australian government's directive that Australian troops were not to become involved in internal political matters. The deepening British commitment in Java and Sumatra made it impossible for British troops to relieve the Australians as soon as had been planned, and the last Australian troops did not withdraw from the NEI until December when they were replaced by Dutch forces (which Mountbatten and Christison had refused to allow to enter Java). Useful as this contribution was, it was peripheral to the central area where the future of the NEI would be decided, Java. Throughout the war, Australia had insisted on the right to be consulted on matters affecting its interests, and when the great powers at Potsdam issued an ultimatum to Japan without reference to the Australian government, the External Affairs Minister, Dr H.V. Evatt, protested sharply.[30] Nevertheless the Australian government decided not to extend its involvement in the NEI, all the while maintaining that it had vital interests there which it was entitled to protect. From the very beginning of the post surrender period, therefore, its position was a weak one, and had been made so by its own actions.

Despite its reluctance to become involved it soon found itself criticised from all sides. In mid September Indonesian seamen working on Dutch ships in Australian ports, together with Indonesian exiles in Australia and Indonesians employed in Dutch administrative units, went on strike or mutinied. Not only was this politically embarrassing to the government, but when the communist dominated Waterside Workers' Federation banned the loading of all Dutch ships destined for the NEI, it threatened not only the return of the NEI government-in-exile but the essential post surrender work about to be undertaken by Mountbatten's forces. Military materiel was undoubtedly part of the cargo that was held up, but so too were medical and food supplies for use in the RAPWI programme. Prompted by the head of the SEAC Liaison Section in Melbourne, Brigadier J. Benoy, Mountbatten sent a personal appeal to Chifley to intervene on behalf of the 'mercy ships' stalled in Australian ports. Benoy also recommended that Mountbatten personally ask Chifley to provide Australian signals staff for Singapore, which would have required a significant change to the already announced demobilisation policy; Blamey thought that even higher channels would have to be used, and that only an approach from Attlee would induce the Australian government to make the required commitment.[31]

Mountbatten chose not to pursue that issue, for a much more immediate problem arose over the 1400 Indonesians whom the government proposed to repatriate from Australia to the NEI on the British ship *Esperance Bay*. Mountbatten was horrified to learn that among the group were a large number of former Indonesian political prisoners held in West New Guinea who had been evacuated to Australia when the Japanese attacked, and he protested to Chifley that their presence in Java would 'tip the scales in favour of the Extremists'. Chifley replied that only about a hundred were extremists, not enough to have any decisive effect on events in the NEI, while for the Australian government, 'if interruption of the movement of the Indonesians or their diversion was embarrassing before it would be doubly so now'. Mountbatten was not convinced, having been told by Van Mook that 'the majority . . . [were] undesirable characters', and being himself in a difficult position through having refused to allow Dutch troops to land for fear that they would inflame the situation in Java. He therefore asked Attlee for a ruling on the course that he was to pursue. Chifley replied to Attlee that Mountbatten was giving far too much weight to the opinions and pressures from the Dutch in the NEI, the first clear sign that the Australian position was moving away from its previous support for the resumption of control by the colonial power, but undertook to divert the ship to Timor where those jointly identified by the Australian and Dutch authorities as extremists would be landed temporarily but with firm undertakings from the Dutch that they would eventually be allowed to move to Java and Sumatra. The compromise, however, was offered on the understanding that Britain would seek to promote a settlement based on substantial political concessions by the Dutch to Indonesian nationalist aspirations.[32]

This dispute underlined the growing divergence between the British and Australian positions on the NEI. The Department of External Affairs suggested that in return for military support in the short term from Britain, it was reasonable to expect the Dutch to acknowledge publicly their obligations to the NEI under the United Nations Charter and to pledge that they would be prepared to place the NEI under international trusteeship. This was a tall order, and was recognised as such by the Department which added:

[I]t is also appreciated that the securing of such a pledge . . . would carry certain implications in regard to Malaya, French Indo-China and of course New Guinea and Papua and other dependent areas in the South East Asia region. . . . It is felt, however, that the situation . . . is so full of explosive possibilities in the future that only fairly drastic remedies applied now will have any hope of successfully meeting the legitimate demands of the native peoples whilst at the same time preserving some order and stability by permitting the return of the previous administration, experienced and skilled in handling these peoples.

'There is no need', it concluded, 'to stress the vital security interests of Australia in fostering a liberal settlement of the problems of the dependent peoples of this area.'[33] The Australian position hardened towards the end of October as it became evident that British policy was to exclude anyone other than the Dutch and the nationalists from a settlement. Australian interests, the Department argued, required that it participate in any final agreement which should be arranged under the auspices of an inter-allied commission of which Australia should be a member. 'In this way', the Department suggested, 'political decisions of the greatest importance would not merely be the responsibility of the United Kingdom and SACSEA [i.e. Mountbatten].' If the Dutch and the Indonesians failed to reach an agreement, the commission should institute an enquiry 'by representatives of powers directly concerned', of which Australia was one.[34] The Australian government therefore protested to London about Dening's statement to the nationalists that the future of the NEI was a matter to be settled between them and the Dutch, on the grounds that Australia had vital interests in the NEI that entitled her to be consulted on developments there. Canberra's fear was that London and SEAC tended to see the problem purely in military terms, not least since the Foreign Office appeared to be unenthusiastic about the trusteeship proposal.[35] Attlee replied that while the British government had kept Australian interests in mind, it was essential to support Mountbatten and his commanders on the spot in their attempts to maintain law and order. In such difficult circumstances it would be inappropriate to raise the possibility of intervention by an outside international body, even the mention of which might well provoke the nationalists into increasing their demands and playing for time.[36]

Attlee's comments were not at all reassuring to the Australian government and confirmed the wisdom of its earlier decision to send an Australian political representative to Mountbatten's staff in Singapore to ensure that Australian interests were not overlooked. When Van Mook eventually heard of this decision, he tried unsuccessfully to have the appointment blocked, but on 7 November W. Macmahon Ball arrived at Batavia.[37] Mountbatten had already advised London that if the forthcoming negotiations between the Dutch and the nationalists broke down there were only two courses open to the British: either there would have to be an increased military commitment, including American forces, or the two external governments most closely concerned – the British and Australian – would have to impose a settlement.[38] The External Affairs Department in Canberra also looked to the United States, but for diplomatic leadership, and in the meantime was hopeful that the British government would act more decisively in bringing the parties to the negotiating table.[39] Sukarno welcomed Macmahon Ball's presence and urged that Australia encourage the United Nations to become involved, a suggestion that Macmahon Ball passed on to Canberra, together with Christison's insistence that only United Nations intervention could solve the NEI problem. Dening was not impressed, fearing that if the matter was referred to outside arbitration both the Soviet Union and China might insist on being included, which would only make the position worse.[40]

British concern that the delicate negotiations between the Dutch and the Indonesians might be affected by outside interference were strengthened by Macmahon Ball's conduct in Batavia and by the Australian reaction to events in the NEI. On the eve of the resumption of talks in Batavia, which had a special significance because they were to be held with the new Sjahrir-led republican cabinet, the British were shocked by several news commentaries on Radio Australia that were critical of the British position in the NEI. Mountbatten's complaint that he could not be criticised for carrying out a policy prescribed by the British government brought an apology from Chifley, who stressed that the broadcasts, which had spoken of British 'hypocrisy', did not represent policy, but British suspicions were not assuaged.[41] Further reports of the irresponsibility of the Australian media came from Christison's political adviser in Batavia, Walsh, who complained to the Foreign Office that Australian journalists in Surabaya were 'tampering with the loyalty' of British troops by suggesting to them that they were suppressing freedom fighters.[42]

It was against this background that Macmahon Ball's mission was viewed with increasing suspicion by Mountbatten's political advisers in SEAC. Macmahon Ball insisted that as a regional power Australia was entitled to be represented at meetings such as those planned between Christison, Van Mook and Sjahrir, and that there could be no repetition of what had happened at the Potsdam conference when decisions affecting Australia's vital interests were made without reference to her government. He also maintained that he had the right to see anyone he wished, and did so. It was on that point that his differences with Dening came to a head. Dening argued, and Christison agreed, that as a member of Christison's staff, Macmahon Ball could only discuss the affairs of the NEI with those approved by Christison, which in effect meant Dening since on political matters Christison was required to act on Dening's (or Walsh's) advice. Dening went even further, and insisted that Macmahon Ball show him the text of all cables he intended to send to the Australian authorities so that Dening could ensure that common (i.e. British) views were reported to Canberra and London. Macmahon Ball rightly objected to this demand ('I feel rather as though my mother had asked to see my letters to my wife', he wrote), although he did show Dening two cables after they had been sent; and the Foreign Office felt that even though technically Dening was correct, it was unwise to insist that Macmahon Ball comply, not least since he could request a reciprocal agreement. Moreover, the Foreign Office pointed out, when the suggestion had been put to the Australian government that it should appoint a political representative at Batavia rather than a consul-general, it had never been envisaged that the arrangement would make the representative subordinate to Christison or to Mountbatten, and that was also the view of External Affairs in Canberra, which according to Benoy was considering recalling Macmahon Ball on the grounds that he had 'less freedom in reporting than a News-paper Correspondent'.[43]

This dispute over procedures reflected a growing divergence between the views of Dening and those of Macmahon Ball who, Dening advised London, with his 'inexperience, his rather fantastic ideas as to the solution of this intricate and delicate problem and his somewhat unfortunate manner can do a lot of harm.' Dening wanted a single political voice, arguing that as long as a system of military administration prevailed, the Australian government had no right to take independent action. This was a feeble defence of Dening's own position; a much stronger argument was Dening's view that at that stage of negotiations between the Dutch and the Indonesians, when both sides were looking to Britain for support, false hopes – and fears – might be raised if the Australian and British political representatives were seen to be acting at cross purposes.[44] According to Macmahon Ball, however, Australian interests were not well served by adhering to the policies articulated by Dening. Christison also opposed Dening's approach and supported a role for the United Nations, but felt obliged to accept Dening's advice since he was the political expert. Macmahon Ball felt no such obligation, and was scathing of Dening's role:

Dening is, I feel, giving Christison and the U.K. Government most unfortunate advice. He is eagerly, if not ably, supported by Walsh. Dening and Walsh have devoted much time to giving me a series of University Extension Lectures on the overwhelming advantages to Australia of restoring Dutch rule here. Dening's qualification seems to be (1) that he has spent many years in the Far East and long ago got to understand the "Eastern Mentality". This is a matter of learning a few simple rules of psychology which will serve you through life; (2) a knowledge of the Foreign Office line. . . . In a word, I think the British political line here shows (1) a complete failure to understand or care about Australia's interests, and (2) an outlook and policy which will increase, and not lessen, all the dangers that lie in the inexorable heightening of national consciousness in South East Asia.

Australia's interests, he maintained, would not be served if European powers such as the Dutch were given control of vital areas of southeast Asia, because 'the ill-will between Dutch and Indonesians [is] so bitter and deep-rooted that the N.E.I. will be a focus of conflict between East and West. . . . That is why, in my view, collective responsibility and collective action is so urgent here.'[45]

Macmahon Ball emphasised a collective approach rather than an individual initiative by the Australian government as Sukarno had urged on him, and he was careful to stress to Canberra that it would be unwise to issue any statement or take any action that might suggest a breach between the British and Australian approach.[46] Evatt was much less cautious. From Washington he pressed Canberra to take the initiative before the stalemate between the Dutch and the Indonesians degenerated into open warfare and to issue a statement outlining Australia's proposals. As an inducement to the British to accept an Australian role in furthering negotiations between the main parties, he suggested that the Australian government offer to prolong the presence of its troops in Borneo, and further, that it offer to provide a military force under Mountbatten's overall command to complete the concentration and evacuation of Japanese surrendered personnel throughout the NEI.[47] Chifley rejected Evatt's advice on the grounds that the Cabinet would not support an extended involvement in Borneo let alone an additional commitment to Java and

Sumatra, and that without a military capability of enforcing the terms of any settlement, Australia could not offer to mediate. Evatt had urged Chifley to take the high moral position of making a statement even if it did not succeed in achieving its goals; Chifley preferred to act only if there was a reasonable chance of success. 'Absence of [a] statement', he advised Evatt, '. . . [does] not mean lack of attention to [the] problem'.[48] Macmahon Ball also fixed on the Australian unwillingness to contemplate a military commitment to Java as a fundamental limiting factor on its ability to act independently. 'I think it useless for us to give advice to the Dutch or Indonesians unless we are prepared to support our words with deeds', he wrote in his final report on returning to Australia in December. 'That is why I feel that if Australia is to participate directly in the Java crisis we should do so, not as an independent nation, but as a member of the United Nations.'[49]

A United Nations initiative was no more welcome to the British than an Australian initiative, and for much the same reason: it threatened to introduce more parties to the negotiating procedure without any promise of lessening the military burden that Britain was required to bear, both in terms of winding up the war against Japan and in policing any agreement that might emerge from successful talks. When the Chiefs of Staff canvassed the possibility of military assistance in Java from the United States and Australian the Foreign Office was unenthusiastic. In a lengthy brief prepared for Bevin the Far Eastern Department argued that American participation would bring with it political intervention that might well inflame rather than assist the situation. Similarly Australian military involvement brought risks. While it would be useful if the Australian government extended its military commitment in Borneo and some of the eastern islands, the department thought that in view of Canberra's attitude the introduction of Australian troops to Java 'would probably lead to undesirable political complications'.[50] The Dominions Office preferred an approach to Australia for military assistance rather than to the United States, but recognised that an Australian involvement would not please the Dutch. The Dominions Secretary of State, Viscount Addison, however, put an end to the discussion by noting that if Canberra was asked to provide troops, 'we should only get a peremptory refusal and the approach would do more harm than good to U.K.-Australian relations.'[51]

Addison was right in that neither Borneo nor Java were realistic possibilities given the domestic political contraints on prolonging the overseas service of Australian troops, but Australian hopes – and British fears – of playing a major role in the Dutch-Indonesian dispute did not disappear overnight. When Clark Kerr's appointment was announced, Macmahon Ball's successor as Australian Political Representative at Mountbatten's headquarters, J.C.R. Proud, advised that a senior Cabinet minister should be sent to southeast Asia 'to discuss matters with him on equal terms'. Such an appointment was all the more necessary because, in Proud's mind, Dening attached little importance to the Australian point of view (which Proud admitted was at least partly understandable since he did not himself know what Canberra's policy was on the major issues).[52] Dening feared that such an Australian initiative might encourage the Indonesians to stall for time and avoid entering into fresh negotiations, and the Dominions Office was horrified at the possibility of Evatt descending on Batavia to put the Australian case. Evatt's energetic interventions at the United Nations conference at San Franscisco in May 1945, usually on behalf of the smaller powers in the face of a perceived threat by the great powers to dominate the new world body, had been widely criticised by British delegation. The Under-Secretary at the Foreign Office, Sir Alexander Cadogan, described him as 'the most frightful man in the world'. 'Evatt', he wrote, 'makes long and tiresome speeches on every conceivable subject, always advocating the wrong thing, and generally with a view to being inconvenient and offensive to us'.[53] Evatt's claims to a special role for Australia in regional affairs were rejected out of hand. 'The Australians cannot be regarded as the principally interested party where Indonesia is concerned, though their general interest is fully recognised on all sides', wrote the Permanent Under-Secretary at the Dominions Office, Sir Eric Machtig. Furthermore, he warned,

for an Australian Cabinet Minister to proceed to Batavia at this stage would be a sensational act most unwelcome to the Dutch as well as ourselves, and would create not only an international situation of some delicacy but might well jeopardise any hopes of Sir A. Clark Kerr's intervention proving successful.[54]

Fortunately the Evatt proposal went no further. Had it done so it would have served only to expose the inconsistencies, not to say the contradictions, in the Australian policy.

The Australian position was essentially a weak one. It rested on self-proclaimed special interests and on the perspective that Australia as a southwest Pacific power, as opposed to the European powers and the United States, could bring to bear on the NEI. The protection of those interests, however, was not pursued with any strength. The government's refusal to prolong its military commitment in Borneo or to extend it to Java (which was formally ruled out by the Cabinet in December 1945) fatally weakened the case for a special Australian role. Evatt had been right when he argued that the possibility of failure was no reason not to act; even more so was Chifley when he replied that without the preparedness to enforce a settlement it might be instrumental in producing, Australia could not put itself forward as a mediator between the rival parties. The harsh reality was that it could not even control its domestic situation. Mountbatten's appeals to Chiefly in October over the shipping bans failed to produce any improvement, and a visit by Mountbatten to Australia in March 1946 was no more successful in persuading Chifley to act decisively.[55] There was undoubtedly some justification for the sense of grievance felt in official Australian circles over the exclusion of the smaller powers from the Potsdam conference and similar meetings, but in the circumstances that prevailed from the Japanese surrender until Mountbatten's departure from SEAC, Australia failed on two counts: its participation in the post surrender activities was minimal, and at a time when the presence of British troops seemed to prevent both sides from resorting to open warfare, it chose to remain on the sidelines even when its own vital interests were at stake. In the process the Australian government came very close to committing what it had always decried in others, the sin of humbug.

Conclusion

Wars rarely end tidily and the war against Japan was no exception. The task confronting Mountbatten following the sudden Japanese surrender and the enlargement of his theatre's boundaries was of staggering proportions. For the next nine months until his departure at the end of May 1946, he was Supreme Commander over an area of one and a half million square miles with a population of some 128 millions. Scattered throughout the territories that lay within SEAC were 738,000 Japanese, including 70,000 in Java, 71,000 in Sumatra, and 71,000 in southern Indochina. They were technically known as 'Japanese Surrendered Personnel' (JSP) but in the early days of the post war period it was not at all clear that the surrender ordered by the Emperor in Japan would be observed by his outlying troops. In the event, while there was no widespread military resistance to the allies from the Japanese, significant numbers of them did not observe the terms of the surrender, but turned their weapons over to nationalist groups and did nothing to prevent attacks (and on occasions participated in them) on French and Dutch civilians, whether free or still confined in camps. The presence of huge numbers of Japanese in SEAC was thought to be politically destabilising and damaging to the efforts of the allies to reassert imperial control. Their evacuation from SEAC and repatiation back to Japan was a high priority for Mountbatten but the numbers involved made it a difficult task, especially since MacArthur initially refused to provide additional shipping. In December 1945, despairing of the situation, Mountbatten told the Chiefs of Staff that with the transport then at his disposal, it would take at least five years before the evacuation had been completed.[1] By the time MacArthur did make extra shipping available in April, the number of JSP within SEAC had been reduced by only 48,000, but the provision of 75 Liberty ships, four LSTs (Landing Ship Tank), and 22 Japanese ships dramatically increased SEAC's capacity for moving the Japanese. By mid May a further 320,000 had been evacuated, followed by an additional 270,000 by the end of June. The remaining 100,000 were due to be retained for labour use until early 1947.[2] It was an impressive achievement, and had the necessary shipping been available earlier, there is no doubt that the great bulk of the Japanese could have been evacuated within several months of the surrender.

There was, however, another side to the problem. Mountbatten had stressed at the surrender ceremony in Singapore that the Japanese were a defeated nation, and to his staff he made it clear that he had 'no intention of allowing ... [them] the slightest latitude in South East Asia Command'.[3] Circumstances made that policy impossible to maintain, especially in Java and Sumatra but also in most parts of SEAC. The breakdown during the war of local police services and the emergence of armed opposition to the return of the allied colonial powers left Mountbatten with no choice but to employ large numbers of Japanese in police roles and at times as active fighting troops. At Semarang, for example, it was necessary to maintain an 18 mile cordon around the perimeter of the city to protect the 240,000 inhabitants including many Dutch and Chinese; lacking sufficient allied troops Mountbatten was forced to use the Japanese. These, he emphasised, were employed in a static defensive role, but in fact when British troops had first arrived at Semarang they had used the local Japanese forces to mount major actions against the armed nationalists in which, as Dening reported, they 'displayed as much gallantry and devotion to duty at the behest of the British as they had in the days of their own arrogant domination'.[4] The forced reliance on Japanese troops undermined the claim that the Japanese had suffered a crushing defeat and the demonstration of allied strength that Dening and others had long argued was essential for the restoration of colonial control. Mountbatten's disquiet was reflected in his diary record of his final visit to Sumatra:

I of course knew that we had been forced to keep Japanese troops under arms to protect our lines of communication and vital areas in Sumatra for which the British Indian troops did not suffice, but it was nevertheless a great shock to me to find over a thousand Japanese troops guarding the nine miles of road from the airport to the town [Palembang], and to find them drawn up in parties of twenty, presenting arms, the officers saluting with swords which long ago should have been souvenirs.[5]

The British press in particular was highly critical of the apparent freedom enjoyed by the Japanese, but for Mountbatten and his commanders in SEAC the protection of former prisoners and internees had a higher priority than the initial insistence on bringing home to the Japanese the magnitude of their defeat. The result was that when Mountbatten left SEAC, there were still more than 64,000 Japanese troops under arms, including 38,000 on guard duty in Sumatra and west Java, and some 25,000 who had allied themselves with the Indonesian nationalists and who were beyond SEAC's immediate control.[6] While the policy of using Japanese troops in both static and active roles was embraced reluctantly by the British, they felt they had no other option given the conditions they encountered in Indochina and particularly in Java and Sumatra. What they would have done had MacArthur provided shipping to make a much earlier evacuation of the Japanese possible is an interesting question.

The RAPWI programme was the most obviously successful of Mountbatten's post surrender tasks. By the time Mountbatten left SEAC more than 96,000 former p.o.w.s and internees had been recovered, 71,000 being evacuated by the end of October 1945.[7] That figure, however, did not include those Dutch civilians who had not been interned during the war but whose lives were subsequently threatened by the outbreaks of nationalist violence, nor those thousands, and eventually hundreds of thousands, of the non-European population who had at least temporarily thrown their lot in with the Dutch and who therefore felt threatened by nationalist ambitions. These so-called IFTUs were a serious embarrassment to Mountbatten. It was difficult to argue the virtues of an allied victory on the grounds that it had saved local peoples from Japanese brutality if the allies' inability to maintain basic law and order exposed those same people to the violence of nationalist groups. After the battle of Surabaya had showed how many wished to identify with a continuing Dutch presence Mountbatten had argued that it would be unconscionable to abandon those who had sought refuge within allied lines, but he found little support in London. The War Office replied that if SEAC was to assume responsibility for the hundreds of thousands of IFTUs Mountbatten's task would become virtually open-ended, and at a time when the British government was trying to limit the British commitment to the NEI. The result was that the whole IFTU problem was simply passed on to the Dutch, and any responsibility that SEAC might have had was rejected on the grounds that the question was an internal political one for the Dutch alone to settle. It was a convenient if not completely satisfying response.

It was the third task allotted to Mountbatten under the Chiefs of Staff directive that proved the most difficult. The maintenance of law and order pushed SEAC into a political arena that no one had foreseen, for the end of the war against Japan was inextricably tied in with the beginnings of other separate, if related, wars against the colonial powers. It was not easy to distinguish between the two, or even to appreciate that what allied forces were encountering in 1945 and 1946 were the first rounds of a prolonged struggle that eventually led to the end of French and Dutch colonial rule in southeast Asia. Certainly the European colonial powers were aware that the war, and especially their disastrous defeats in 1942, had irrevocably changed conditions in their respective colonial territories, but in the case of the French and Dutch the political concessions they were prepared to offer were grudging and minimal. British policy was more liberal, both because of a quite different concept of empire in which self-government was always an eventual however distant aim and because Britain's ability to withstand invasion during the course of the European war made the recovery of colonial territory less essential to the restoration of national pride and integrity. The British government's view of the problems in SEAC immediately following the Japanese surrender was tempered by two main preoccupations: it was acutely aware of the potential effect that actions in Indochina and the NEI might have on its own colonial territories, and it was anxious to establish a close and firm relationship with its European allies, in particular with France. These long term considerations clashed with the immediate problems faced by Mountbatten and SEAC in their attempt to bring the war against Japan to a conclusion: to rescue p.o.w.s and internees, to restore a semblance of law and order, and to do it with a minimum of troops.

Mountbatten was given little guidance on how he should approach the chaotic situation that confronted him. It cannot be said that his political advisers – at whatever level – were wiser or had keener insights into the nature of the changes that he encountered in southeast Asia. Indeed, on occasions military men, without any expert advice or special training, grasped the fact that political conditions had fundamentally changed well before their advisers could bring themselves to acknowledge that the war had swept away the comfortable assumptions of pre war colonial policy. Dening's acceptance of the strength of Indonesian nationalism was gradual and reluctant, while Walsh, originally despatched to keep Christison on the political rails, never did come to terms with the reality of the independence movement and proved incapable of offering political guidance of any utility whatever. In July 1946 the British consul-general in Batavia, Gilbert MacKereth, whose appreciation of the situation in the NEI was otherwise well-informed, wrote to the Foreign Office that a 'great deal of my time is taken up with trying to keep the soldiers out of political trouble.'[8] It was a comment that could well have been made by any of the political advisers in SEAC during Mountbatten's time as Supreme Commander. By and large the criticism was unfounded. Certainly Gracey's actions soon after his arrival had political implications that he did not appreciate, but then neither at the time did anyone else in SEAC or in the British government. The need to give him a political adviser was not thought to be a high priority, so that in the critical days following his arrival in Saigon Gracey could act only on the basis of his directive, or else according to his own lights, and it must be said that the Nelsonic blind eye does not always produce heroic outcomes. Had Christison followed the political advice he was given and interpreted his directive strictly, British and Indian forces might well have been faced with widespread armed opposition on the scale that occurred at Surabaya, with incalculable consequences for the RAPWI programme. Critics of British policy in this period, and especially of British military involvement, all too easily forget the great and pressing humanitarian task that was the first duty of Mountbatten and his forces to accomplish.

It was the men on the spot who bore the brunt of bringing the war against Japan to a close, and if they did not fully understand or necessarily sympathise with the political forces confronting them, their record of achievement in the post surrender period was no less creditable on that account. What they and their political advisers failed to appreciate was that not only were the fundamental changes that were occurring in non-British territories beyond their power to direct, but that even the rate of change was hardly theirs to control. Little more than a year after Mountbatten left SEAC, he was appointed by the same Labour government to preside over the dissolution of the British empire in India, and his decision there that the timetable for the British withdrawal from the subcontinent had to be accelerated could hardly have been unaffected by his experiences in southeast Asia and especially in the NEI.

Mountbatten was determined that history should record his achievements, that his central role in great events should be recognised. His version of those events did not always accord with the evidence. He had no monopoly of insight into or sympathy with the aims of the various nationalist movements SEAC encountered: Christison, Slim and others were no less aware of the new political atmosphere in which they had to operate. His claim that he kept a tight control over his commanders (and that he had to do so) was countered by Pyman's admission that it 'would be wrong to say that the machinery of command in Kandy is really efficient', or by Dening's charge that SEAC headquarters 'has now attained a standard of inefficiency which makes it a byword'.[9] Indeed, the criticism that the lavish scale of his wartime headquarters at Kandy provoked – criticism which his official biographer shrugs off with the comment that 'If his panache, enthusiasm, flamboyance were thought desirable in the interests of morale, then they had to be paid for. Mountbattens do not come on the cheap.'[10] – continued after it was moved to Singapore in November. Pyman and others were irritated by Mountbatten's tendency to involve himself in every aspect of SEAC's affairs and to interfere in operational matters that properly concerned his commanders-in-chief, but it was as much as anything Mountbatten's drive and energy at every level that inspired SEAC when even Dening, one of his strongest critics, conceded that 'Mountbatten was not . . . given the tools to finish the job'.[11] That said, the pity of it was that he was unwilling to share the credit with others. When it came to producing the despatches from SEAC, Mountbatten insisted that those of his commanders-in-chief be held back until his own were completed, with the result that Air Chief Marshal Sir Keith Park, Allied Air C-in-C, SEAC, had to wait until April 1951 before the report he had written in November 1945 appeared in the *London Gazette*.[12] Even when Mountbatten's despatches were published in 1951, there was some feeling that he had not been sufficiently generous towards his former senior subordinates. It was, in fact, only as a result of considerable pressure that he agreed to include a brief section paying tribute to them: he admitted that he 'had been reluctant to write in a catalogue of names, scratching all their backs in turn, as this is a proceeding that always seems to me to defeat its object, by appearing like a mutual admiration society.'[13]

These, however, were ultimately minor failings and it would be a carping critic who lent too much weight to them. More important were his achievements, and those of SEAC, and it is on them that a considered judgment must be based. Reflecting on the situation in the NEI in December 1945, Mountbatten wrote, 'although it may all look a bit confused at the moment, I hope historians reading my telegrams, memos and minutes will not find too much to pick holes in. . . .'[14] In this historian's view, he was not far wrong.

Notes

References with the prefix CAB, DO, FO, PREM and WO are to documents in the Public Record Office, London. All other archival citations include the appropriate depository reference (AA, NA etc.).

Chapter one: From war to peace

1   See especially Christopher Thorne, *Allies of a Kind: The United States, Britain and the war against Japan, 1941–1945* (London: Hamish Hamilton, 1978), and *The Issue of War: States, Societies, and the Far Eastern Conflict of 1941–1945* (London: Hamish Hamilton, 1985); and Wm Roger Louis, *Imperialism at Bay: The United States and the Decolonization of the British Empire, 1941–1945* (New York: Oxford Univesity Press, 1978).
2   David A. Day, 'Promise and Performance: Britain's Pacific Pledge, 1943–5', *War & Society*, 4:2 (September 1986), 71–93.
3   Sir H. Seymour to J.C. Sterndale Bennett, 12 December 1944, FO 371/46325 F214/127/61.
4   Dening to Mountbatten, 14 July 1944, CAB 122/1162.
5   Sterndale Bennett, minute, 22 February 1945, FO 371/46304 F1113/11/G61.
6   Sterndale Bennett, minute, 23 February 1945, ibid.
7   Halifax to FO, 6 March 1945, FO 371/46325 F1415/127/61.
8   Field Marshal Sir Henry Maitland Wilson (Joint Staff Mission, Washington) to General Sir Hastings Ismay (Secretary, War Cabinet), 27 March 1945, FO 371/46325 F1987/127/61.
9   Dening to FO, 6 March 1945, FO 371/46325 F1417/127/61.
10 Ibid.
11 Memorandum of a conversation between General Wedemeyer and Consul Max W. Bishop, 12 June 1944, enclosure no. 1 to despatch no. 481, CCS 000.1 SEAC (8-7-44), RG 218, NA.
12 V.F.W. Cavendish-Bentinck, minute, 22 February 1945, FO 371/46304 F1113/11/G61.
13 Roger Allen, minute, 10 March 1945, FO 371/46325 F1415/127/G.
14 Sterndale Bennett, minute, 7 April 1945, FO 371/46325 F2144/127/61.
15 Major General S. Woodburn Kirby, *The War against Japan*, vol V, *The Surrender of Japan* (London: HMSO, 1969), pp. 224–6.

16 Dening to FO ('Top secret and personal'), 31 July 1945, *Documents on British Policy Overseas*, Series 1, vol. 1 (*1945*) (London: HMSO, 1984), Calendar i to no. 599.
17 Browning to Mountbatten, 31 July 1945, ibid.
18 Kirby, *The Surrender of Japan*, pp. 233–4.
19 Mountbatten to COS, SEACOS 448, 20 August 1945, CAB 105/162.
20 Mountbatten to COS, SEACOS 450, 21 August 1945, ibid.
21 John Ehrman, *Grand Strategy*, vol. V (London: HMSO, 1956), pp. 244–5, 249–52.
22 Mountbatten to COS, SEACOS 417, 9 June 1945, CAB 105/162.
23 General Sir Charles Lane (SACR), minute on meeting with C-in-C, India, 20 August 1945, WO 203/4327.
24 Kirby, *The Surrender of Japan*, pp. 86–7.
25 Auchinleck to Mountbatten ('Top Secret and Personal'), 24 August 1945, WO 203/4327.
26 Mountbatten to Auchinleck, 30 August 1945, ibid.
27 Wilson to Ismay, 23 August 1945, CAB 122/1036.
28 James C. Dunn (Director, Office of European Affairs) to J.C. Hilldring (Director of Civil Affairs Division, War Office), 24 February 1944, *FRUS, 1944*, vol. V (Washington: Government Printing Office, 1965), p. 1195.
29 JSM to COS, 16 October 1945, CAB 122/1068.

Chapter two: The allied re-entry to southern Indochina

1 The question of French Indo-China is discussed inter alia in Walter La Feber, 'Roosevelt, Churchill, and Indochina: 1942–45', *American Historical Review*, LXXX (December 1975), 1277–95; Thorne, *Allies of a Kind*; and John J. Sbrega, *Anglo-American Relations and Colonialism in East Asia, 1941–1945* (New York: Garland Publishing, 1983).
2 L.H. Foulds, minute, 5 March 1945, FO 371/46304 F1269/11/G61.
3 See François Kersaudy, *Churchill and De Gaulle* (London: Collins, 1981).
4 Roosevelt to Stettinius, 1 January 1945, *FRUS, 1945*, vol. VI (Washington: Government Printing Office, 1969), p. 293.
5 Halifax to FO, 9 January 1945, FO 371/46304 F190/11/G61.
6 Sterndale Bennett, minute, 9 January 1945, FO 371/46304 F163/11/G61.
7 Dening to Eden, 6 January 1945; to Sterndale Bennett, 12 January 1945; FO 371/46304 F163/11/G61 and F586/11/G61.
8 Hollis to Cavendish-Bentinck, 24 January 1945; to Sterndale Bennett, 25 January 1945: FO 371/46304 F381/11/G61 and F190/11/G61.
9 Cadogan, minute, 27 February 1945, FO 371/46304 F1271/11/G61.
10 La Feber, 'Roosevelt, Churchill, and Indochina', pp. 1292–4.

11 N. Brain (SEAC HQ) to Sterndale Bennett, 11 April 1945, FO 371/46306 F2234/11/G61; La Feber, 'Roosevelt, Churchill, and Indochina', p. 1294.
12 Stettinius to Grew, 8 May 1945, DSR 851 G.01/5–845, RG 59, NA.
13 Marcel Vigneras, *Rearming the French* (Washington: Office of the Chief of Military History, 1957), pp. 391–4.
14 Dening to Sterndale Bennett, 2 February 1945, FO 371/46304 F956/11/G61.
15 Ibid.
16 De Gaulle to Truman, 15 May 1945, *FRUS, 1945*, vol. VI, pp. 308–9.
17 St. Didier to Marshall, 29 May 1945, OPD 336.2 TS, RG 319, MMB, NA.
18 François de Langlade, 'La situation de l'Indochine: Sommaire au 22 mai 1945', 'Etats associés, 1945–1957', Box 20, Série A, Sous-section 3, Dossier A 333, AMAE.
19 Marshall, memorandum, 6 July 1945, OPD 336.2 TS, RG 319, MMB, NA.
20 Lt General W.B. Smith (Chief of Staff to Eisenhower) to Secretariat, JCS, 9 June 1945; J.E. Hull, memorandum, 6 July 1945: ibid.
21 St. Didier to Marshall, 6 July 1945, ibid.
22 Hull, memorandum, 6 July 1945, ibid.
23 Brig. T.D. Daly (British Military Attaché, Paris), Report No. 7, 16 July 1945, FO 371/49135 Z9016/219/17.
24 Lt General W.B. Smith to Secretariat, JCS, 9 June 1945, OPD 336.2 TS, RG 319, MMB, NA.
25 J.J. McCloy (Assistant Secretary of War) to Major General T.T. Handy (Assistant Chief of Staff, Operations Division, War Department), 1 June 1945, ibid.
26 Vigneras, *Rearming the French*, p. 398.
27 Ibid., p. 399.
28 Massigli to Affaires Etrangères, 11 and 14 August 1945, 10 H 125, Dossier 'TO des Attachés Militaires',' SHAT.
29 J. Balfour (British Embassy, Washington) to FO, 16 August 1945, FO 800/464.
30 'Journal de Marche du Général Leclerc, 1 juil–31 déc 1945' [hereafter 'Journal de Marche' (1)], entry for 10 August 1945, 10 H 161, Dossier 2, SHAT.
31 WO to SACSEA, 17 August 1945, WO 203/4271.
32 Leclerc to d'Argenlieu, 28 August 1945, FL.
33 Ibid.; 'Journal de Marche' (1), 26 August 1945, 10 H 161, Dossier 2, SHAT.
34 General A. Juin (Chief of Staff, National Defence) to Minister of War, 29 August 1945, 10 H 782, untitled Dossier (brown buckle), SHAT; Memorandum of a meeting between Leclerc and MacArthur, 29 August 1945, CEFEO François 1°, 'Redition Japonais', FL.
35 Peter M. Dunn, *The First Vietnam War* (London: C. Hurst, 1985), p. 45.
36 Gracey to Terauchi, 4 September 1945, WO 203/5608.

37 Rivier to Leclerc, 7 September 1945, 10 H 599, Dossier 'septembre 1945', SHAT.
38 Martin to Leclerc, 7 September 1945, 10 H 161, Dossier 4, SHAT.
39 Adrien Dansette, *Leclerc* (Paris: Flammarion, 1952), p. 186; 'Journal de Marche' (1), 4 September 1945, 10 H 161, Dossier 2, SHAT; Leclerc to Lt Colonel de Guillebon (Chief of Staff, CEFEO), 6 September 1945, FL.
40 Gracey to Mountbatten, 21 September 1945, WO 203/4020.
41 Ibid.
42 ALFSEA Operational Directive no. 12, 'Masterdom' (occupation of French Indochina), WO 203/2066.
43 Gibbons, memorandum, 7 September 1945, WO 172/1782.
44 Dening to FO, 10 September 1945, FO 371/46308 F6636/11/61.
45 ALFSEA to Control Commission No. 1 (Saigon), 12 September 1945, WO 203/5644.
46 'Conférence du 21 septembre 1945', CEFEO François 1°, 'Redition Japonais', FL.
47 Leclerc to d'Argenlieu, 28 August 1945, FL.
48 Mountbatten to Gracey, 24 September 1945, WO 203/4020.
49 Mountbatten to COS, SEACOS 490, 24 September 1945, CAB 105/162.
50 Leclerc to de Guillebon, 6 September 1945, FL.
51 Lt Colonel Stagnard (Paris), 'La situation en Indochine au 17 septembre d'après les télégrammes reçus par la D.G.E.R.', 17 September 1945, 10 H 599, Dossier 'Septembre 1945', SHAT.
52 Juin to French ambassadors in London and Washington, 9 September 1945, 10 H 95, Dossier '1945', SHAT.
53 Leclerc to Mountbatten, 18 September 1945, FL.
54 Kimmins, memorandum; Browning to Mountbatten, 19 September 1945: WO 203/5611.
55 'Conversation entre le Major Général Kimmins et le Commandant Weil', 18 September 1945, 10 H 161, Dossier 3, SHAT.
56 'Journal de Marche' (1), entries for 19 and 21 September 1945, 10 H 161, Dossier 2, SHAT.
57 Dening to FO, 19 September 1945, FO 371/46308 F7161/11/61.
58 Bevin to Seymour, 17 September 1945, FO 800/461.
59 Dening to FO, 19 September 1945, FO 371/46308 F7160/11/61.
60 Mountbatten to War Office, SAC 23210, 24 September 1945, WO 203/4020.
61 Rivier to Leclerc, 17 September 1945; Etat-Major Général, Défense Nationale (Paris), 'Situation de l'Indochine à la date du 8 septembre 1945', 8 September 1945; 'Notice sur les événements récents d'Indochine et la situation politique en Indochine à la date du 12.9.45', 13 September 1945: 10 H 599, Dossier 'septembre 1945', SHAT.
62 Rivier to Leclerc, 17 September 1945, 10 H 599, Dossier 'septembre 1945', SHAT.
63 See Dunn, *The First Vietnam War*, chapter 8, especially for Gracey's and Cédile's motives.

Chapter three: Consolidation and expansion in southern Indochina

1 Gracey to Mountbatten, SGN 99, 25 September 1945, WO 203/ 4273.
2 Pyman to Gracey; Gracey to Pyman, 23 September 1945: WO 203/4271.
3 Gracey to Mountbatten, SGN 99, 25 September 1945, WO 203/ 4273.
4 Cédile to Leclerc, 28 September 1945, 'Etats associés, 1945–1957', Box 20, Série A, Sous-section 3, Dossier 386, AMAE; Cédile, 'Instruction No. 1: Principes à observer à l'occasion de la réprise du travail', 23 September 1945, 10 H 161, Dossier 1, SHAT.
5 D'Argenlieu to Paris, 29 September 1945, Télégrammes, arrivées 1945: 900, no. 61, AOM.
6 Gracey to Mountbatten, COS 30, 26 September 1945, WO 203/ 4020.
7 Gracey to Mountbatten, SGN 99, 25 September 1945, WO 203/ 4273.
8 SACSEA, 27th miscellaneous meeting, 22 September 1945, WO 172/1785.
9 Dunn, *The First Vietnam War*, is an extended apologia for Gracey. Gracey's own unpublished defence of his actions, written in October 1946 in response to a draft report by the Recorder for SEAC, is by no means entirely convincing: Gracey to Recorder, SEAC, 3 October 1946, Gracey Papers 36, KCL.
10 Lt Colonel Roos (Service des Renseignements) to Leclerc, 3 September 1945, 10 H 161, Dossier 5 'Télégrammes 1945, SHAT; Cédile to d'Argenlieu, 20 September 1945, 'Etats associés, 1945–1957', Box 20, Série A, Sous-section 3, Dossier 386, AMAE; Cédile to Leclerc, 25 September 1945, 10 H 599, Dossier 'Octobre 1945', SHAT.
11 SACSEA, 28th miscellaneous meeting, 22 September 1945, WO 172/1785. There is a French record of the meeting in FL.
12 Leclerc to d'Argenlieu, 22 September 1945, FL.
13 Leclerc to de Gaulle, 23 September 1945, FL.
14 Mountbatten to COS, SEACOS 491, 25 September 1945, CAB 105/162.
15 Leclerc to Kimmins, 25 September 1945, WO 203/4271.
16 Mountbatten to COS, SEACOS 494, 29 September 1945, CAB 105/162.
17 Cadogan to Col C.R. Price (Cabinet Office), 25 September 1945, FO 371/46308 F7161/11/61.
18 Brain to FO, 27 September 1945, FO 371/46309 F8420/11/61.
19 Massigli to Affaires Etrangères, 28 September 1945, 10 H 125, Dossier 'TO des Attachés Militaires', SHAT.
20 'Journal de Marche' (1), entry for 29 September 1945, 10 H 161, Dossier 2, SHAT.
21 COS to Mountbatten, COSSEA 366, 1 October 1945, CAB 105/165.
22 Joint Planning Staff, 'French Indo-China – Measures for

Responsibility for Internal Security by SACSEA', 30 September 1945, JP(45)258 (Final), CAB 84/75.

23 COS to Mountbatten, COSSEA 366, 1 October 145, CAB 105/165; Dening to FO, 25 September 1945, FO 371/46308 F7445/11/61.
24 Mountbatten to COS, SEACOS 500, 2 October 1945, CAB 105/162.
25 Auchinleck to COS, 7 October 1945, WO 203/4271.
26 SACSEA, 287th meeting, 2 October 1945, WO 172/1786.
27 Cadogan to Price, 25 September 1945; R. Lambert, minute, 28 September 1945: FO 371/46308 F7161 and F7489/11/61.
28 Leclerc to Lt Colonel Vezinet, 24 September 1945, FL.
29 COS to Mountbatten, COSSEA 366, 1 October 1945; Mountbatten to COS, SEACOS 500, 2 October 1945: CAB 105/162; Leclerc to Guillebon, 6 September 1945, FL; Lt Colonel Stangard (Paris), 'La situation en Indochine au 17 septembre d'après les télégrammes reçus par la. D.G.E.R.', 17 September 1945, 10 H 599, Dossier 'Septembre 1945', SHAT: SACSEA to HQ East Africa Command, 24 September 1945, WO 203/4271; Cadogan to Price, 25 September 1945, FO 371/46308 F7161/11/61.
30 COS to Mountbatten, COSSEA 368, 4 October 1945, CAB 105/162.
31 Cédile to Leclerc, 28 September 1945, 10 H 140, Dossier 'Pieces de Base', SHAT.
32 Brain to FO, 27 September 1945, FO 371/46309 F8420/11/61.
33 Gracey to Mountbatten, COS 30, 26 September 1945, WO 203/4271.
34 Brain to FO, 27 September 1945, FO 371/46309 F8420/11/61.
35 'Journal de Marche' (1), entry for 30 September 1945, 10 H 161, Dossier 2, SHAT.
36 Gracey to Mountbatten, COS 30, 26 September 1945, WO 203/4271; Brain to FO, 27 September 1945, FO 371/46309 F8420/11/61.
37 Gracey to Mountbatten, 1 October 1945, WO 172/1786.
38 Mountbatten to COS, SEAC(RL) 119, 3 October 1945, CAB 105/178.
39 Mountbatten to COS, SEACOS 497, 1 October 1945, CAB 105/162.
40 RAF Mission to France to Air Ministry, 3 October 1945, FO 371/46309 F7886/11/61; COS (45), 242nd meeting, 5 October 1945, CAB 79/40.
41 Myers to Mountbatten, 3 October 1945, WO 172/1786.
42 De Gaulle to Leclerc, 29 September 1945, FL.
43 Defence Committee meeting, 5 October 1945, CAB 69/7.

Chapter four: First encounters in the Netherlands East Indies

1 Leahy, quoted in Thorne, *Allies of a Kind*, p. 613.
2 CCS to SHAEF, 8 February 1945; minute by R. Allen, 2 March 1945: FO 371/46354 F/1037/1037/61.
3 Halifax to FO, 30 May 1945, FO 371/46354 F3327/1037/61.
4 'Note on Future Operations against the N.E.I.', 5 June 1945, WO 172/1772.

5   Mountbatten to COS, SEACOS 447, 19 August 1945, CAB 105/162.

6   Major General Charles Harrison to Mountbatten, 24 August 1945, WO 203/3862.

7   'Dutch and French Forces available for S.E.A.C.', 7 September 1945, WO 203/4024.

8   Van Oyen to Mountbatten, 12 September 1945, WO 203/4025.

9   Netherlands Staff Section, Kandy, to HSD, 23 September 1945, WO 203/2312.

10 'Memorandum by Under-Secretary of the Navy on Training of Netherlands Marines in the U.S.', 19 September 1945, SWNCC 189/2, RG 353, NA.

11 John D. Hickerson, Acting Chairman, SWNCC, to Secretary of State, 24 September 1945, SWNCC 189, RG 353, NA.

12 Correspondence between Lieutenant General E.K. Smart (Australian military representative, London) and Major General F.E.W. Simpson (Assistant Chief of the Imperial General Staff), on basing Dutch troops in Australia, 20 September 1943, AWM 54, 16/2/3, AWM.

13 Van Aerssen to External Affairs, 4 September 1944, in Advisory War Council agendum no. 22/1944, 20 September 1944, CRS A2679, AA.

14 Notes on Advisory War Council agendum no. 22/1944, 20 September 1944, CRS A2679, AA.

15 Ibid.

16 War Cabinet minute no. 3807, 21 September 1944, CRS A2676, AA.

17 N.J.O. Makin to van Aerssen, 24 September 1944, in Advisory War Cabinet agendum no. 30/1945, CRS A2680, AA.

18 Australian Military Mission, Washington, to Land Head Quarters, Melbourne, 18 April 1945, Blamey Papers, Box 8.4; telegram, External Affairs to High Commissioner, London, 17 March 1945, AWM 54, 16/2/3: AWM.

19 AMM, Washington, to LHQ, Melbourne, 18 April 1945, Advisory War Council agendum no. 30/1945, CRS A2679, AA.

20 Report of the Joint Administrative Planning Sub-Committee, 17 March 1945, AWM 54, 16/2/3, AWM.

21 Lieutenant General E.K. Smart to Major General F.E.W. Simpson, 19 June 1945, ibid.

22 LHQ, Melbourne, to Australian Army Staff, London, 30 April 1945, ibid.

23 War Cabinet Minute no. 4293, 28 June 1945, CRS A2676, AA.

24 Chifley to van Aerssen, (?) September 1945, Shedden Papers, Box 562, AA.

25 Harrison to SEAC, 27 August 1945, WO 203/3862.

26 Report by Major General F.G.L. Wijeman, Chief Staff Officer, NICA, 25 August 1945, WO 203/3862; Kirby, *The Surrender of Japan*, p. 311.

27 Yong Mun Cheong, *H.J. van Mook and Indonesian Independence: A Study of His Role in Dutch-Indonesian Relations, 1945–48* (The

Hague: Martinus Nijhoff, 1982), pp. 25–30; Thorne, *Allies of a Kind*, pp. 218–19.

28 The speech is reproduced in Yong, *Van Mook and Indonesian Independence*, pp. 200–2.

29 Ibid., pp. 29–30.

30 *Enquètecommissie Regeringsbeleid 1940–1945* Part VIII: *Militair beleid 1940–1945, Terungkeer naar Nederlandsch-Indië* ('s Gravenhage: Staatsdrukkerig, 1956), q. 68885.

31 Charles Cruickshank, *SOE in the Far East* (Oxford: Oxford University Press, 1983), p. 149.

32 *Enquètecommissie Regerinsbeleid*, Part VIII, q. 99828.

33 Ibid., q. 60324.

34 The work of Dutch Intelligence regarding the NEI is dealt with in Colonel J.J. Nortier, *Acties jin de archipel, de intelligence-operaties van NEFIS-III in de Pacific-Oolog* (Franeker: Uitgeverij T. Wever BV, 1985).

35 *Enquètecommissie Regerinsbeleid*, Part VIII, p. 535.

36 Ibid., q. 99828.

37 Ibid., q. 94170.

38 Van Mook to J.H.A. Logemann, Minister of Overseas Territories, 12 and 17 August 1945, in S.L. van der Wal (ed.), *Officiële Bescheiden*, vol. 1 ('s-Gravenhage: Martinus Nijhoff, 1971), pp. 13–14, 36–8.

39 'Situation in the Netherlands East Indies', 19 February 1944, AWM 54, 423/11/6, part 24, AWM.

40 F.S.V. Donnison, *British Administration in the Far East 1943–46* (London: HMSO, 1956), p. 423.

41 Vice Admiral The Earl Mountbatten of Burma, *Report to the Combined Chiefs of Staff by the Supreme Allied Commander, South East Asia 1943–1945* (London: HMSO, 1951), pp. 181, 183.

42 R. Harris Smith, *OSS, The Secret History of America's First Central Intelligence Agency* (Berkeley: University of California Press, 1972), p. 251.

43 Yong, *Van Mook and Indonesian Independence*, pp. 30–1; *Officiële Bescheiden*, vol. 1, p. 3, n. 2.

44 Donnison, *British Administration in the Far East 1943–6*, pp. 415–17.

45 Ibid., pp. 417–18; SACSEA, 20th miscellaneous meeting, 4 September 1945, WO 172/1781; Van Mook, 'Memorandum on the Organization of Civil Affairs in the N.E.I.', 2 September 1945, *Officiële Bescheiden*, vol. 1, pp. 79–81.

46 There are many studies of the Indonesian revolution. Among the most useful are G. McT. Kahin, *Nationalism and Revolution in Indonesia* (Ithaca: Cornell University Press, 1952); B.R.O'G. Anderson, *Java in a Time of Revolution: Occupation and Resistance, 1944–1946* (Ithaca: Cornell University Presss, 1972); Anthony Reid, *The Indonesian National Revolution* (Hawthorn: Longmans, 1974).

47 Mountbatten to COS, SEACOS 461, 3 September 1945, CAB 105/162.

48 SACSEA, 278th Staff meeting and 20th miscellaneous meeting, 4 September 1945, WO 172/1781.
49 Mountbatten to COS, SEACOS 465, 5 September 1945, CAB 105/162.
50 Dening to FO, 6 September 1945, FO 371/46392 F6409/6398/61.
51 Joint Logistical Planning Committee, SEAC HQ, 'Administrative Plan: Law and Order', 31 August 1945, WO 203/3862.
52 Mountbatten, personal diary, 4 September 1945, WO 172/1781.
53 David Wehl, *The Birth of Indonesia* (London: George Allen & Unwin, 1948), pp. 37–8. Yong, *Van Mook and Indonesian Independence*, p. 34, is less critical of the narrowness of Greenhalgh's report, arguing that within his terms of reference he had no reason to make contact with the nationalists. However, given that essential services, including transport, were being maintained by the nationalists, albeit somewhat sporadically, Greenhalgh's failure to appreciate the importance of their cooperation in any programme to repatriate p.o.w.s and internees is astonishing.
54 Van der Plas to Van Mook, undated (received in Brisbane, 22 September 1945), *Officiële Bescheiden*, vol. 1, p. 150.
55 C.S.5 to SACSEA, 18 and 21 September 1945, WO 203/2312.
56 Van Straten to Van Mook, 20 September 1945, *Officiële Bescheiden*, vol. 1, pp. 146–8.
57 Bevin to Mountbatten, 13 September 1945, WO 203/3863.
58 Hawkins (Batavia) to Medical Directorate, ALFSEA, and SACSEA, 20 September 1945, WO 203/4024.
59 Aide-memoire by the Dutch Ambassador, 15 September 1945, FO 371/46392 F6991/6398/61.
60 Mountbatten to Bevin, 17 September 1945, WO 203/3863.
61 HQ ALFSEA to 14th Army, 6 RAPWI Control Staff, 13 September 1945, WO 203/4024.
62 CS5 to SACSEA, 14 September 1945, WO 203/2312.
63 Van Kleffens to Bland, 20 September 1945, FO 371/46392 F7608/6398/61.
64 Christison, handwritten 'memoir', p. 173. A typed copy is now available at the Imperial War Museum.
65 Philip Ziegler, *Mountbatten: The Official Biography* (London: Collins, 1985), p. 334.
66 Ibid.

Chapter five: Deeper into Java

1 Van der Plas to Van Mook, 28 September 1945, FO 371/46392 F7665/6398/61.
2 SACSEA, 286th meeting, 28 September 1945, WO 172/1785.
3 SAC's diary, 30 September 1945, ibid.
4 Van der Plas to Van Mook, 28 September 1945, FO 371/46392 F7665/6398/61.

5 F.R. Hyns, minute, 4 October 1945, FO 371/46392 F7758/6398/61.
6 Attlee to Lawson, 29 September 1945, ibid.
7 Lawson to Attlee, 1 October 1945, ibid.
8 Bevin to Attlee, 6 October 1945, ibid.
9 DO 45(8), 10 October 1945, CAB 69/7.
10 Report by Van der Plas (undated, received 2 October 1945), *Officiële Bescheiden*, vol. 1, p. 229.
11 The most careful account is by Yong, *Van Mook and Indonesian Independence*, pp. 35–6.
12 Van Mook to Mountbatten, 30 September 1945, *Officiële Bescheiden*, vol. 1, p. 193.
13 Mountbatten to Christison, 30 September 1945, WO 172/1785.
14 Christison, 'Memoirs', p. 176.
15 SACSEA, 30th miscellaneous meeting, 28 September 1945, WO 172/1785.
16 Mountbatten to Van Mook, SEAC 415, 28 September 1945, FO 371/46392 F7629/6398/61.
17 Mountbatten to COS, SEACOS 495, 29 September 1945, CAB 105/162.
18 Van Mook to Mountbatten, 29 September 1945, WO 203/4024.
19 Yong, *Van Mook and Indonesian Independence*, pp. 38–42.
20 Record by Wilson Young of conversation with Netherlands Ambassador and Minister of Overseas Territories, 29 September 1945, FO 371/46392 F7663/6398/61.
21 Ibid; see also the official Dutch statement on the NEI monitored by the BBC, 26 September 1945, FO 371/46392 F7607/6398/61. The irony of the British position *vis-à-vis* Java and Indochina has attracted relatively little attention from historians. One who has pointed to the curious position in which Britain found herself is D.C. Watt:

> The case of Indonesia was particularly odd in that, whereas in Vietnam the leaders of the Indo-Chinese communist party whom the Americans took to be the spokesmen for the nascent Vietnamese independence movement had collaborated with OSS against the Japanese, while their French opponents were at least tarred with the stigma of defeat and collaboration with both Germany and Japan, the leaders of the Indonesian nationalists had collaborated with the Japanese. They had seized power with Japanese aid and arms, while the Dutch had fought valiantly to defend the East Indies against Japan and had stood up to the severest Japanese diplomatic pressure before the attack had begun.

Succeeding John Bull: America in Britain's Place 1900–1975 (Cambridge: Cambridge University Press, 1984), p. 245.
22 Mountbatten to Leese, 27 February 1945, in Hugh Tinker (ed.), *Burma: The Struggle for Independence 1944–1948*, vol. 1, *From Military Occupation to Civil Government, 1 January 1944 to 31 August 1946* (London: HMSO, 1983), p. 96.
23 Mountbatten to C-in-C, ALFSEA, 2 June 1945, ibid., pp. 189–91.

24 Record of a meeting with Civil Affairs Officers in Government House, Rangoon, 16 June 1945, ibid., pp. 203–4.
25 Frank Siegfried Vernon Donnison CBE, 'Narrative of Events', ibid., p. 1004.
26 Penney to Browning, 15 October 1945, Penney Papers 5/26, KCL.
27 Mountbatten to Driberg, 4 October 1945, C91, BA.
28 Kirby, *The Surrender of Japan*, p. 429.
29 Wilson Young, 'Situation in Java', 20 September 1945, FO 371/46392 F7656/6398/61.
30 Minute by Sterndale Bennett, 19 September 1945, ibid.
31 Sterndale Bennett to Major General L.C. Hollis (COS Secretariat), 30 September 1945, FO 371/46392 F7655/6398/61.
32 Schermerhorn to Helfrich, 29 September 1945, Helfrich Papers, AMH.
33 Minute by Bevin, 29 September 1945, FO 371/46392 F7663/6398/61.
34 Sterndale Bennett to Hollis, 30 September 1945, FO 371/46392 F7655/6398/61.
35 Minutes, 1 (Wilson Young) and 2 (F.R. Hyns) October 1945, FO 371/46392 F7649/6398/61.
36 Orme Sargent to Sterndale Bennett, 4 October 1945, FO 371/46393 F8066/6398/61.
37 COS to Mountbatten, COSSEA 367, 1 October 1945, CAB 105/165.
38 Slim to Mountbatten, 4 October 1945, C 247A, BA.
39 Mountbatten to Christison, 4 October 1945, WO 172/1786.
40 Dening to FO, 30 September 1945, FO 371/46392 F7649/6398/61.
41 Dening to FO, 3 October 1945, FO 371/46392 F7845/6398/61.
42 Joint Planning Staff, 'Situation in Java', 30 September 1945, JPS(45) 265 (Final) in FO 371/46392 F7663/6398/61.
43 Memorandum by Sterndale Bennett on meeting with the Dutch Ambassador and the Minister for Overseas Territories, 1 October 1945, FO 371/46392 F7702/6398/61.
44 The official English translation of the Dutch statement of their position was sent by Bland (Hague) to Foreign Office, 1 October 1945, FO 371/46392 F7668/6398/61.
45 Memorandum by Sterndale Bennett on meeting between Bevin and representatives of the War Office and Chiefs of Staff, 30 September 1945, FO 371/46392 F7657/6398/61.
46 Sterndale Bennett to Hollis, 3 October 1945, FO 371/46392 F7663/6398/61.
47 Ibid.
48 COS to Mountbatten COSSEA 365, 1 October 1945, CAB 105/165.
49 COS to Mountbatten, COSSEA 364, 30 September 1945, CAB 105/165. For the text of the proclamation, see *Officiële Bescheiden*, vol. 1. pp. 173–4.
50 COS to Mountbatten, COSSEA 370, 4 October 1945, CAB 105/165.
51 Mountbatten to Christison, 4 October 1945, CAB 105/178.
52 SACSEA, 288th meeting, 5 October 1945, WO 172/1786.

53   Mountbatten to COS, SEACOS 504, 5 October 1945, CAB 105/162.
54   Mountbatten, conversation with the author, 25 June 1979.
55   Pyman, diary entry, 5 October 1945, Pyman Papers 5/1, KCL. Pyman's recommendations to Slim are in his signal, 4 October 1945, WO 172/1786.
56   Pyman, diary entry, 7 October 1945, Pyman Papers 5/1, KCL.
57   Pyman, diary entry, 9 October 1945, ibid.
58   Slim to CIGS, 6 October 1945, annex to COS (45) 607(0), CAB 80/97.
59   Slim to Mountbatten, 9 October 1945, WO 203/4024.
60   Christison to Slim, 7 October 1945, WO 172/1786.
61   Christison, 'Memoirs', entry for 4 October 1945.
62   Christison to Mountbatten, 7 October 1945, C49, BA.
63   SAC's diary, 10 October 1945, WO 172/1787.
64   Samuel Eliot Morison, *History of United States Naval Operations in World War II*, vol. III, *The Rising Sun in the Pacific 1931–April 1942* (Boston: Little Brown and Company, 1965), pp. 376–77.
65   Helfrich to Mountbatten, 25 September 1945, Helfrich Papers, AMH.
66   Christison quoting Helfrich, SACSEA, 35th miscellaneous meeting, 11 October 1945, WO 172/1787.
67   DO(45), 8th meeting, 10 October 1945, CAB 69/7.
68   Minute by Sterndale Bennett, 9 October 1945, FO 371/46393 F7947/6398/61.
69   Minute by Sargent, 6 October 1945, FO 371/46392 F7845/6398/61.
70   Minute by Sargent, 9 October 1945, FO 371/46394 F8422/6398/61.
71   DO(45), 8th meeting, 10 October 1945, CAB 69/7.

Chapter six: To Surabaya and beyond

1   Mountbatten to COS, SEACOS 498, 1 October 1945, CAB 105/162. For a brief account of the INA, see Louis Allen, *The End of the War in Asia* (London: Hart-Davis, MacGibbon, 1976), Book 1, Chapter 5.
2   SACSEA, 34th miscellaneous meeting, 10 October 1945, WO 172/1787.
3   Mountbatten to COS, SEACOS 511, 11 October 1945, CAB 105/162.
4   FO to Dening, 11 October 1945, FO 371/46393 F 8202/6398/61.
5   Dening to FO, 11 October 1945, FO 371/46393 F 8219/6398/61.
6   Van der Post, 'The Pressing Situation in Java', 6 October 1945, FO 371/46395 F8696/6398/G61.
7   Attlee, minute, 12 October 1945, PREM 8/71.
8   Van Kleffens to Dutch Ambassador, London, 12 October 1945, FO 371/46394 F8366/6398/61.
9   Mountbatten to Christison, 13 October 1945, C49, BA.
10   COS to SACSEA, COSSEA 377, 10 October 1945, CAB 105/162; Mountbatten to Christison, 12 October 1945, C49, BA.

11 Sargent to Bevin, 14 October 1945, FO 371/46393 F8426/6398/61;
   Dening to FO, 16 October 1945, FO 371/46394 F8484/6398/61.
12 Dening to FO, Sargent to Dening, 16 October 1945, FO 371/46394
   F8423/6398/61.
13 Joint Planning Staff, 'French Indo China and Netherlands East Indies
   – Letter from General Sir William Slim', JP(45) 273 (Final), 14
   October 1945 in FO 371/46309 F8661/11/G.
14 DO(45) 9th meeting, 15 October 1945, CAB 69/7.
15 Penney to Browning, 15 October 1945, Penney Papers 5/26, KCL.
16 Mountbatten to COS, SAC 25506, 16 October 1945, CAB 105/178.
17 Mountbatten to COS, SEACOS 519, 16 October 1945, CAB
   105/162. Since SEACOS 519 had been seen by Dutch staff members
   at Kandy, Mountbatten simultaneously sent SAC 25506 on a
   GUARD (i.e. restricted) basis which enabled him to express much
   more freely his feelings about the intransigence of the Dutch and the
   reasonable attitude of Sukarno.
18 Penney to Browning, 12 October 1945, WO 203/4024.
19 SSU report no. XL 20489, 11 October 1945, RG 226, MMB, NA.
20 Mountbatten to COS, SEACOS 515, 13 October 1945, CAB
   105/162. The Foreign Office distrust of Christison's judgment was
   displayed in Sterndale Bennett's request to Dening to provide specific
   examples of the actions to which Christison had taken exception, 14
   October 1945, FO 371/46394 F8433/6398/61.
21 Christison to Mountbatten, 19 October 1945, WO 203/4024.
22 Auchinleck to Private Secretary, Viceroy, 17 October 1945,
   Auchinleck Papers, JRULM.
23 Auchinleck to Mouuntbatten, 18 October 1945, WO 203/4024.
24 Mountbatten to Auchinleck, 19 October 1945, ibid.
25 DO(45) 10th meeting, 19 October 1945, CAB 69/7.
26 This was a common theme in Dutch statements on the situation in the
   NEI. See, for example, the text of the broadcast on 5 October 1945
   by the Minister for Overseas Territories, J.H.A. Logemann, who said
   that while it could be understood that there was natural war fatigue
   among peoples who had fought so far from home, 'we cannot
   suppress our bitterness that the common work is remaining uncom-
   pleted, at our cost.' P.F. Grey (Hague) to FO, 6 October 1945, FO
   371/46393 F8084/6398/61.
27 These details are from ALFSEA signal 1483, relayed to London in
   Mountbatten to COS, SEACOS 532, 2 November 1945, CAB
   105/162.
28 Mountbatten, *Post-Surrender Tasks*, para. 55.
29 Kirby, *The Surrender of Japan*, p. 336.
30 DO(45) 12th meeting, 5 November 1945, CAB 69/7.
31 The quotation is from Chifley's letter to Attlee cited in note 32 below.
   See also Margaret George, *Australia and the Indonesian Revolution*
   (Carlton: Melbourne University Press, 1980), chapter 2, and M.T.P.
   Herbert, 'Asking Too Much: Australia, The Netherlands and the
   Netherlands East Indies, 1942–1945' (BA Hons. thesis, Department

of History, Faculty of Military Studies, University of New South Wales, 1985).

32 Chifley to Attlee, 31 October 1945, CRS A4355, item 7/1/3/2, AA; also DO 35/1577.

33 Attlee to Chifley, 5 November 1945, PREM 8/68.

34 Pyman, 'Review of situation in NEI as seen at ALFSEA HQ on 20 Oct 45', Pyman Papers 5/1, KCL.

35 Pyman, diary, 4 November 1945, ibid.

36 Joint Planning Staff, HQ SEAC, 'SEAC Commitments in NEI', 3 November 1945, WO 172/1790.

37 SACSEA, 293rd meeting, 2 November 1945, ibid.

38 Mountbatten to COS, SEACOS 538, 5 November 1945, CAB 105/162.

39 Dening to Sterndale Bennett ('Top Secret and Personal'), 30 October 1945, FO 371/46400 F9991/6398/61.

40 JP(45) 289(Final), 22 October 1945; COS to JSM (Washington), 24 October 1945; Marshall to Wilson, 30 October 1945: CAB 122/1068.

41 Memorandum, J.H. Morgan, Office of European Affairs, Department of State, 15 October 1945, DSR, 856d.20/10–1545, RG 59, NA.

42 See for example the suggestions put out by the Information Office in the Washington embassy ('Guidance for British Officials'), 29 October 1945: 'While the history of *colonial development* should not be painted in too rosy colours, it is necessary to emphasize that the Colonial Empire is not a kind of imperial real-estate project run and exploited for the benefit of Britain.': CAB 122/1036. On the need to inform US officials on Britain's role in the war against Japan, particularly on the 'magnitude of the Burma campaign', see JSM(S)(45)91, 7 November 1945, ibid.

43 Helfrich to MacArthur, 20 October 1945, Helfrich Papers, AMH.

44 Bevin referred in the Tokyo incidents as another example of the unhelpful pressures on Britain. DO(45) 12th meeting, 5 November 1945, CAB 69/7. Equally unwelcome, though in another direction, was Field Marshal Jan Smuts' insistence that Dutch claims for British support in the NEI were 'overwhelming. They must not be allowed to succumb to this Quisling movement'. Smuts to Attlee, 3 November 1945, FO 371/46398 F9688/6398/61.

45 COS to Mountbatten, COSSEA 398, 1 November 1945, CAB 105/165; Mountbatten to COS, SEACOS 533, 2 November 1945, CAB 105/162.

46 COS to Mountbatten, COSSEA 408, 9 November 1945, CAB 105/166; Nye to Browning, 10 November 1945, WO 203/4024. In a personal message on November 12th, the Chiefs of Staff told Mountbatten: 'We are being considerably embarrassed by not having had a single official report on the progress of military operations in Sourabaya since they began on 8th November.' WO 203/4024.

47 Dening to Sterndale Bennett, 9 November 1945 ('Personal. Top Secret'); minutes by Wilson Young, 9 November 1945: FO 371/46399 F9767/9780/6398/G61.

48 At the end of October, for example, General Yamamoto, Chief of Staff of the 16th Japanese Army, and Admiral Yameda, Japanese Naval Commander-in-Chief, had submitted reports urging the allies to recognise Indonesian independence. A member of the Foreign Office described them as 'among the most impudent documents I have ever seen': B.W.A. Plunkett, minute, 3 November 1945, FO 371/ 46394 F8632/6398/61.

49 Wehl, *The Birth of Indonesia*, p. 66. Christison later claimed ('Memoirs', p. 186) that German officers, as well as Japanese, fought at Surabaya, but there is no evidence to support this.

50 Weekly Intelligence Review No. 60, 1 December 1945, WO 172/ 1793.

51 Political Warfare Division to all Commands, 1 December 1945, WO 172/1793. For an earlier example of the fears about the local Japanese see Major General C.G.G. Nicholson's comment to Penney that Japanese encouragement of the nationalist movement was 'undoubtedly caused by the Japanese desire to make the return of the Allies difficult and to lay the foundation of their own future return.' SEAC(RL) 163, 19 October 1945, CAB 105/178.

52 COS to Mountbatten, COSSEA 406, 9 November 1945, CAB 105/166.

53 Pyman to Christison, 9 November 1945, WO 172/1791.

54 SACSEA, 294th meeting, 13 November 1945; Mountbatten to C-in-Cs, naval, land, air forces, ALFSEA, WO 172/1791.

55 Christison, 'Memoirs', p. 188.

56 'Extract of Monthly Intelligence Survey for November 1945', 17 November 1945, Pugh Papers, IWM.

57 SACSEA, 294th meeting, 13 November 1945, WO 172/1791.

58 Mountbatten to COS, SEACOS 546, 13 November 1945: SEACOS 561, 3 December 1945, CAB 105/162.

59 COS to Mountbatten, COSSEA 407, 9 November 1945, CAB 105/166.

Chapter seven: A British policy for Java?

1 Dening to FO, 21 October 1945, FO 371/46395 F8701/6398/61.

2 Dening to FO, 24 October 1945, FO 371/46396 F8889/6398/61.

3 Dening to FO, 27 October 1945, FO 371/46396 F9031/6398/61.

4 Bland (Hague) to FO, 4 November 1945, FO 371/46397 F9454/6398/ 61: *Officiële Bescheiden*, vol. 1, pp. 505–6.

5 Dening to FO, 3 November 1945, FO 371/46397 F9447/6398/61.

6 For more details on the November changes, see Anderson, *Java in a Time of Revolution*, chapter 8; Reid, *The Indonesian National Revolution*, chapter 4.

7 Dening to Mountbatten, 5 November 1945, WO 172/1790.

8 Christison to Slim, 7 November 1945, WO 203/4024.

9 Mountbatten to COS, SEAC(RL) 209, 9 November 1945, CAB 105/178.

10   Helfrich to Mountbatten, 18 November 1945, in SEAC(RL) 229, 21
     November 1945, CAB 105/178.
11   Hawthorn to Slim, 21 November 1945, copy in Helfrich Papers,
     AMH. Van Oyen angrily rejected Hawthorn's charges, arguing that
     since Dutch troops were not under his operational control, he could
     not be held responsible for their behaviour. The specific incident on the
     night of 18 November, which had given rise to Hawthorn's adverse
     report, was, according to Van Oyen, caused by Indonesians shooting at
     Dutch soldiers who returned the fire in self defence. He was probably
     closer to the truth of the whole matter when he suggested that it was his
     constant pressure to have ex-p.o.w. battalions deployed in Java which
     put him offside with Christison and his staff. Van Oyen to Helfrich, 2
     December 1945, copy in Helfrich Papers, AMH.
12   Walsh to FO, 21 November 1945, FO 371/46401 F10364/6398/61.
13   Christison to Helfrich, 23 November 1945, Helfrich Papers, AMH.
14   Dening to FO, 26 November 1945, FO 371/46402 F10633/6398/61.
15   Helfrich to Mountbatten, 18 November 1945, in SEAC(RL) 229, CAB
     105/178; 26 and 28 November 1945, WO 172/1793.
16   Brigadier N.D. Wingrove (COS, C-in-C, ALFNEI) to Helfrich, 29
     November 1945, Helfrich Papers, AMH.
17   B.W.A. Plunkett, minute, 3 December 1945, FO 371/46403 F11025/
     6398/61.
18   Christison, 'Circular No. 6', December 1945, copy in Helfrich Papers,
     AMH.
19   The minutes of the meeting are in WO 172/1793. For the comment by
     the Dutch observer, see *Officiële Bescheiden*, vol. II ('s Gravenhage:
     Martinus Nijhoff, 1972), pp. 214–15. The Australian Political Repre-
     sentative at Christison's headquarters, W. Macmahon Ball, similarly
     observed that Sjahrir had noted that 'Dening did most of the talking
     and made him, Sjahrir, feel like a small boy being questioned by a
     policeman.' Quoted in Walsh to FO, 17 November 1945, in DO
     35/1579.
20   Mountbatten to Christison, 19 November 1945, WO 172/1792.
21   Walsh to FO, 20 November 1945, FO 371/46401 F10298/6398/61.
22   Mountbatten to Dempsey, 20 November 1945, WO 203/4024.
23   SACSEA, 296th meeting, 20 November 1945, WO 172/1792.
24   FO to Dening, 23 November 1945, WO 172/1792.
25   Dening to FO, 24 November 1945, FO 371/46402 F10475/6398/61.
26   For the text of the broadcast, see FO 371/46403 F10974/6398/61.
27   Christison to Mountbatten, 30 November 1945, WO 172/1793.
28   Dening to FO, 1 December 1945, FO 371/46403 F10974/6398/61.
29   FO to Bland, 2 December 1945, FO 371/46403 F11006/6398/61.
30   'Netherlands East Indies: Memorandum by the Secretary of State for
     Foreign Affairs', 30 November 1945, DO(45)43, CAB 69/7.
31   Mountbatten to Bevin, 25 November 1945, FO 800/461 FE/45/59.
32   Pyman to Dempsey, 30 November 1945, WO 172/1793.
33   Helfrich to Mountbatten, 30 November 1945, *Officiële Bescheiden*,
     vol. II, p. 257.

34 Mountbatten to COS, SEACOS 561, 3 December 1945, CAB 105/162.
35 Mountbatten to COS, SEACOS 562, 3 December 1945, CAB 105/162.
36 Mountbatten to Wavell, 5 December 1945, WO 172/1793.
37 Mountbatten to COS, SEACOS 579, 17 December 1945, CAB 105/162. Christison subsequently told Sjahrir and other Indonesian leaders that 'It is in no way my policy that reprisals should be taken in cold blood as a matter of principle', but that hardly carried much conviction after the destruction of Bekasi. 'Points discussed with the Indonesian leaders by Lt.-Gen. Sir Philip Christison . . . 27 December 1945', Helfrich Papers, AMH.
38 Mountbatten to Dempsey, 29 December 1945, C83, BA.
39 Christison, 'Memoirs', p. 188; Wehl, *The Birth of Indonesia*, pp. 77–81; SACSEA, 298th meeting, 3 December 1945; Mountbatten to Christison, 3 December 1945: WO 172/1793; Mountbatten, *Post-Surrender Tasks*, p. 295.
40 SACSEA, 298th meeting, 3 December 1945, WO 172/1793.
41 'Report of War Office Liaison Officer After a Visit to Java, November 1945', 30 November 1945, DO(45)42, CAB 69/7.
42 COS, 'Long Term Policy in Netherlands East Indies', 5 December 1945, DO(45)41, CAB 69/7; COS to Mountbatten, COSSEA 424, 5 December 1945, CAB 105/165.
43 Far Eastern Department, 'Defence Committee. Java: Brief for the Secretary of State', 6 December 1945, FO 371/46408 F12362/6398/61.
44 DO(45), 15th meeting, 7 December 1945, CAB 69/7.
45 Ibid.
46 J.C.R. Proud (Australian Political Representative, SACSEA) to Acting Minister of External Affairs, Canberra, 12 December 1945, CRS A1066, Item P45/47/10/1, AA.
47 Mountbatten to COS, SEACOS 545, 13 November 1945, CAB 105/162.
48 SACSEA, 301st meeting, 6 December 1945, WO 172/1793.
49 *Officiële Bescheiden*, vol. II, p. 325.
50 Proud to Acting Minister of External Affairs, 12 December 1945, CRS A1066, Item P45/47/10/1, AA.
51 Bevin to Mountbatten, 5 December 1945, FO 800/461.
52 Secretary of State, Dominions, minute, 6 December 1945, DO 35/1581.
53 Ismay to Mountbatten, 12 December 1945, Ismay Papers, IV/Mou/4BA, KCL.
54 Mountbatten to COS, SEACOS 575 and 579, 14 and 17 December 1945, CAB 105/162.
55 Mountbatten to Christison, 15 December 1945, WO 172/1794.
56 COS (45) 285th meeting, 17 December 1945, CAB 79/42; COS to Mountbatten ('personal'), 19 December 1945, WO 172/1795.
57 Information and Civil Affairs Committee, SEAC HQ, 20th meeting, 17 December 1945, WO 172/1795.

58 After Bland at the Hague criticised the thrust of several articles on the NEI ('Is it right that such a man [Morrison] should be allowed a free hand to insult the Dutch and inflame the Indonesians?'), the News Department of the Foreign Office indicated to *The Times* that a more positive approach would make it easier for London to urge a 'generous and liberal policy' on the Dutch. Wilson Young, however, suggested that Morrison's articles probably reflected Dening's own views on the situation. Bland to Sterndale Bennett, 9 November 1945; Sterndale Bennett to Dening, 13 November 1945; minute by Wilson Young, 12 November 1945: FO 371/46399 F 9832/6398/61.

59 FO to Walsh, 9 January 1946, FO 371/46409 F12432/6398/61.

60 Walsh to FO, 29 December 1945, ibid.

61 W. Ridsdale (News Department), minute, 2 January 1946, FO 371/46409 F12432/6398/G61.

62 Macmahon Ball, 'Report on the N.E.I.', 17 December 1945, CRS A1838, Item 401/1/2/1, AA.

63 Mountbatten to COS, SEACOS 577, 15 December 1945, CAB 105/162.

64 Mountbatten to COS, SEACOS 584, 20 December 1945, CAB 105/162; Brain (Dening's deputy, Batavia) to FO, 20 December 1945, FO 371/46407 F12056/6398/61; Dening to FO, 19 December 1945, FO 371/46407 F11999/6398/6; Pyman, diary, 22 December 1945, Pyman Papers 5/3, KCL.

65 COS to Mountbatten, COSSEA 441 and 442, 21 and 23 December 1945, CAB 105/166; Mountbatten to COS, SEACOS 587, 21 December 1945, CAB 105/162.

66 COS to Mountbatten, COSSEA 441, 21 December 1945, CAB 105/166.

67 Dening to Sterndale Bennett, 13 December 1945, FO 371/46405 F11654/6398/61.

68 Yong, *Van Mook and Indonesian Independence*, pp. 68–9.

69 Sterndale Bennett, record of a conversation between Bevin and the Dutch ambassador, 10 December 1945, FO 371/53769 F154/1/61.

70 'Record of a Meeting held at Chequers on 27th December to Discuss the Situation in Indonesia', PREM 8/71; also in *Officiële Bescheiden*, vol. II, pp. 453–69.

71 Mountbatten to COS, SEACOS 553, 21 November 1945, CAB 105/162.

Chapter eight: The British withdrawal from Indochina

1 De Gaulle to Leclerc, 29 September 1945, FL.

2 'Journal de Marche' (1), entries for 22 September and 2 October 1945, 10 H 161, Dossier 2, SHAT.

3 Ibid., entry for 2 October 1945.

4 Ibid., entry for 5 October 1945.

5 The text of Cédile's broadcast is in 10 H 599, Dossier 'octobre 1945', SHAT.

6   Dening to Bevin, 5 October 1945, FO 371/46309 F7907/11/61.
7   Pyman diary, entry for 8 October 1945, Pyman Papers, KCL.
8   Slim to Brooke, 6 October 1945, annex to COS(45) 607(O), CAB 80/97.
9   Hirst to Gracey, 10 October 1945, Gracey Papers 48, KCL.
10 SACSEA, 33rd miscellaneous meeting, 9 October 1945, WO 172/1787; 'Journal de Marche' (1), entry for 9 October 1945, 10 H 161, Dossier 2; the French record of the meeting is in 10 H 599, Dossier 'octobre 1945': SHAT; Col. Roos (head of the liaison section, CEFEO, Calcutta), 'Rapport', 12 October 1945, 'Etats associés, 1945–1957', Box 20, Série A, Sous-section 3, Dossier A 335, AMEA.
11 Mountbatten to COS, SEACOS 513, 12 October 1945, CAB 105/162.
12 Gracey to Slim, 13 October 1945; Major General E.M. Bastyan (ALFSEA) to Gracey, 15 October 1945: WO 203/4020.
13 Gracey to Browning, SGN 204, 14 October 1945, WO 203/4273.
14 SSU report no. XL 20704, 12 October 1945, RG 226, MMB, NA.
15 SSU report no. XL 34155, 5 January 1946, RG 226, MMB, NA.
16 Cédile to Leclerc, 25 September 1945, 10 H 599, Dossier 'octobre 1945', SHAT; 'Rapport du Colonel Roos', 12 October 1945, 'Etats associés, 1945–1957', Box 20, Série A, Sous-section 3, Dossier A 335, AMAE. See also 'Journal de Marche' for 18 October 1945, a typical entry: 'Diner chez le Général Gracey au Gouvernement Cochinchinois. Excellent diner, très cordiale. Tous les Anglais sont extrémement sympathiques': 10 H 161, Dossier 2, SHAT; and the comments made in 1981 by General Guillebon: Institut Charles de Gaulle, *De Gaulle et l'Indochine* (Paris: Plon, 1982), p. 167.
17 Juin to Military Attaché, London, 25 October 1945, Télégrammes 900 arrivée, Londres, no. 248, AOM.
18 Gracey to Mountbatten, 19 October 1945, WO 203/4273.
19 Mountbatten to Gracey, 31 October 1945, Gracey Papers 40, KCL.
20 Auchinleck to Mountbatten, 14 October 1945, Auchinleck Papers MUL 1104, JRULM.
21 COS to Mountbatten, COSSEA 381, 15 October 1945, CAB 105/165.
22 Mountbatten to Gracey, 31 October 1945, Gracey Papers 40, KCL.
23 Gracey to Mountbatten, 9 November 1945, WO 203/4271.
24 Gracey to Slim, 5 November 1945, Gracey Papers 38, KCL.
25 BBC monitoring, 7 November 1945, in FO 371/46309 F9806/11/61.
26 Gracey to Mountbatten, 9 November 1945, WO 203/4271.
27 Ibid.
28 Mountbatten to Slim, 15 November 1945, WO 172/1791; Mountbatten to COS, SEACOS 579, 17 December 1945, CAB 105/162.
29 Leclerc to Gracey, 12 November 1945, 10 H 161, Dossier 4, Folder 'novembre 1945'; 'Journal de Marche' (1), entry for 17 November 1945, 10 H 161, Dossier 2; Leclerc to Commanding Officer, Air

(Indochina), 18 December 1945, 10 H 706, Dossier 'Journal de Décembre 1945': SHAT; Gracey to Slim, 5 November 1945, Gracey Papers 38, KCL.

30 D'Argenlieu to Juin, 7 December 1945, 10 H 140, Dossier 'SACSEA Conference interalliée 1945'; 'Journal de Marche' (1), entries for 31 October and 17 December 1945 ('The Admiral thinks that it is time to ... talk of independence. Idiot. No sense of the situation. The General is disgusted.'), 10 H 161, Dossier 2: SHAT.

31 'Weekly operational report no. 4, 14–21 December 1945', 10 H 106, Dossier 'Décembre 1945', SHAT.

32 Record of meeting, Saigon, 30 November 1945, WO 172/1792.

33 SACSEA, 300th meeting, 6 December 1945, WO 172/1792; 'Journal de Marche' (1), entry for 6 December 1945, 10 H 161, Dossier 2, SHAT.

34 Gracey to Leclerc, 12 December 1945, Gracey Papers 40, KCL.

35 SSU report no. XL 32194, 22 December 1945, RG 226, MMB, NA; Squadron Leader E. de Baglion (Head of French delegation, Control Commission No. 1, Saigon) to Gracey, 20 November 1945, 10 H 138, 'Télégrammes, Octobre à Décembre 1945', SHAT.

36 'Conférence publique', 11 December 1945, 10 H 138, 'Télégrammes, Octobre à Décembre 1945', SHAT.

37 'Report on F.I.C. by Col. Chapman Walker', December 1945, annex to Charles S. Millet, US Consul, Canton, to Secretary of State for War, 8 March 1946, DSR 851G.00/3–846, RG 59, NA; Mountbatten to COS, SEACOS 662, 17 March 1946, CAB 105/163.

38 Mountbatten, *Post-Surrender Tasks*, p. 298; JCS to SWNCC, 28 January 1946; SWNCC Secretariat, Note, 31 January 1946: SWNCC 35/13/D, RG 353, NA.

Chapter nine: Breakthrough in Java?

1 Mountbatten to Helfrich, 5 January 1946, Helfrich Papers, AMH.

2 Helfrich to Christison, 8 January 1946, ibid.

3 Helfrich, Order of the Day, 7 January 1946, ibid.

4 Helfrich to Mountbatten, 24 January 1946, ibid.

5 Bland (Hague) to FO, 8 January 1946, FO 371/53770 F413/1/61.

6 Mountbatten to Dening, 15 January 1946, WO 172/1798; SACSEA, 309th meeting, 8 January 1946, WO 172/1797.

7 Sargent to Dening, 2 January 1946, FO 371/53769 F82/1/61. Christison's reputation for blundering into politically sensitive areas by making public statements was confirmed by a report in the *Evening Standard* (13 January) which quoted a circular letter Christison had issued to all British and Indian officers of the rank of major and above:

    We have suffered 1200 casualties rescuing Dutch men, women and children, and, as far as the man-in-the-street is concerned, we have received no thanks. Our officers' 'release' has been deferred and young Britishers are still being conscripted to come here and assist us. . . . We must continually remind ourselves that the majority of the unfortunate Dutch are mentally sick.

8   Browning to Penney, 2 January 1946, Penney Papers 5/41, KCL.
9   CIGS to Mountbatten ('personal and private'), 10 January 1946, WO 172/1797; Mountbatten to Christison, 25 January 1946, WO 172/1799.
10 Browning to Weld, 26 January 1946, FO 371/53776 F1610/1/61; Mountbatten to CIGS, 14 January 1946, WO 172/1798.
11 Dening to Sargent ('strictly personal and very confidential'), 14 January 1946, FO 371/53771 F750/1/61.
12 Dening to Bevin ('personal'); minute by Wilson Young, 15 January 1946, FO 371/53772 F1012/1/61. Willing as they were to uphold Mountbatten's status as Supreme Commander, the COS drew the line at his more extreme displays of sensitivity, rejecting his protests that 'the tone and wording . . . [of low level signals] is inappropriate as coming from a department of the War Office to a Supreme Headquarters.' Browning to VCIGS, VCIGS to Browning, 22 January 1946, WO 203/4397.
13 Dening to Sterndale Bennett, 19 January 1946, FO 371/53772 F1086/1/61.
14 Dening to Mountbatten, 22 January 1946, Dening FEP File, BA.
15 Mountbatten to Bevin, 25 January 1946, WO 172/1799.
16 Dening to Bevin ('Top Secret and Personal'), 29 January 1946, FO 800/461.
17 Bevin to Dening ('to be deciphered personally by Mr Dening'), 29 January 1946, ibid.
18 Mountbatten to Bevin, 9 February 1946, C212, BA.
19 Browning to Lane (SACSEA[RL]), 17 January 1946, WO 203/4220.
20 Browning to Mountbatten, 26 June 1946, C32, BA.
21 Browning to Mountbatten, 29 June 1946, ibid.
22 Christison to Mountbatten, 2 February 1946, C212, BA.
23 Bevin to Dening, 19 January 1946, FO 371/53775 F1395/1/61.
24 Attlee to Mountbatten, 18 January 1946, FO 371/53772 F1090/1/61.
25 Entries, 4 and 11 February 1946, Killearn Diaries 1946, vol. 1, MECSAO.
26 Bevin to Killearn, 12 February 1946, FO 371/54017 F2441/333/61.
27 SACSEA, 309th meeting, 8 January 1946, WO 172/1797. In deciding to use the term terrorist, Mountbatten wanted to emphasise that in his view only the moderates constituted a political party with whom any sort of settlement could be reached.
28 DO(46), 2nd meeting, 18 January 1946, CAB 131/1.
29 John Thompson, *Hubbub in Java* (Sydney: Currawong Publishing Company, 1946), pp. 49–50. Thompson was a war correspondent in Java for the Australian Broadcasting Commission, and had been one of the reporters singled out for criticism by Walsh (see p. 158).
30 Helfrich to Mountbatten, 24 January 1946, Helfrich papers, AMH. Helfrich sent Mountbatten selections from a report by John Bowers of

United Press, which largely confirmed Thompson's later account.
31 'Report on Activities of 5 Parachute Brigade Group in Semarang January–May 1946', copy in Darling papers, Imperial War Museum.
32 Browning to Denning (Principal Administrative Officer, SEAC HQ), 1 February 1946, CAB 105/179.
33 Mountbatten, *Post-Surrender Tasks*, pp. 297–8.
34 P. Noel Baker, 'Record of a Conversation with The Netherlands Ambassador on January 7th, 1946', FO 371/53770 F419/1/61.
35 Mountbatten to COS, SEACOS 619, 11 January 1946, CAB 105/163; Walsh to FO, 9 January 1946, FO 371/53770 F477/1/61.
36 Dempsey to Mountbatten, 12 January 1946, WO 172/1798.
37 CM 5(46), 15 January 1946, CAB 128/5.
38 Dening to Walsh, 15 January; Wilson Young to Walsh, 17 January 1946, F 371/53771 F811/1/61.
39 Bevin to Clark Kerr, 25 January 1946, FO 371/53722 F 1089/1/61; Lane (SACR) to Auchinleck, 5 February 1946, WO 203/4327; Clark Kerr to FO, 8 February 1946, FO 371/53777 F2049/1/61.
40 For the Dutch proposals see *Officiële Bescheiden*, vol. III, pp. 703–4.
41 Van Mook to Logemann, 13 February 1946, *Officiële Bescheiden*, vol. III, p. 388.
42 Clark Kerr to FO, 23 Ferbruary 1946, FO 371/53781/ F2887/1/61
43 Clark Kerr to FO, 25 February 1946, FO 371/53781/ F2980/1/61.
44 Browning to Mountbatten, 24 February 1946, WO 172/1803.
45 Pyman, diary entry for 28 February 1946, Pyman Papers 5/3, KCL.
46 Clark Kerr to FO, 13 March 1946; minutes by Sterndale Bennett and Sargent, 22 and 23 March 1946: FO 371/53783 F3801/1/61.
47 Clark Kerr to FO, 9 March 1946, FO 371/53783 F3643/1/61.
48 Mountbatten to COS, SEACOS 660, 14 March 1946, CAB 105/163.
49 COS, 'Future Policy in Netherlands East Indies', 20 March 1946, COS (46)92 (O), CAB 80/100.
50 Wilson Young, minute, 13 March 1946, FO 371/53783 F3643/1/61.
51 Sterndale Bennett, minute, 21 March 1946, FO 371/53784 F54371/1/ G.
52 Sargent, minute, 22 March 1946, ibid.
53 COS to Mountbatten, COSSEA 493, 15 March 1946, CAB 105/166; Bevin, 'Policy in the Netherlands East Indies', 26 March 1946, FO 371/53787 F5379/1/G.
54 DO(46), 7th meeting, 27 March 1946, CAB 131/1.
55 Browning to Mountbatten, 27 March 1946, WO 172/1807.
56 Clark Kerr to FO, 23 March 1946, FO 371/53784 F4528/1/61; 26 March 1946, FO 371/53785 F4609/1/61.
57 Clark Kerr to FO, 29 March 1946, FO 371/53785 F4888/1/61.
58 The negotiations are covered in Oey Hong Lee, *War and Diplomacy in Indonesia 1945–1950* (Townsville: James Cook University of North Queensland, South East Asian Monograph Series no. 10, 1981), pp. 70–3.
59 Ibid., pp. 74–5.
60 The minutes of the meeting, 12 April 1946, are in PREM 8/263; also

in *Officiële Bescheiden*, vol. IV ('s Gravenhage: Martinus Nijhoff, 1974), pp. 109–13.

61 I.N. Djajadiningrat, *The Beginnings of the Indonesian-Dutch Negotiations and the Hoge Veluwe Talks* (Ithaca: Cornell Modern Indonesia Project, 1958).

62 Mountbatten to COS, SEACOS 643, 4 May 1946, CAB 105/163.

63 MacKereth to FO, 24 April 1946, FO 371/53789 F6148/1/61.

64 Bevin, minute, 27 April 1946, FO 371/53789 F6278/1/61; SACSEA, 329th meeting, 28 April 1946, WO 172/1810; Mountbatten to COS, SEACOS 688, 30 April 1946, CAB 105/163.

65 SACSEA, 322nd meeting, 6 May 1946, WO 172/1811. Mountbatten agreed, and used Browning's words to convey to the Chiefs of Staff his own sense of outrage at the Dutch action: SEACOS 694, 7 May 1946, CAB 105/163.

66 COS to Mountbatten, COSSEA 522, 8 May 1946 quoting minute by Attlee, CAB 105/166.

67 Entry for 27 April 1946, Killearn Diaries 1946, vol. 1, MECSAO.

68 Entry for 28 April 1946, ibid.

69 Entry for 2 May 1946, ibid.

70 SACSEA, 332nd meeting, 7 May 1946, WO 172/1811.

71 SACSEA, 331st meeting, 3 May 1946, WO 172/1810.

72 Mountbatten to COS, SEACOS 689, 3 May 1946, CAB 105/163.

73 Bevin to Attlee, 5 May 1946, FO 800/482 NE/46/7.

74 COS to Mountbatten, 30 May 1946, COSSEA 529, CAB 105/166.

75 Killearn to FO, 19 May 1946, FO 371/53793 F7439/1/61.

76 Entry for 15 May 1946, Killearn Diaries 1946, vol. 1, MECSAO.

77 FO to Killearn, 18 May 1946, FO 371/53792 F702/1/61.

78 MacKereth to FO, 11 May 1946, FO 371/53792 F7032/1/61. For Mountbatten's last defence against Dutch charges that he was undermining their authority and promoting the aspirations of the nationalists, see SEACOS 700, 21 May 1946, CAB 105/163, in which Mountbatten's comment that the Dutch were 'unduly sensitive' summed up his attitude.

79 SACSEA, 45th miscellaneous meeting, 25 May 1946, WO 172/1812. Mountbatten sent his proposals to the Chiefs of Staff in SEACOS 703, 25 May 1946, CAB 105/163.

80 SACSEA, 45th miscellaneous meeting; SAC, 335th meeting, 25 May 1946, WO 172/1812.

81 Killearn to FO, 28 May 1946, FO 371/53795 F7988/1/61.

Chapter ten: From the sidelines

1 Memoranda for the President: 'Indochina and Southeast Asia' and 'Southeast Asia: British Attitudes', 8 September 1944, DSR, 856D.01/10–544, RG 59, NA.

2 Stettinius to John G. Winant (US Ambassador, London), 21 November 1944, *FRUS, 1944*, vol. V, pp. 11285–6.

3 Dening to FO, 16 January 1945; FO to Halifax, 27 January 1945: FO 371/46304 F381/11/61.

4 La Feber, 'Roosevelt, Churchill and Indochina', pp. 1292–4.

5 Memorandum by Grew, 16 May 1945, *FRUS, 1945*, vol. VI, pp. 307–8.

6 Robert J. McMahon, *Colonialism and Cold War: The United States and the Struggle for Indonesian Independence, 1945–49* (Ithaca: Cornell University Press, 1981), pp. 72–3.

7 Oakes to State Department, 6 September 1945, DSR, 851G.00/9–645, RG 59, NA.

8 Acheson to American Mission, New Delhi, 6 September 1945, ibid.

9 Acheson to SWNCC, 5 October 1945, in McMahon, *Colonialism and Cold War*, pp. 100–01; Vincent, memorandum with comments by Matthews and Acheson, 28 September 1945, DSR, 851G.00/9–2845; Matthews, memorandum, 2 October 1945, DSR, 851G.00/10–245: RG 59, NA.

10 Stanley K. Hornbeck (US Ambassador, The Hague) to State Department, 5 and 14 October 1945, DSR, 856D.01/10–545 and 856D.00/10–1445, RG 59, NA.

11 Byrnes to Winant, 13 October 1945, *FRUS, 1945*, vol. VI, p. 1164; J.H. Morgan, memorandum, 15 October 1945, DSR, 856D.20/10–1545, RG 59, NA; McMahon, *Colonialism and Cold War*, pp. 101–4.

12 Dening to FO, COS to JSM, 17 October 1945, FO 371/46394 F8514/8531/6398/61.

13 Hornbeck to State Department, 3 and 8 November 1945, DSR, 856D.24/11–345/385, RG 59, NA.

14 COS(45) 275th meeting, 23 November 1945, CAB 79/41; Joint Chiefs to SWNCC, 4 January 1946, DSR, 856D.56/1–446, RG 59, NA.

15 Mountbatten to COS, SEACOS 572, 11 December 1945, CAB 105/162; COS to Mountbatten, COSSEA 452, 4 January 1946, CAB 105/166.

16 Mountbatten diary, entry for 15 June 1945, WO 172/1768.

17 Wilson (JSM) to Mountbatten, 19 December 1945, WO 172/1795; also Wilson to Mountbatten, 17 November 1945, WO 172/1792.

18 Halifax to FO, 10 November 1945, FO 371/46399 F9862/6398/61; also Winant to State Department, 7 November 1945, *FRUS, 1945*, vol. VI, p. 1168–9.

19 Memorandum of conversation between Moffat and a British Embassy official, 8 November 1945, *FRUS, 1945*, vol. VI, pp. 1167–8; Byrnes to Winant, 8 November 1945, ibid., p. 1173.

20 Winant to State Department, 24 November and 1 December 1945, ibid., pp. 1174–5.

21 McMahon, *Colonialism and Cold War*, p. 111.

22 Record of conversation between Miss Jane Foster (OSS) and A.L. Moffat and J.F. Cady (State Department), 12 December 1945, DSR 851G.00/12–1245, RG 59, NA.

23 Dunn, *The First Vietnam War*, chapter 9, is a detailed and extremely critical account of Dewey's activities in Saigon.
24 Captain Phelan, Field Mission into F.I.C., 17 October 1945, DSR 851G.00/10–1745, RG 59, NA. Patti's account, *Why Vietnam?* (Berkeley: University of California Press, 1981), is tendentious and self-serving.
25 SSU report no. XL 24742, 10 November 1945, RG 226, MMB, NA.
26 Deuxième Bureau, 'La Situation en Extrême-Orient', 3 October 1945, 10 H 599, Dossier 2, 'Situation en Extrême-Orient: Etudes août-déc 1945', SHAT.
27 SSU report no. XL 29090, 6 December 1945, RG 226, MMB, NA.
28 Acheson, minute, 18 January 1946, DSR 851G.00/1–1846, RG 59, NA.
29 Speech in the House of Representatives, 29 August 1945, quoted in George, *Australia and the Indonesian Revolution*, pp. 35–6.
30 Paul Hasluck, *The Government and the People, 1942–1945* (Canberra: Australian War Memorial, 1970), p. 593.
31 Benoy to Mountbatten, 3 October 1945, WO 203/4429; Mountbatten to Chifley, 6 October 1945, WO 172/1786; Benoy to Browning, 9 October 1945, WO 203/4429.
32 Mountbatten to Chifley, 20 October 1945; Chifley to Mountbatten, 20 October 1945: CRS A1838, Item 401/3/1/1 pt. 1, AA; Mountbatten to Attlee, 22 October 1945, CAB 105/178; Chifley to Attlee, 23 and 24 October 1945, CRS A2937, Item 110/45, AA; George, *Australia and the Indonesian Revolution*, pp. 38–9. For a sympathetic treatment of the dock strikes and the *Esperance Bay* episode, see Rupert Lockwood, *Black Armada* (Sydney: Australasian Book Society, 1975). Lockwood was editor of *Tribune*, the official organ of the Australian Communist Party, at the time of the strikes.
33 J.W. Burton (Acting Secretary, External Affairs) to Evatt, 14 October 1945, CRS A1838, Item 401/3/1/1 pt. 1, AA.
34 N.J.O. Makin (Acting Minister of External Affairs), 'Considerations affecting Australian policy', 29 October 1945, CRS A4355, Item 7/1/3/2, AA.
35 Chifley to Attlee, 31 October 1945, CRS A4355, Item 7/1/3/2; J.D.L. Hood (External, London) to External (Canberra), 25 and 26 October 1945, CRS A2937, Item 110/45: AA.
36 Attlee to Chifley, 4 November 1945, PREM 8/68.
37 Principal Staff Officers' (HQ SEAC) meeting, 1 November 1945, comment by H.N. Brain (Deputy Chief Political Adviser), WO 172/1790.
38 Mountbatten to COS, SEACOS 538, 5 November 1945, CAB 105/162.
39 External (Canberra) to External (London), 4 November 1945, CRS A2397, Item 110/45, AA.
40 Macmahon Ball to Burton, 10 and 11 November 1945, CRS A1838, Item 401/1/2/1, AA; Dening to Mountbatten, 12 November 1945, FO 371/46400 F9981/6398/61.

41 Mountbatten to Benoy, 16 November 1945, WO 172/1791; Chifley to Mountbatten, 22 November 1945, FO 371/46402 F10525/6398/61.
42 Walsh to FO, 20 November 1945, FO 371/46401 F10298/6398/61.
43 Dening to FO, 18 November 1945; Walsh to FO, 19 November 1945; FO to Dening, 23 November 1945: DO 35/1579; Benoy to Browning, 21 November 1945, WO 203/4429.
44 Dening to FO, 18 November 1945, DO 35/1579.
45 Macmahon Ball to Burton, 22 November 1945, CRS A1838, Item 401/1/2/1, AA.
46 Macmahon Ball to Burton, 15 November 1945, ibid.
47 Evatt to External Affairs, 23 November 1945, CRS A4355, Item 7/1/3/2, AA.
48 Chifley to Evatt, 28 November 1945, ibid.
49 Macmahon Ball, 'Report on the N.E.I.', 17 December 1945, CRS A1838, Item 401/1/2/1, AA.
50 Far Eastern Department, 'Brief for the Secretary of State', 6 December 1945, FO 371/46408 F12362/6398/61.
51 J.E. Stephenson (Assistant Under-Secretary) to Addison; minute by Addison, 6 December 1945: DO 35/1581.
52 Proud to Burton, 14 January 1946; to Evatt, 22 January 1946: CRS A 1066, Item P45/47/10/2, AA.
53 David Dilks (ed.), *The Diaries of Sir Alexander Cadogan O.M., 1938–1945* (London: Cassell, 1971), p. 745.
54 Dening to Foreign Office, 23 January 1946; minute by Machtig, 28 January 1946: DO 35/1579.
55 'Report of a meeting between the Supreme Allied Commander, South East Asia, and the Prime Minister of Australia', 25 March 1946, WO 172/1808.

Conclusion

1 Mountbatten to COS, SEACOS 596, 28 December 1945, CAB 105/162.
2 'Concentration and Repatriation of JSP in SEAC: Briefs for SAC returning to London 30 May 1946', WO 172/1813.
3 SACSEA, 17th miscellaneous meeting, 20 August 1945, WO 172/1777.
4 Mountbatten to WO, 3 April 1946, WO 172/1808; Dening, 'Review of Political Events in South-East Asia 1945 to March 1946', WO 172/1807.
5 SAC, personal diary, 26 April 1946, WO 172/1810.
6 'Concentration and Repatriation of JSP in SEAC', WO 172/1813.
7 'Statistical Data on the Recovery of RAPWI: Briefs for SAC returning to London 30 May 1946', WO 172/1813.
8 MacKereth to Wilson Young, 25 July 1946, FO 371/53806 F11563/1/61.

  9 Pyman to Dempsey, 29 October 1945, Pyman Papers 5/1, KCL;
      Dening to Bevin, 29 January 1946, FO 800/461.
 10 Ziegler, *Mountbatten*, p. 280.
 11 Dening, 'Review of Political Events in South-East Asia 1945 to March
      1946', WO 172/1807.
 12 Park to Air Commodore L.T. Pankhurst, 3 May 1949; Mountbatten
      to Hollis, 20 April 1949: AIR 2/7926.
 13 Mountbatten to Driberg, 17 December 1945, C91, BA.

Bibliography

Archival sources

Australia

Australian Archives, Canberra
  A461 Prime Minister's Department, Correspondence Files, Multi-numbered Series, Third System: 'Netherlands East Indies – General Reps', 1945–1946
  A1066 Correspondence Files, Multiple Number Series 1945
  A1838 External Affairs: Correspondence Files
  A2680 Advisory War Council Agenda Files
  A2937 External Affairs (London): Correspondence Files
  A4355 Australian Mission, Netherlands East Indies (Batavia), Correspondence Files
Australian War Memorial, Canberra
  AWM 54 Written Records: War 1939–1945

Britain

Public Record Office, London
  AIR 2 Correspondence
  CAB 69 War Cabinet Defence Committee (Operations)
  CAB 79 Chiefs of Staff minutes
  CAB 80 Chiefs of Staff memoranda
  CAB 105 War Cabinet telegrams (pieces 162–166 for telegrams between Mountbatten and the Chiefs of Staff, SEACOS and COSSEA)
  CAB 122 British Joint Services Mission, Washington Office Files
  CAB 131 Defence Committee minutes and papers
  DO 35 Dominions Office, General Correspondence
  FO 371 Foreign Office, General Correspondence
  FO 800 Papers relating to Bevin as Foreign Secretary
  PREM 8 Prime Minister's Office
  WO 172 War Diaries of South East Asia Command
  WO 203 Military Headquarters papers, Far East

France

Archives du Ministère des Affaires Etrangères
  Etats associés 1945–57
Archives nationales, section d'Outre-Mer

Télégrammes 1940–1946
Service historique de l'Armée de Terre
  10H 86–336 Corps Expéditionnaire d'Extrême Orient, Cabinet du
  Général, Commandant en Chef

United States of America
National Archives, Washington
  RG 59   Department of State Records
  RG 218   Records of the Joint Chiefs of Staff
  RG 226   Records of the Office of Strategic Services
  RG 319   Army Staff: Plans and Operations Division
  RG 353   Records of the State-War-Navy Coordinating Committee

Private Papers

General T.W. Blamey papers, Australian War Memorial, Canberra
Lt General Sir Philip Christison papers, private possession, copy in
  Imperial War Museum, London
General Sir Kenneth Darling papers, Imperial War Museum, London
Major General Sir Douglas Gracey Papers, Liddell Hart Centre for
  Military Archives, King's College London.
Admiral C.E.L. Helfrich papers, Afdeling Maritieme Historie, The Hague
General H.L. Ismay papers, Liddell Hart Centre for Military Archives,
  King's College London
Lord Killearn papers, Middle East Centre, St Antony's College, Oxford
Général Leclerc papers, Fonds historique du Général Leclerc de Haut-
  clocque, Maréchal de France, Saint-Germain-en-laye
W. Macmahon Ball, 'Batavia diary', private possession
Mountbatten papers, Broadlands Archives
Major General W.R.C. Penney papers, Liddell Hart Centre for Military
  Archives, King's College London
Major General H. Pyman papers, Liddell Hart Centre for Military
  Archives, King's College London
Major General L.H.O. Pugh papers, Imperial War Museum
Sir Frederick Shedden papers, Australian Archives, Canberra

Published documents

Burma: The Struggle for Independence 1944–1948. Vol. 1: *From Military
  Occupation to Civil Government, 1 January 1944 to 31 August 1946.*
  Ed. by Hugh Tinker. London: HMSO, 1983.
Documents on British Policy Overseas. Series 1, Vol. 1: *1945.* London:
  HMSO, 1984.
Enquètecommissie Regeringsbeleid 1940–1945, Part VIII: *Militair beleid
  1940–1945, Terungkeer naar Nederlansch-Indië.* 's Gravenhage:
  Staatsdukkerig, 1956.

Foreign Relations of the United States, 1944 , vol. V; *1945*, vol. VI. Washington: Government Printing Office, 1965, 1969.

Mountbatten, Earl. *Report to the Combined Chiefs of Staff by the Supreme Allied Commander, South East Asia 1934–1945*. London: HMSO, 1951.

——. *Post Surrender Tasks. Section E of the Report of the Combined Chiefs of Staff by the Supreme Allied Commander, South East Asia 1943–1945*. London: HMSO, 1969.

Officiële Bescheiden Betreffende de Nederlands-Indonesische Betrekkingen 1945–1950. Ed. by S.L. van der Wal. Vols. 1–4. 's Gravenhage: Martinus Nijhoff, 1972–4

Secondary sources

Bullock, Alan. *Ernest Bevin: Foreign Secretary (1945–1951)*. London: Heinemann, 1983.

Barclay, Glen St. J. *Friends in High Places: Australian-American Diplomatic Relations since 1945*. Melbourne: Oxford University Press, 1985.

Buttinger, Joseph. *Vietnam: A Dragon Embattled*. Vol. 1: *From Colonialism to the Vietminh*. London: Pall Mall Press, 1967.

Cruickshank, Charles. *SOE in the Far East*. Oxford: Oxford University Press, 1983.

Day, David A. 'Promise and Performance: Britain's Pacific Pledge, 1943–5', *War & Society*, 4:2 (September 1986), pp. 71–93.

Densette, Adrien. *Leclerc*. Paris: Flammarion, 1952.

Devillers, Philippe. *Histoire du Vietnam de 1940 à 1952*. Paris: Eds du Seuil, 1952.

Dilks, David (ed). *The Diaries of Sir Alexander Cadogan O.M., 1938–1945*. London: Cassell, 1971.

Djajadiningrat, Idrus N. *The Beginnings of the Indonesian-Dutch Negotiations and the Hoge Veluwe Talks*. Ithaca: Cornell University Modern Indonesia Project, 1958.

Donnison, F.S.V. *British Military Administration in the Far East 1943–46*. London: HMSO, 1956.

Doulton, A.J.F. *The Fighting Cock*. Aldershot: Gale & Polden, 1951.

Dunn, Peter M. *The First Vietnam War*. London: C. Hurst, 1985.

Edwards, P.G. *Prime Ministers and Diplomats: The Making of Australian Foreign Policy 1901–1949*. Melbourne: Oxford University Press, 1983.

Ehrman, John. *Grand Strategy*. Vol. VI. London: HMSO, 1956.

George, Margaret. *Australia and the Indonesian Revolution*. Carlton: Melbourne University Press, 1980.

Harris, Kenneth. *Attlee*. London: Weidenfeld & Nicolson, 1982.

Hasluck, Paul. *The Government and the People, 1942–1945*. Canberra: Australian War Memorial, 1970.

Horner, D.M. *High Comand: Australia and Allied Strategy 1939–1945*.

Sydney and Canberra: George Allen & Unwin/Australian War Memorial, 1982.

Institut Charles de Gaulle. *Le Général de Gaulle et l'Indochine.* Paris: Plon, 1982.

Irving, R.E.M. *The First Indochina War.* London: Croom Helm, 1975.

Isoart, Paul (ed.). *L'Indochine Française 1940–1945.* Paris: Presses Universitaires de France, 1982.

Kahin, George McT. *Nationalism and Revolution in Indonesia.* Ithaca: Cornell University Press, 1952.

Kersaudy, François. *Churchill and De Gaulle.* London: Collins, 1981.

Kirby, S. Woodburn. *The War against Japan.* Vol. V. *The Surrender of Japan.* London: HMSO, 1969.

La Feber, Walter. 'Roosevelt, Churchill and Indochina, 1942–45', *American Historical Review,* 80:5 (December 1975), 1277–95.

Legge, J.D. *Sukarno: A Political Biography.* London: Allen Lane, 1972.

Lockwood, Rupert. *Black Armada.* Sydney: Australasian Book Society, 1975.

Long, Gavin. *The Final Campaigns: Australia in the War of 1939–1945.* Canberra: Australian War Memorial, 1963.

Massu, Jacques. *Sept Ans avec Leclerc.* Paris: Plon, 1974.

McMahon, Robert J. *Colonialism and Cold War: The United States and the Struggle for Indonesian Independence, 1945–49.* Ithaca: Cornell University Press, 1981.

Morison, Samuel Eliot. *History of United States Naval Operations in World War II.* Vol. III: *The Rising Sun in the Pacific 1931–April 1942.* Boston: Little Brown and Company, 1965.

Oey Hong Lee. *War and Diplomacy in Indonesia 1945–50.* Townsville: Committee of South-East Asian Studies, James Cook University, 1981.

Orange, Vincent. *A Biography of Air Chief Marshal Sir Keith Park GCB, KBE, MC, DFC, DCL.* London: Methuen, 1984.

Ovendale, Ritchie (ed.). *The Foreign Policy of the British Labour Governments, 1945–1951.* Leicester: Leicester University Press, 1984.

Reid, Anthony J.S. *The Indonesian National Revolution 1945–1950.* Hawthorn: Longman, 1974.

Robertson, John. *Australia at War 1939–1945.* Melbourne: Heinemann, 1981.

Rosie, George. *The British in Vietnam: How the twenty-five year war began.* London: Panther Books, 1970.

Sbrega, John J. *Anglo-American Relations and Colonialism in East Asia. 1941–1945.* New York: Garland Publishing, 1983.

Thompson, John. *Hubbub in Java.* Sydney: Currawong Publishing Co., 1946.

Thorne, Christopher. *Allies of a Kind. The United States, Britain and the War against Japan, 1941–1945.* London: Hamish Hamilton, 1978.

——. *The Issue of War: States, Societies and the Far Eastern Conflict of 1941–1945.* London: Hamish Hamilton, 1985.

——. 'Engeland, Australië en Nederlands Oost-Indië 1941–1945', *Inter-*

nationale Spectator, XXIX:8 (August 1975), pp. 493–505.

Vigneras, Marcel. *Rearming the French*. Washington: Office of the Chief of Military History, 1957.

Wehl, David. *The Birth of Indonesia*. London: George Allen & Unwin, 1948.

Yong Mun Cheong. *H.J. van Mook and Indonesian Independence: A Study of His Role in Dutch-Indonesian Relations, 1945–48*. The Hague: Martinus Nijhoff, 1982.

Ziegler, Philip. *Mountbatten: The Official Biography*. London: Collins, 1985.

Theses

Herbert, M.T.P. 'Asking Too Much: Australia, The Netherlands and the Netherlands East Indies, 1942–1945'. (BA Hons. thesis, Department of History, Faculty of Military Studies, The University of New South Wales, 1985)

Squire, Clifford William. 'Britain and the Transfer of Power in Indonesia 1945–46'. (PhD thesis, School of Oriental and African Studies, University of London, 1979)

Newspapers

The Times (London), *Manchester Guardian, Sydney Morning Herald*

Index